SOMEWHERE ELSE

The universities are no longer on the frontiers of knowl-edge. A lot of students are leaving, professors are leaving. The universities won't die or disappear, but they'll lose their charisma and their imaginative capacity to innovate, which means that they will become the kind of places where you learn the past, where you consolidate, and then, when you're ready to really get into things, then you'll say, "O.K. I'm gonna go and work with Soleri, or I'm gonna work with Piaget, or I'm gonna study with Gopi Krishna, or I'm gonna go to India or go to the Lama Foundation in New Mexico –"

—WILLIAM I. THOMPSON
Time, August 27, 1972

a
living-learning
catalog

SOMEWHERE ELSE

Edited by

Center for Curriculum Design

Foreword by

JOHN HOLT

THE **SWALLOW PRESS** INC.
CHICAGO

First Edition
  First Printing

Published by
The Swallow Press Incorporated
1139 South Wabash Avenue
Chicago, Illinois 60605

This book printed on 100% recycled paper

ISBN 8-8040-0609-1 (cloth)
ISBN 0-8040-0610-5 (paper)
LIBRARY OF CONGRESS CATALOG CARD NUMBER 72-91916

Back cover art courtesy LNS/UPS

TO LEO
who said
"Go where your mind blows"

We are students without teachers. . . . We study, but we are not taught. . . . No one will admit that we are the real foundation of the university.

–Homage to Ortega y Gasset
from Spanish students, spoken
at his graveside, February, 1956

Contents

Whoever wants to know a thing has no way of doing so except by coming into contact with it, that is, by living (practicing) in its environment. If you want knowledge, you must take part in the practice of changing reality. If you want to know the taste of a pear, you must change the pear by eating it yourself.

                        —MAO TSE-TUNG

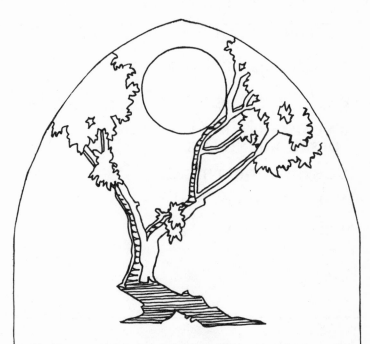

" The whole culture is out there. What I urge is
that a child be free to explore and make sense
of that culture in his own way. "

John Holt
Rasberry Excercises

Foreword

When I say, as I do whenever I can, that young people—what we now call "minors" or "children"—should have, if they want it, the legal right to work, to travel, to live away from their parents, to be financially independent, to plan and direct their own learning; or when I say that attendance at school should not be compulsory, I usually get for a response two anxious, angry, horrified questions:

Where would they go?

What would they do?

Well, as it happens, there are, even now, plenty of places to go, and plenty of interesting, instructive, useful things to do. There should be and someday will be a great many more. But there are already a great many, and a great many young people would go to them and use them if they were more free to do so.

That is what this book is about. It is a guide or directory to some of the places where people (of whatever age) can go to live, work, and learn (they are all one) in ways not ordinarily provided for by conventional schools and workplaces, which like to draw clear and sharp lines between work, play, and learning.

The book reminds me of another anxious question someone once asked me. This was at a meeting—very pleasant—of (mostly) sociologists at Harvard, with whom I had been discussing some of my ideas about education. At one point someone said to me, "But if we educate children in the way you propose, how are they later going to fit on the tracks laid down by society?"

The question showed me that he understood very clearly what

1

schools are for—to make people think, as they had made him think, that the tracks that make a society at any particular moment are not only the best tracks, but the only possible tracks. His remark was a perfect illustration of what Ivan Illich was to say some years later about how the institutions of our society dominate not only our lives but our imaginations, not only what we do but what we even think we might or could do.

I didn't say any of this to my questioner. What I said was, "They'll make new tracks!" From their expressions it was clear that most of them had never thought of this. "And after all," I went on, "where do you think the present tracks in society came from? They weren't always there. They didn't fall from the sky. Somewhere, back in the past, someone *made* a track, did something *that had not been done before*—usually because everyone who considered doing it, if anyone did, thought it was impossible or crazy."

Societies are constantly making new tracks. If they don't they freeze up, get hardening of the arteries and joints, corrode, decay, and die. All of which our society is quite clearly in the process of doing. The question is, can people, the kind of people this book writes about, make enough new tracks, and fast enough? Can we find new ways of living, thinking, learning, working to replace those which have quite obviously ceased to work? Nobody knows. Time will tell.

Meanwhile, here are some new tracks, some new ways in which people are trying to make a different and better world. Here are some roads to the future, if we have a future.

JOHN HOLT

"Find out what kind of world you want to live in, what you are good at, and what to work at to build that world. What do you need to know? Demand that your teachers teach you that."
                                    PETER KROPOTKIN
                                "A Letter to the Young"

Introduction

This is a catalog of places to learn for those who can't bring themselves to go to college, for those who shouldn't go to college, or those who don't want to go to college.

And it is for anyone of any age interested in learning-places that are an alternative to grades, credits, credentials, and competition.

Learning, as most of us know, takes place everywhere, not just within the four walls of a classroom or within the confines of an institution. And when we succeed in freeing ourselves from the "necessity" of credentials, and realize that many of the things we want to know about aren't being taught in schools, even in the free schools, then we have taken a first step toward kicking the schooling habit.

When we realize and act upon our belief that learning doesn't have to be structured into compulsory institutions, then we have taken another step toward assuming responsibility for our own education.

Hence this catalog of learning-places and resources.

Our main criteria for entries were 1) no grades, no credit, no credentials; 2) an ongoing program open democratically to all ages and colors and persuasions; and 3) a place not easily found by persons searching for alternative learning-places. We've included many entries that we consider "establishment," but there's no reason non-establishment versions couldn't be set up by people interested in alternatives to some of these higher-priced places.

3

We worry about regular colleges and schools shipping off their most restless and challenging students to these learning-places for extra credits granted for "experiential education." These schools and colleges talk of classrooms without walls, learning in the world, etc. We trust in the integrity of the non-establishment places to resist co-optation by well-heeled, well-intentioned institutions and their students.

We are also worried about the *deluge* of inquiries that may break upon the people we have listed. So we urge you *not* to drop in or to send inquiries out of idle curiosity. Visits should be arranged by prior notice and should reflect real need for more information. These people are serious, and too busy to accommodate "spectators." It will be most helpful to all concerned if written inquiries include a statement describing the basis of your interest.

But *do* write to the people you are interested in. *Don't* write to The Center. We just don't have the staff time to handle inquiries, and we are giving you all the information we can through this catalog and future supplements.

A number of places which otherwise qualify for inclusion are not listed in the catalog because our requests for information didn't get an answer. We figure that if they treat us that way, they'll treat you that way too. Also, some places are not listed simply because we didn't have room. Where there are obviously hundreds of such places (e.g., growth centers), we purposely listed only a few as representative.

Somewhere Else is organized into two parts: Centers and Networks. Centers are places, people, or things (such as publications) to go to for *instruction;* Networks are people, places, or things to go to for *information about* instruction. Under Centers and Networks, the categories (Alternative Futures Centers, Artisan Centers, Awareness Centers, etc.) appear in alphabetical order. Under the categories, the entries themselves are alphabetized by country or state or city, *not* by the title of the entry; foreign entries are placed at the beginning of each category and U.S. listings follow. Finally, the cross references and the Index should assure that you don't miss out on any information, wherever it is in the book.

We've tried hard to verify the information in *Somewhere Else* and to make it as up-to-date as possible. In most cases we have presented listings in the individual's/organization's own words or attempted to capture the tone of their literature. We've added our own commentary or evaluation in a few cases. But we depend on you to confirm or revise our work so far.

A feedback page is included at the end of the catalog, for whatever corrections, comments, advice, or new information you can pass along to us. We would like to hear about how a supplement can be most useful to you, and what we might do or cease doing to make it more effective. And if we have included something that you feel we shouldn't, please let us know that, too, along with the reasons why.

This is a catalog of alternative learning-places, not a wish book or a collection of products to be consumed in the hopes of achieving a "together" state of mind.

Place Magazine, a journal for "hip" travelers, cautions its readers against the boll weevil mentality when they discover a friendly, sympathetic, or beautiful place, in these words:

"Consider the boll weevil, if you will. This is one bug that never could fit in. He kept moving on and messing over every farm that seemed like a pretty place to settle down. . . .

"The weevil will remain strung-out and bewildered. He lacks reverence for and deference to the wilds. He does not know that the relationship of a being to a place is the cornerstone of every value and virtue, that it determines the worth of life and work and love and art.

"His consciousness will allow only one obsessive I-it demand: 'Fields of bobbing balls of cotton all for me to eat.' And he is astonished to find that places too make their demands; that a place will say: 'Only those worthy may have me.'"

—from *Place* Magazine
855 High Street
Palo Alto, Ca. 94301
$8 a year

"Somewhere else" is of course a different place, but even more it is a *different way of being* in the same place—or any place. Realistically, we recognize that many of the persons who use this catalog are unlikely to go to any of the places we list. But we are sure that the catalog will help them to see numerous possibilities for creating new alternatives right where they are. This is what the catalog is really for, helping "somewhere else" to find you.

ROGER WICKER
PATTY BAKER
NOEL McINNIS
MIKE LUISI
THE CENTER FOR CURRICULUM DESIGN

ON BEING SOMEWHERE ELSE

"Every place I go, there I am."

These are the words of a fellow who spent many years, going to many different places, trying to find himself. One day, having had no success, he finally recognized the obvious. Having been found by himself, he went back to where he started.

Many people want to go somewhere else, assuming things will be better there. Sometimes they are better: something *does* get left behind, or something sought *is* found. Frequently, however, new places become the same place because they all have one thing in common: yourself.

If you bought this catalog for wish-fulfillment, don't shelve it when you have finished it. Give it to someone who is seeking self-fulfillment. He's the one it's intended for. He wants to *be* somewhere else, not go there.

PART I

CENTERS

Places to learn directly rather than vicariously; places to learn
to be a whole thing rather than to be a cog in a mass
production process.

... the future isn't what it used to be ...

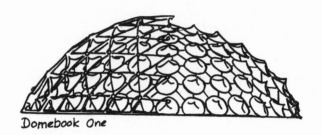

Domebook One

ALTERNATIVE FUTURES CENTERS

We understand that John McHale originally coined the term "alternative futures," but we first heard it from Robert Theobald when he said, "We must invent an alternative future which will replace our current future by making it irrelevant."

Until recently the acceptable models for thinking about the future were all in terms of a continuance of present trends with no dramatic changes. But it is now becoming obvious, both from studies of the environment and from studies of human psychology, that a continuation of present patterns of behavior would lead to the destruction of the human race.

As we have recognized the impossibility of continuing present trends, we have often tended to swing to the opposite extreme and to argue that we can invent any future that we like. There are some futurist thinkers who believe that there are no limitations on man— whether cultural or genetic. This belief seems as naive as the belief that man's future is totally constrained by his past.

In reality, our future is determined by our past history, our future dreams, and our present attitudes and resources. Studies of alternative futures are designed to study what futures are possible and desirable and to consider the ways in which these futures can be brought into existence.

CENTRO INTERCULTURAL DE DOCUMENTACION
Apartado 479
Cuernavaca, Morelos, Mexico
This is Ivan Illich's "think-tank" where the ex-Jesuit and his colleagues have been spinning out the concept of deschooling for the past several years. Rather than reform schools, Illich maintains that it is necessary to create new institutions and forms for learning. Seminars are offered every year in February, at $30 per course. Currently CIDOC is concerning itself with alternative approaches to school, transportation, design, and medical care.

There are anywhere from 100 to 200 people attending various seminars on Latin America and the alternatives seminars: an incredible melange of people.

For information on times, dates, and seminars, write to Señorita Esperanza Godot, Apartado 479, Cuernavaca, Morelos, Mexico. (*See also*, Cuauhnahuac.)

PAOLO SOLERI
COSANTI FOUNDATION
6433 E. DOUBLETREE ROAD
SCOTTSDALE, ARIZ, 85253

Paolo Soleri is the architect who envisions cities in structures that sit lightly upon the land, vertically, instead of being sprawled for miles in every direction.

Arcosanti is a visionary model city for 3,000 people that Soleri, students, and helpers are building in the Arizona desert. The entire city will sit on 1/10th of the total piece of land, and will be entirely self-sufficient. Everything is being built from scratch using precast concrete, ferro cement over dirt forms, free-form buildings, and specialized structures.

Anyone is welcome to work on the city, but you must apply to Cosanti Foundation Workshops, and the fee is based on whether you want to work for one session of six weeks or for the whole summer.

AQUARIUS PROJECT
Box 4013
Berkeley, Ca. 94704

Aquarius Project is interested in the counter-technology branch of the counterculture, as expressed in the proliferation of *Whole Earth Catalog/Radical Software*-type publications, and looks for ways to utilize the skills of overground society's drop-outs as well as pushed-outs (the victims of unemployment in the technical professions).

Aquarius Project rejects the Movement denial of science and technology, and the naive longing on the part of many for a simple return to the supposedly idyllic conditions of past societies. They foresee technologically sophisticated intentional communities as an advance guard developing knowledge crucial to a society undergoing radical social change. Contact them if you are planning a community, or interested in areas such as hydroponics, or "technological guerrilla warfare."

MOUNTAIN INSTITUTE FOR MAN
Gold Hill
Boulder, Colo. 80302
Winter address: 201 East Chestnut
     Chicago, Ill. 60611
     c/o Charles G. Arnold

Mountain Institute for Man is a newly gathered community of generalists seeking answers to social, ethical, and biological problems. It provides weeklong seminars in a setting of mountains, domes, and hydroponics, with both "teachers" and "learners" drawn from all academic levels and disciplines. The Institute seeks to disseminate new information which will initiate constructive political action, and to develop creative life styles in harmony with the planet. Leisure time can be spent backpacking in Roosevelt National Forest, horseback riding (costs extra), or with crafts and theater.

Membership is $25, applicable toward a seminar fee. Seminars are: $125/wk for adults, covering food and housing; $100/wk for students with food and housing; or $50/wk for anyone wishing to cook their own food and bring a tent. Some scholarships are available.

There is also a day camp on the Institute property (250 acres) for kids up to 8 years and a coed residential camp (Lazy A Ranch) for kids 9-18, so they can live and learn too. (*See also*, Sight Point Institute.)

THE NEW ALCHEMY INSTITUTE
Box 432
Woods Hole, Mass. 02543
c/o John Todd

The New Alchemists are a group of scientists, artists, and humanists with the common goal of finding new "ways in which science and the individual can come to the aid of man and his stressed planet."

They seek to develop a biotechnology based on an ecological ethic, as well as to develop decentralized communities where people can live in a manner consistent with this philosophy and be relatively self-contained in terms of

power and production. They recoil from uniformity through chemistry.
Projects underway include:
—Harvest Garden Research—for personal production of food, "using sophisticated, ecologically sane practices".
—Pure Energy for Powering the Communities of the Future—for regional
power production based on utilization of "clean" sources such as wind,
sun, waves, and tides.
—The Creation of Communities—for totally planned, ecologically designed
"villages of the future" where practices enhancing individual stature and
communal relationship will be encouraged.
—Experimental and Teaching Centers—for the study of "all phases of de-
centralist technology and land skills" in tropical and temperate climates.
—The New Alchemy Knowledge Center—for compiling materials collected
worldwide from all cultures.

PLANNED TOTAL ENVIRONMENT, INC.
GPO Box 620
New York, N.Y. 10001
Planned Total Environment is "working toward establishing decentralized
intentional communities through functional human engineering and progressive
sane housing" with a humanized pro-scientific attitude.
They are tax exempt and non-profit, and finance projects through sale of
land in New York's Adirondack Mountains. On land suitable for natural home-
sites they have built semi-underground homes and human potential labs from
junk/surplus materials.
In the summer of 1972 they organized a scientist/artist/poet co-op on an
island off the coast of Canada and by the winter they'll be offering weekend
workshops integrating encounter and sensory awareness techniques using videotape and bio-feedback.
"We are particularly interested in hearing from radical scientists." (*See
also*, Bio-Meditation Society)

FUTURE SHOCK, INC.
2307 Flora
Cincinnati, Ohio 45219
(513) 241-3428
A course/project designed for "the change-agents in Cincinnati's businesses
and schools," Future Shock, Inc. offers an experience in "actualizing Consciousness III" a la Charles Reich's book *The Greening of America*. They
invite you to "explore, experiment, experience your new electronic-age mind"
in six two-hour sessions for $18. "Our methods of instruction were developed in
classes at the University of Cincinnati within the past two years. Please understand that our sessions are *not* encounter groups. No therapy, either personal or
group, is involved. No hypnotism, drugs, smoking, or occult practices are em-
ployed. . . ."
The sessions offer opportunities to "enjoy guided experiences which teach
you to control body processes previously considered involuntary, expand awareness of the non-verbal signals you constantly give and receive, and take home
additional instructions so you can put your new skill into practice at once in your
home, office, or school."

DENNIS LIVINGSTON
2460 Dartmoor Road
Cleveland Heights, Ohio 44118
(216) 932-3334
Dennis Livingston has done teaching and research at the University of California, Davis, Case Western Reserve University, and Scripps Institution of Oceanography, on the interrelated subjects of alternative world futures, global pollution, world order, and science fiction. He is currently being a college (teacher) drop out and is generally willing to aid students and teachers—grade school through graduate school and non-school—in developing curricula and programs on these topics, probably for a fee. He has bibliographies on world futures and science fiction, and is developing an inventory of science fiction stories relevant to social policy issues.

ALTERNATIVE FUTURES CENTERS:
See also, The Life Center; Minnesota Experimental City; Ontario College of Art; SOCIAL AND POLITICAL CHANGE CENTERS.

We can only live these changes; we cannot think our way to humanity. Every one of us, and every group with which we live and work, must become the model of the era which we desire to create.

—IVAN ILLICH

ARTISAN AND SKILLS CENTERS

DUMAS PERE
School of French Cooking
1129 Depot Street
Glenview, Ill. 60025
(312) 729-4823

This French cooking school offers free apprenticeships to high school graduates "who desire training to work professionally as Chef (men) or Cordon Bleu (women)." It's tuition-free and the apprenticeships usually last a year. You'll be working with Chef John Snowden. An interview is required before the apprenticeship, so write or call for details and an appointment.

TURLEY FORGE
WROUGHT IRONWORK
SANTA FE, N. M., 87501
TELEPHONE 505 -983-6986

Blacksmithing isn't quite a lost art. Owner Frank Turley takes five students at a time for six weeks in a course that provides a groundwork in blacksmithing technique and theory. His forge is the type that was in operation around 1915. His course material includes discussions of shop layout, ferrous metals, and forge equipment. His students practice the smithing essentials of drawing, upsetting, hot rasping, forge welding, punching, bending, and tempering. After basic techniques are mastered, students work on projects they are personally interested in. He doesn't lean heavily on horseshoeing, though students who wish can learn to make all classes of horseshoes and several of the essential tools.

Frank Turley says the work is physically demanding and concentrated. The course costs $350, on a first-come first-served basis. The Forge provides all materials needed in the class, though supplies for projects beyond basic lessons are furnished by the students. Students make their own arrangements for housing and meals. Visitors are welcomed at the Forge.

Bookbinding

CAPRICORNUS
3167 College Avenue
Berkeley, Ca. 94705

Bookbinders through the ages have had the responsibility for making books beautiful and lasting. But there aren't many bookbinders left, and books aren't quite as beautiful or permanent as they used to be.

But, the art is coming back. Anne Henning and Theo Kahle offer classes in fine hand bookbinding. It's an ancient and painstaking, and highly rewarding craft.

Classes are held once a week for three to four hours, and the fee is $25 a month. The San Francisco *People's Yellow Pages* says: ". . . you get your money's worth. These people won't let you get away with shoddy work, although the atmosphere is patient and fairly relaxed."

RICHARD MINSKY

BOOKBINDING   AND   REPAIRING

105-21 Metropolitan Avenue
Forest Hills, N.Y. 11375   (212) 441-1537

Originally, Richard Minsky started out to get a Ph.D. at Brown University, but the good smells of leather and books in the basement workroom of the university bookbinder seduced him into bookbinding. He learned the craft by working with a master bookbinder, and he is now offering classes.

There are beginning classes which include the history of bookbinding, lessons in techniques for cloth binding, leather binding, and lettering with gold foil. Classes are limited to six students, and cost $50 for a 12-week course meeting once a week, for two hours, or $50 for an eight-week course, meeting once a week for three hours.

Advanced bookbinding classes include library research into binding problems, rebacking and rebinding books from different periods, saving as much of the old leather as possible, and various techniques for marbling paper. These are private lessons at $12 per hour. Another course, Problems of Materials and Design on Modern Bindings, includes tooling with colored foils on leather and vellum, inlaying and onlaying leather and objects (stones, jewels), molding leather, and inlaying stained glass. "In this stage of his studies, the student looks at the book as a medium for self-expression, and is in a position to develop new techniques to fit problems arising in the realization of an artistic conception. Private lessons, $25 per hour."

Crafts

AEGINA ARTS CENTRE

136 West 52nd St., New York, New York 10019

AEGINA ARTS CENTRE
24 Kiniskas St.
Athens, Greece
739-536

On a sunny isle in the Aegean Sea, just an hour or two from Athens is an international center for people of all ages. Aegina Arts Centre offers workshops in music, musicology, acting, dance (Greek folk dances, Indian dances, yoga and modern dance), painting and drawing, poetry, archeology, photo-communications, and modern Greek.

Two sessions run from July through August, and the cost per session is $300, or both for $500.

No academic credit is offered, unless by special arrangement with the school to which you want the credit transferred. Enrollment is limited, so AAC recommends early registration. They will help you find housing, which ranges from $65 to $85 (double) per session. They suggest that $100 a month over room and board and tuition should be adequate unless you're planning expensive travel outside of Greece.

"The Centre encourages a free-flow of movement between various workshops, studios and lectures in music, poetry, archeology, literature, drama and painting. . . .Informal lectures as a background to the summer festivals of music and drama in the ancient theatres of Athens and Epidaurus are . . . an integral part of the program.

"The school is situated on the island of Aegina, between Attica and Peloponnesus, about one and a half hours from Athens by ferry. The island has been inhabited for over five thousand years, and has been famed both as an artistic and commercial centre."

ARTAUD
499 Alabama Street
San Francisco, Ca. 94110
(415) 864-9160

Artaud isn't strictly a craft school, although the building is full of artists and craftsmen. It's run as a "container commune" with 111,000 square feet of warehouse space for 53 groups who pay 6½c per square foot. The people at Artaud use the space for photography, art studios, dome designing, creating mime, printing, leather craft, dance, film, a mechanics school, chemical work on organic soaps, and creative arts in general.

Some of the people will teach what they know. An information booklet is available. Please ask for the booklet either by mail or phone before you visit Artaud; they're serious people who don't mind talking, but they do mind being "visited" to death by "learning groupies."

One of the components of Artaud is:

CREATIVE ARTS SCHOOL OF SHASTA AT ARTAUD
499 Alabama
San Francisco, Ca. 94110
c/o Donna Ottosen
Shasta School describes itself as attempting to prove that "education can be taught with art." In a flexible arrangement with students and teachers, the students choose an education that makes sense to them, with classes running in creative writing, drama, cookery, photography, potting, and voice, among others. The cost is $40 per month for those who can pay, and no one who is really serious about learning is turned away for lack of money. Shasta is primarily for high school age students, and work done there may be given credit at public high schools.

Shasta School is also interested in seeing free art schools spring up all over the country. Write before visiting—they are busy people.

THE ANDERSON RANCH
Box 5225
West Village
Aspen, Colo. 81611
A bunch of nice people recently moved into an old farm and turned it into a really crafty place. "Last summer [1970] we offered metals, pottery, drawing, kiln building, and glass blowing. Winter saw the addition of photo silkscreen, raku pottery, natural dyeing, and weaving." In 1971, they added special workshops in welding, glassblowing, and serigraphy.

"Our emphasis is on the development of independence in the use of tools and process, consequently, extensive studio time, one-on-one contact, and considerable tool making are integral to the program."

Tuition, including materials, is $130 for in-state people, $180 for out-of-state. Workshops range from $60 to $80. Housing is available from $75 per month and up. Courses begin in late June and go for eight weeks.

HAYSTACK MOUNTAIN SCHOOL OF CRAFTS
Deer Isle, Me. 04627
Haystack Mountain is the grandmother of the crafts schools, and consequently, like Penland in North Carolina, it tends to be a little more expensive than some lesser known craft centers.

"Haystack is not patently a school, although it conforms to the principle and purpose of all institutions of serious learning. It functions as a catalyst of ideas and people by encouraging a climate where diverse, and even conflicting, opinion and expression are allowed to reflect the differences in the people— young and older, vanguard and conservative, radical and doctrinaire—who make up the Haystack community." Classes are offered only during the summer from the last week in June to the middle of September. Most classes are three weeks long, although you can stay all summer if you can afford it.

The major concentrations at Haystack are ceramics, glass, jewelry, graphics, and weaving.

Applicants for Haystack must be 18 or older, and there are openings for 55 residents and 10 day students. Their catalog is published each year in February. Priority is given to applications received before April 1.

Prices range from $50 to $160 per week, including room, board, and tuition.

TROUT FISHING IN AMERICA
353 Broadway
Cambridge, Mass. 02114
(617) 876-7791
   Our friends at the People's Yellow Pages of Cambridge describe TFIA as "a good, open place for people to get together and share. Presently in progress: The Rainbow Trout Coffee House, a music workshop, pottery, batik, weaving, candlemaking, silkscreening, dulcimer building [for lots of information on dulcimers, see the *Whole Earth Catalog* supplement for January, 1971, page 21], wilderness survival, photography, massage, flute, poetry, astrology, music theory. A place to start your own thing, if you like. Potluck suppers every Sunday night—all welcome."

CAPE COD CRAFTS COOPERATIVE
Box 454
North Eastham, Mass. 02651
(617) 255-2029
   This is a place for low-income people to work and to learn crafts. It opened in the summer of 1971, and is also a place to market wares at lower commissions than profit-making stores.

LOS LLANOS
Old Santa Fe Trail
Santa Fe, New Mexico 87501

   "Believing that part of the generation gap has been caused by the lack of opportunity for people of all ages and backgrounds to study subjects of mutual interest together, classes are open to everyone from high school age to octogenarians. The only requirement is a desire to continue to challenge one's mind."
   Los Llanos is a two-part operation:
1) The School of Arts and Crafts offers an all-year program which includes weaving, pottery and art courses. The Spring semester includes photography, elementary woodworking, guitar, seminars such as "The Influence of Mexican Prehistoric Ceremonialism on the Southwest," classes in Navajo weaving and cookery, and conversational Spanish and French. Classes are limited to a maximum of 15. Each class is two hours long, during a nine-week "semester." Prices range from $5 for the cookery classes to $51 for pottery and weaving classes.
2) The high school offers "an educational challenge to the student who has been unable to achieve success academically or socially. The current pressure of requirements for a high school degree or entrance to college have left many students with no confidence in themselves or in their abilities." Boarding tuition is $4,500 inclusive, which covers a trip to Mexico taken by the entire school. Day students pay $1,650 inclusive, plus $250 for the Mexico trip.
   Located ten minutes from Santa Fe, Los Llanos has a complex of buildings that house all the activities, including two kilns, a swimming pool, and many gardens and patios.

CRAFT STUDENTS LEAGUE
West Side "Y"
840 8th Avenue at 51st Street
New York, N.Y. 10019
(212) 246-4712
   This New York City craft center offers year-round instruction in leather working, batik, macramé, guitar construction, jewelry and enameling, picture framing, stained glass, fabric construction, gem-cutting, ceramics, painting, sculpture, woodworking, weaving, and twelve other fields. Their prices are reasonable, but since it's in New York City, there are no housing facilities.

JOHN C. CAMPBELL FOLK SCHOOL
Brasstown, N.C. 28902
(704) 837-2775
   The Campbell Folk School has been around for over 40 years: "its educational purpose has been to stimulate a belief in the natural, cultural, and personal resources which are the heritage of all. A variety of programs are a result: a demonstration farm, a woodcarving enterprise, short courses in crafts, and service-learning programs for youth."
   They offer classes in woodcarving, weaving, simple woodworking, and other handcrafts.
   Courses/workshops are also offered in Appalachian, Anglo-American, and Danish folk dances, folk songs, dulcimer, and folklore. Their program runs from early spring through late fall, and their prices are nice: $175 for tuition, room and board was the highest price we saw in their craft listing section. They grow and cook their own food, and some work scholarships are available on the farm in exchange for craft classes. (See listing under SOCIAL AND POLITICAL CHANGE CENTERS)

PENLAND  SCHOOL OF CRAFTS

Penland, N.C. 28765
(704) 765-2359
   One of the granddaddies of the craft schools, Penland attracts a faculty of world-known craftsmen every summer to teach pottery, weaving, metalsmithing, jewelry, enameling, lapidary, graphics, woodworking, sculpture, vegetable dyeing, plastics, and glassblowing.
   Classes are in session during the summer months, from the end of May through the middle of September. Penland is expensive: a whole summer there can run around $1000, but there are sessions that last from two to three weeks, and it's possible to get by for around $300, including all fees, tuition, room and board. Scholarships are available and details on how to get them are in the catalog. There's an April 1 deadline for scholarship applications. College credit, undergraduate and graduate, is possible too.
   Penland also has two 8-week sessions, one in the spring and one in the fall called "concentration." "These sessions are in weaving, ceramics, glassblow-

ing, and metal jewelry. The instructors select the students, and the classes are limited in number." As with all Penland facilities, the studios are open for use 24 hours a day, seven days a week.

center for art and ecology
Route 1, Box 20A
Otis, Ore. 97368

From their literature: "Sitka Center is devoted to the arts and crafts and their interrelationship with the coastal environment. The Center building is located on the south side of Cascade Head at the mouth of the Salmon River, three miles from US 101 on Three Rocks Road."

Sitka's programs focus interest towards the arts and crafts and provide a basic understanding of the sea and shoreline. Day programs are conducted in pottery, weaving, photography, painting, drawing, and natural dyeing, with other offerings such as this: ". . . because of the extremely fine tides during this week (June 12-16), the program will be primarily devoted to the study of the marine environment, using cameras, tape recorders, and drawing."

Age limits reach all the way down to 7. Most of these programs are designed for older children and teenagers, but adults are welcome in some.

There are also workshops that allow for residency at the center: "Participants will camp or make arrangements to stay in the area. Tents and good meals will be provided for residents." Facilities are open at all times. Specific workshops offered are: pottery and pinhole cameras, with focus on the processes of raku and stoneware ceramics and kiln building plus the construction of pinhole cameras; natural dyes of the coast area; raku, painting, and non-loom weaving; and workshops with the Oregon Museum of Science and Industry. Tuition ranges from $17 for the dyeing workshop to $140 for resident programs in pottery.

THE HILLSIDE CENTER
617 N.W. Culpepper Terrace
Portland, Ore. 97210
(503) 227-4146

Craft classes are only part of the good things at Hillside Center. The whole place is located in fine old buildings on a wooded hilltop near downtown Portland. Studio space is sometimes available on a co-op basis: you pay a small fee for studio space and help make cooperative decisions on how Hillside is run. Crafts classes are offered in bookbinding, weaving and textiles, macramé, basketry, vegetable dyeing, and more.

ARROWMONT

BOX 567 — GATLINBURG, TENNESSEE 37738

"Arrowmont School is an outgrowth of the Settlement School established in 1912 by Pi Beta Phi collegiate sorority. In 1970 the name was changed to the Arrowmont School of Crafts and the new craft building complex containing over 38,000 square feet of floor space was completed.

"Arrowmont attracts students from the ages of 18 to 80, and from all parts of the U.S. Many students from foreign lands also have attended.

"Classes begin in mid-June and continue through August. Faculty members are nationally recognized as outstanding teachers and excellent craftsmen. Undergraduate and graduate credit is offered through the University of Tennessee, as well as non-credit courses. These include beginning and advanced ceramics, stitchery, vegetable dyeing, spinning, weaving, silk screening, block printing, batik, jewelry, macramé, enameling, and design.

"Expenses range from $100 to $120 per week. Tuition, room and board, application and registration fees are included in the cost. Studio fees and cost of materials are extra, though not expensive."

Field trips are organized to visit local Appalachian craftsmen in the great Smoky Mountains area, Indian craftsmen, and the Craftsmen's Fair of the Southern Highlands Handicraft Guild, in nearby Asheville, North Carolina.

FLETCHER FARM CRAFT SCHOOL
Ludlow, Vt. 05149
(802) 685-4863

Fletcher Farm Craft School is located in the heart of the Green Mountains of Vermont, and is housed in a converted sugarhouse, barn, and carriage house. Sponsored by the Society of Vermont Craftsmen, Fletcher offers classes in two and three-week cycles with college and high school credit available if you want it.

Courses offered include pottery, weaving, spinning and dyeing, design and printing, sculpture, jewelry, enameling, drawing and painting, cut and pierced lampshades, Early American decoration, and rosemaling.

A three-week course costing from $200 up, depending on how fancy you want your sleeping quarters. Scholarships are available for Vermont crafts teachers, who must be "legal" residents of Vermont. For information, contact Mrs. Harriet Turnquist, Chelsea, Vt. 05038.

See also, Nordenfjord World University (Asgard); Tail of the Tiger.

Graphics

CHICAGO PRINTMAKERS WORKSHOP
3335 North Halsted
Chicago, Ill. 60614
(312) 929-2811
    This is a cooperative printmakers workshop with all the equipment you could probably want. Classes are offered evenings and weekends. They have a gallery where they hang members' work for sale. Classes are in etching, silkscreen, woodcuts, and lithography, and run 8 weeks. Costs are about $75-85, including supplies.

THE PAUPERS PRESS PRINTMAKING WORKSHOP & GALLERY
2743 N. Sheffield Avenue·Chicago 60614

(312) 348-0469
    The Paupers Press is a nice, low-key operation teaching etching, engraving, lino or wood cuts, and edition printing, among other techniques.
    Classes are taught by Howard Albert in the evenings from 7 to 10 p.m., and on Saturday and Sunday from 1 to 4 p.m., start and end when you want. The cost is fantastically low: $6 per three-hour session.

PRATT GRAPHICS CENTER
831 Broadway
New York, N.Y. 10003
(212) OR 4-0603
    Regular classes and workshops are taught here in silkscreen, etching, woodcut, lithography, and photo-printing techniques.
    Workshops run daily, days and evenings.

THE PRINTMAKING WORKSHOP
248 West 23rd Street
New York, N.Y. 10011
(212) 989-6125
    "The Printmaking Workshop provides instruction for the young potential printmaker as well as the mature painter and sculptor. An independent, non-profit professional studio, the Workshop is open to artists who wish to work in the lithography, etching or woodcut media.
    "Classes are given at the Workshop by well-known artist-printmakers. The fees are nominal and scholarships are available on the basis of ability and need." You can become a member of the Workshop, in addition to taking classes, by review of your portfolio or by professional recommendations.

pacific northwest graphics workshop

box 78 star route   cheshire, oregon 97419

Nick de Matties, a young printmaker who has set up the Pacific Northwest Graphics Workshop, believes that it is better to provide "an alternative style of study in which print skills are circulated and reciprocated."

The Workshop is located on ten acres of woodland in the coast range of mountains. It has a studio building, and boating, fishing, and swimming are nearby. Students live in large four-man tents on wooden platforms, and meals are served in the main building, family-style.

"The prime objective of the workshop is to free the students of daily routines so that they may spend the maximum time available studying the manifold possibilities of the print media. Although providing instruction and direction is a basic part of the workshop, students with previous experience in printmaking will find a challenging and stimulating atmosphere where an underlying concern for technical excellence allows a full range of visual expression." Lectures, slide presentations, demonstrations, and critiques will take place between 8:30 and 3:30 Monday through Friday, but the studio itself is open at all times. Tuition is $750 for an eight-week summer session, with tent and meals included.

De Matties hopes to have about 25 students each summer and hopes eventually to have novices and masters working together, recreating the learning relationship which recreated artists during the Renaissance. De Matties had previously taught in universities and colleges, but left that style of teaching for the workshop model he has now in Oregon. "I think there's an urban aesthetic," he says. "It's perpetuated by urban papers, consumed by urbanites and shown in urban museums. I just began to question the value of those aesthetics. I wanted to get out of the city. . . . The only place most people can do printmaking is in a college or university, some large, meek, bureaucratic institution, and that always puts you right in the middle of the urban aesthetic."

See also, New Thing Art and Architecture Center; Omega Graphics.

Jewelry

THE SNARLING IRON

Mars Hill, North Carolina

c/o Judith Angus
(704) 645-7635

In her jewelry and metal design workshop-studio, Judith Angus teaches a ten-week course "devoted to learning fundamental skills and processes related to jewelry or metal design depending on individual interests." Workshops are offered in the spring and summer months (and eventually in the winter, too), with classes meeting Monday, Wednesday, and Friday from 1 to 4 p.m.

"Students are urged to register for the entire course as a continuity of processes is desirable for a maximum learning experience. However, students may elect to work on a per diem basis as their schedules permit. . . ."

Tuition is $300 for the full course, or $10 per class session, payable at the time of the class. Living is cheap in Mars Hill, with a few apartments scattered around the downtown area and houses in the surrounding mountains renting in the $45-100 range. The college in the town is Mars Hill College, a four-year liberal arts college with a fairly good Appalachian studies program as well as traditional subjects.

Music and Instruments

Ali Akbar College of Music

P.O. Box 956
San Rafael
CA 94902

(415) 924-1530

Short of going to India to study Indian music, the Ali Akbar College may be the best place anywhere to learn it since it's the school of Ali Akbar Khan, master Indian musician. Located in San Rafael, near San Francisco, the College offers instruction in plucked string instruments: sarod, sitar, guitar; bowed strings: violin, cello, dilruba, sarangi, chandra sarang; classical Indian flute; tabla; pakhwadj and tala. All beginning students attend two vocal classes, which include dhrupad, kheyal, and thumri; Indian classical dancing is also offered:

kathak dance, folk and children's dances, as well as orchestra and dance-drama productions, and Hindi language classes.

Founded in 1967, Ali Akbar College of Music is set up so that "During the three yearly 12-week sessions the student learns hundreds of traditional rhythmic and melodic compositions, many newly created in class, and thereby absorbs the centuries of form and style out of which he will express his own musicianship."

Tuition for continuous study is $200 per session; part-time is $225. Housing is available at the College, and the residence hall serves organic natural foods in balanced meals, vegetarian and meat.

WEST BANK SCHOOL OF MUSIC
1813 Sixth Street South
Minneapolis, Minn. 55404
> As they say in their advertisement in *Rolling Stone:*
>> Wanted: world's greatest unknown musicians to teach and/or study at West Bank School of Music. Any instrument, style (classical, folk, rock, blues, jazz, country, etc.). Also theory, jazz harmony, composition, arranging, etc. No grading, testing, academism, competition, just pure learning.

GEORGE KELISCHEK

MASTER VIOLIN MAKER
Brasstown. North Carolina   28902

George Kelischek is a master violin maker who has just finished building a studio in the mountains of Western North Carolina, next door to the John C. Campbell Folk School. He offers year-round courses for amateur instrument makers, and summer courses in the art of playing historical instruments, mostly Renaissance woodwinds such as the krummhorn, rauschpfeiff, kelhorn, kortholt, cornetti, etc.

"For the first time there is a place where anyone interested may go to build himself a musical instrument such as a viola da gamba, harpsichord, rebec, lute, hurdy-gurdy, psaltery, dulcimer, krummhorn, kelhorn, violin, guitar or others from kits in our workshops." George Kelischek will also set up workshops for high school or college music departments to enable students to gain experience in "a practical workshop making their own instruments for use in your school."

Costs are $35 per week for use of workshop facilities, tools, books, drawings, advice. You can bring your own kits, or purchase kits or raw materials from the workshop. Guests cook their own meals in a variety of housing arrangements available, from furnished self-contained two-room and bath apartments ($60 a week) to self-contained one-room and bath apartments ($50 a week) to lodging in Fiddlers Hall. There are also nearby motels and local residents who offer guest rooms.

HAL RIEGGER POTTERY WORKSHOPS
Experiment-A-Workshops
5835 Bowness, N.W.
Calgary 45, Alberta
Canada

Hal Riegger and Gillian Hodge are conducting primitive pottery workshops in five locations around the world ranging from Tubac, Arizona to Corfu, Greece.

"All workshops are conducted in a physical environment that is more or less primitive. The equipment, tools, and materials of the potter's studio are absent, and instead, people attending the workshops must be perceptive and inventive, using what the surroundings provide in the pursuit of making pottery. It must also be realized that the workshops are based on exploration and discovery. The materials, tools, and equipment, such as they are, will be different from what you may be used to. An open mind that permits you to discover how best you can handle the situation will be the way to learn and grow. It would be best to approach the workshop as primitive man, knowing nothing, but learning throughout the workshop how you can cope successfully with the situation."

Minimum age is 15. Tuition ranges from $50 to $450. Hal Riegger is also the author of *Primitive Pottery* published by Van Nostrand Reinhold.

BIG CREEK POTTERY
DAVENPORT, CALIF. 95017

c/o Bruce McDougal
(408) 423-4402

Located on an old dairy farm 60 miles south of San Francisco, with the Pacific Ocean on one side and the Santa Cruz Mountains on the other, Big Creek Pottery offers "serious students a unique opportunity to live and work together in a beautiful rural environment.

"Life at Big Creek is simple and centers around a full day's work in the studio with Bruce McDougal instructing. The session is structured to emphasize development of skills at the wheel, glazing (including calculation), firing of kilns (cone 10 stoneware, salt and raku), clay processing and kiln construction. A wheel is provided each student and the studio is open in the evenings and weekends."

Students share the little chores of the Pottery, and the food is fresh, raised on the farm. "The gardens, animals, ocean, streams, and mountains are very much a part of every day at Big Creek."

Tuition covers room, board, instruction and all materials. Previous experience in pottery is not required. There are three sessions: spring (six weeks), $600; summer (nine weeks), $850; and fall (nine weeks), $850. Advanced workshops, also.

OPUS 4
791 South Corona
Denver, Colorado 80209

Located in the foothills of the Rockies, Opus 4 offers "a total ceramic experience . . . designed for everyone interested in pottery, from the beginner to the advanced student."

Consisting of two three-week seminars in traditional pottery and contemporary ceramic sculpture, Opus 4 will have five professional potters as instructors. They offer instruction on three levels: handbuilding, basic wheel throwing, glazing, and basic firing theory; ceramic sculpture, special projects in hand-building and wheel throwing, glaze composition and application, kiln loading and firing, high temperature and Raku kiln building and theory; and independent projects, including advanced throwing techniques, glaze formulation, and high temperature and Raku kiln building and theory.

Tuition, room and board range from $295 for residents, and $275 for non-residents, for the three week period. Students must be at least 18.

THE POTTERY SHOP
Lookout Mountain
Route 2
Rising Fawn, Ga. 30738
(404) 657-4444

Charles and Rubynelle Counts run a unique crafts center in Rising Fawn, Ga. Rubynelle is into weaving, and Charles is a potter *par excellence*. He offers an intensive six-week course for "potters/skills at the wheel" that begins in mid-June.

His tuition is $300. A $50 deposit is required before May 15 and an interview is necessary before registration. Class size is limited to fifteen people. You work at potting from 9 to 5, Monday through Friday. Housing is available in the area and is the responsibility of the student. When you can throw a pot to Charles Counts' satisfaction you know it's good. We've heard from friends who have been through the course that he's a real taskmaster, though.

CLAY PEOPLE
3345 North Halsted
Chicago, Ill. 60657
(312) 528-5156

The Clay People offer three basic courses: handbuilding, wheel throwing, and stoneware sculpture.

"The main idea is to offer a college level education without the hassle of college (i.e. prerequisites, grades, etc.) taught by someone who has college teaching experience. Students are encouraged to learn by doing. . . . Also, students are advised to take notes during the lectures, some of which are 1½ hours long.

"At first students are to keep everything they construct (if the craftsmanship is acceptable) so they have something on which they can experiment applying glazes. After a few classes, the craftmanship requirements go up, and design is brought into the discussion. From that point on, students are no longer allowed to keep their pots solely on the basis that 'it's beautiful because I made it.'"

The adult handbuilding course, "Fundamentals and Handbuilding," is "designed for people who have little or no experience with stoneware clay. Emphasis will be placed on physical properties of clay, craftsmanship, design and glazing. Each lesson begins with a lecture and demonstration after which each student is given a project." Classes are limited to 15 and are offered as ten three-hour sessions.

An advanced handbuilding course deals with new techniques of glazing and construction and all work will be discussed in "class participation critiques".

The adult wheel throwing course is designed "to teach the art of 'throwing'. It does not include any of the basic fundamentals of clay or any glazing techniques." These classes are limited to six, so each student has his own wheel to work on.

The "Stoneware Sculpture" course is "designed for people who desire to explore the use of stoneware clay as a sculpture medium."

Tuition for the handbuilding and stoneware sculpture classes is $75, which includes all clay used during the class, all·glazes, all firing of work done in class, and use of the tools and equipment. Tuition for the wheel throwing class is $100, and includes all materials used in class.

THE POT SHOP
604 Dempster Street
Evanston, Ill. 60202
(312) 864-7778

"A craft, particularly ceramics, is supposed to be a joyful experience, a joining of an imaginary conception with a physical enactment. We learn the muscular control to carry out an idea in clay. We create objects about which we should be incapable of making verbose conceptual statements. We make self-justifying, contained spaces for humble uses.

"The key to understanding a craft is in the knowledge that *we*, as opposed to a group of hidden machines, are capable of making things. The workshop then becomes a place where simple skills are passed on to people interested in mastering clay and feeling for themselves what it is to take ordinary earth and transform it into good, unpretentious pottery.

"In a wider sense, The Workshop is an experiment with the concept of a crafts community. We would like to investigate the possibilities of forming a context in which people may learn to explore the aspects of crafts in general. I do not know exactly what that will mean. If I did, the experiment would be unnecessary, but I am suggesting that such a need exists. . . . "

The Workshop offers eight-week classes in wheel throwing and handbuilding. Classes meet three hours weekly and additional practice is encouraged. Classes cost $60.

MUDFLAT
196 Broadway
Cambridge, Mass. 02139
(617) 354-9626
    Potter Bob Fenton of Wakefield, Massachusetts, says this of Mudflat: "Mudflat, a pottery school located in Cambridge, is in my estimation one of the best pottery schools in the country. It's new, young, enthusiastic, non-bureaucratic, and involved with just one thing—teaching pottery. Courses are six weeks long.
    Classes meet twice a week for three hours a class. A student may use the facilities from 10 in the morning till 10 at night all week long while attending classes. The course costs $60. Work-study is available.
    "Mudflat has helped put two working pottery cooperatives into being . . . rent is low and everybody's in the same building on the same floor. There's still plenty of space available in the building and anybody's welcome to some of it. We're looking for all types of craftsmen and hope to, one day, have a huge mother of a crafts collective."

BOB FENTON
45 Pitman Ave.
Wakefield, Mass. 01880
    Bob Fenton, a potter, will teach beginners the art of throwing pots. He only "charges enough to exist."

TUSCARORA

RETREAT & SUMMER POTTERY SCHOOL

TUSCARORA, ELKO COUNTY, NEVADA

(702), ask for operator in Tuscarora, then give number 5732
Winter address 'til June 1:
    c/o Dennis Parks
    545 North Indianhill
    Claremont, Ca. 91711
    Director Dennis Parks describes Tuscarora as ". . . not a quickie remedial program for the novice—rather as an intensified pragmatic approach toward developing a craftsman. A school where a beginner might build a kiln, construct a wheel, dig his clay, then learn to make pots; where experienced potters could return to the basics of clay, water and fire."
    Located in the small, almost-ghost-town of Tuscarora in northeastern Nevada, Tuscarora Retreat and Summer Pottery School takes between eight and

twelve students, ranging in age from 15 to 50. Formal instruction is kept to a minimum. At least three hours a day a potter is in the studio to help, answer questions, and guide according to the students' individual needs. "The situation is more like a co-op than a classroom studio."

"In prospecting, digging and processing clay and in making bricks, building and firing kilns there is necessarily a good deal of cooperation among the students. This has been a successful way to introduce beginners to ceramics. Knowledge of the primitive aspects of the craft seems to be a natural way to preface and supplement learning the skills of making objects out of clay. . . .

"For the month of July a fee of $365 is charged. This covers everything— instruction, materials, firing and studio space as well as room and board. In order to keep the fees down, it is understood that everyone will take turns sharing the different, necessary chores to keep the school running, in the studio, the houses and the kitchen."

BALDWIN POTTERY
540 La Guardia Place
New York, N.Y. 10012
(212) 475-9742

"Baldwin Pottery is a workshop for professional and semi-professional potters and a school for adults and children." They offer year-round beginning and advanced classes in throwing, handbuilding, and glaze chemistry which meet for 15 three-hour sessions, once or twice a week. Cost is $90. An intensive course covering the same areas is offered "periodically," meeting daily for three weeks (15 sessions) from 10 a.m. to 4 p.m., for $150. In addition, special classes are set up on demand in raku, porcelain, cookware, etc.

Students may use the workshop for practice outside class periods for 50c an hour, with a time estimate submitted in advance. The Pottery also fires the work of outside potters (for a fee), and provides consultation for those who want to set up their own studios.

BOWERY POTTERY
163 Bowery at Delancey
New York, N.Y. 10002
(212) WA 5-8478

Janine Sade, instructor at Bowery Pottery, says, "Bowery Pottery is unique in specializing in handbuilding methods rather than production-oriented methods such as molding or throwing on the potter's wheel. The basic techniques of handbuilding are easier for the beginner while the varieties of form possible are more challenging for the advanced student. The classes are small and informal, held in a large and sunny studio filled with plants."

Classes are offered for twelve weeks at a time for $75, which includes the cost of all clay and glazes, Firing costs are 1c per cubic inch. You have a choice of morning, afternoon, or evening classes.

"We generally do some raku firing too, and every spring and sometimes fall we drive out to the country and do a pit firing. The classes are small: from seven to eleven students in a class, so we all become friends and often go to museums or skating with each other when we're not making pots."

MULBERRY STREET CERAMICS CO.
280 Mulberry Street
New York, N.Y. 10012
(212) 966-5136
    Potter George Pock takes two students at a time, and takes them through a two-month course for beginners. We don't know any more; please fill us in, if you know.

JUGTOWN POTTERY

Route 2
Seagrove, N.C. 27341
c/o Nancy Sweezy
    The Jugtown Pottery is a continuation of a Piedmont Carolina potting tradition dating back to 1750. The original English settlers of the area brought with them a need for practical pottery.
    Built in 1921 in an effort to revive the pottery tradition, Jugtown Pottery is essentially a Pottery like those operating in the 18th century.
    "We dig our own clays locally and process them. A horse turns the pug mill which grinds the clay. The pottery is all handturned on a wheel, dried, bisque fired to harden, glazed and burned a second time. . . . Some of the forms we make here today are linked way back to early English pottery, some were the development of a settler's life, some have evolved in these 200 years and some are being designed now for present needs. The chicken pie dishes we make are identical to the ones being excavated at Jamestown, Virginia which are considered to be the earliest (non-Indian) pottery form made in America."
    Nancy Sweezy says, "We have four apprentices at all times and many young people are interested in coming here. Entertainment is self-made, work is vigorous, and it's hard to get the kids to go away."
    Write before you visit, so you don't interrupt their work. And inquire about apprenticeships before you get there, since there's probably a waiting list.

POTTERY NORTHWEST
305 Harrison Street
Seattle, Wash. 98109
(206) MA 4-9504
    Classes are $120 per quarter, use of facilities $44 a month, including clay and glazes.

See also, ARTISAN AND SKILLS CENTERS: Crafts.

Theater and Dance

en/emble

the only repertory company in Chicago

4520 North Beacon
Chicago, Ill. 60640
(312) 769-0601
   The Ensemble, Chicago's only professional repertory and dance company, has an ongoing apprenticeship program for dancers and actors. "The four-month apprenticeship includes training in both modern dance and acting with the professional company members. Allied work in production and assisting at performances gives the apprentice the unique opportunity to become involved in the total work of a professional company.
   "The Ensemble covers tuition costs for the apprentice's professional training. Admission to the program is by audition with the Company's directors. . . . Openings occur periodically . . . the program involves a full commitment and allows little time for jobs, school or performing on the side." For more information contact Kathy Richards, company manager.

Theatre Workshop Boston, Inc.
The Boston· Center for the Arts
549 Tremont Street
Boston, Massachusetts 02116

(617) 482-4778
   Theater Workshop is "an environmental theater company, producing original works. Professional non-equity company under the artistic direction of Barbara Linden. Comprehensive improvisation workshop program including professional actor training, teacher training to develop curricula with improvisational

techniques, and all age groups of children and teens. Work in movement, mime, sound, sensory awareness, psycho-drama techniques, and esoteric practices of yoga and Sufism as they relate to theater."

The company has produced four "critically acclaimed theater pieces" and worked with the Boston Philharmonic and public television station.

Adult and young adult workshops for actors run 10 weeks, one evening a week, for $75. Children's workshops, for age groups for four to 17 years, run for 12 weeks and cost $85. There are also workshops for parents of participating children. Workshops are limited to fifteen at present, with plans for expansion. Write Marilyn Bentov.

See also, Aegina Arts Centre; Bridge Mountain Foundation; Nethers Community School.

Weaving and Textiles

ALBION HILLS FARM SCHOOL OF SPINNING
R.R. 3
Caledon East, Ontario
Canada
c/o Edna Blackburn

Edna Blackburn offers instruction in spinning, dyeing, and weaving all year around. Write for details.

SUMMER WORKSHOP FOR WEAVERS
Big Creek Pottery
Davenport, Ca. 95017

The summer workshop for weavers at Big Creek, a restored dairy ranch 60 miles south of San Francisco on the Pacific Coast, is taught by Mary Ellen Cranston-Bennett.

"This year's workshop centers around a nine-week study of weaving during which the student works full-time in the studio learning traditional and contemporary techniques. Although some time will be devoted to the art of spinning yarns from various raw materials and dyeing yarns with native plants, the main emphasis will be weaving.

"Students will learn the essentials of weaving, including how to warp, dress a loom, weave on floor, table or frame looms, and draft patterns. Each student will be encouraged to develop his own artistic capabilities within the general field of weaving, whether his own area of interest be yardage, rugs, tapestry, etc."

The ranch is a cooperative venture with students invited to participate in the chores. Food is grown on the ranch.

Tuition for the nine weeks of instruction, fresh air, ocean, and mountains is $800, which includes room, board, instruction, and all materials for spinning and first weaving projects.

WEAVING WORKSHOP
3300 North Halsted Street
Chicago, Ill. 60657
(312) 929-5776

A very friendly place where you can learn the whole business of weaving, beginning with wall hangings and progressing through a coverlet with the "Whig Rose" pattern.

Classes are six weeks long, and each class is three hours a week. Classes are limited to ten people.

Beginners work on wall hangings, while learning the basics of yarn, warp and woof, and eight or nine basic weaves. A beginners' class on the loom is $35, with a $5 fee for a small hand loom that's yours when the class is over. There are advanced classes in tapestry and rugs, also.

HARTLAND AREA CRAFTS
Hartland, Mich. 48029
c/o Mrs. Edwin C. Ochs

Handweaving fundamentals taught here. For day or residential students. Information on request from Mrs. Ochs.

KOGO STUDIO / GALLERY

32 Greene Street
New York, N.Y. 10013
(212) 966-1408

Yoshiko Kogo, also a member of the New School faculty, runs a series of classes in her well-equipped studio/gallery in designing and printing fabrics by hand.

She teaches hand-painting, batik, tie-dye, and block printing on fabric. The classes are offered in monthly sessions beginning on the first Tuesday of each month. Tuition is $30 a month (four sessions, one day per week) including lab fee, excluding individual art supplies such as brushes and fabrics. The $5 registration fee enables you to take any set of classes as many times in a year as you wish without paying a registration fee each time.

THE SPINSTER
34 Hamilton Avenue
Sloatsburg, N.Y. 10974
c/o Ruth Castino
(914) 753-5105
   Ruth Castino teaches spinning in wool, mohair, camelhair, alpaca, silk; and dyeing with flowers, berries, grasses and roots. She also helps you create your own yarns, sells spinning wheels, gives demonstrations, and repairs old spinning wheels. Ms. Castino comes highly recommended by a friend of ours in nearby Pomona, N.Y.

JIM'S STUDIO CRAFTS
121 Decatur Road
Oak Ridge, Tenn. 37830
(615) 483-4148

   This is a small craft school specializing in original textile crafts: knotted, stitched, or woven of natural or synthetic fibers. Owner-instructor James Gentry also offers workshops in macramé techniques. He's a member of the Southern Highland Handicraft Guild and the Foothills Craft Guild.
   For workshop information, and a catalog of macramé supplies, drop a postcard.

THE LOOMERY
201 1st Avenue South
Seattle, Wash. 98109
(206) MA 2-6527
   Sells spinning wheels, looms, etc, and gives instruction in weaving and other yarn crafts.

See also, ARTISAN AND SKILLS CENTERS: Crafts; ARTISAN AND SKILLS NETWORKS: List of Weaving Resources.

ARTISAN AND SKILLS CENTERS:

See also, Bridge Mountain Foundation; Center for Urban Encounter; Cuauhnahuac; Cold Mountain Institute; Cosanti Foundation Workshops; Cowichan Centre for Gestalt Learning; Ft. Wayne Folk School; The McDowell Colony; MEDIA CENTERS; *Moonlighter's Manual;* NEW LEARNING CENTERS; Next Step; Nordenfjord World University (Asgard, Writing Farm); Pendle Hill; Sunrise Hill Free School; Symbas.

GAY LIBERATION CENTERS

THE TANGENT GROUP
3473½ Cahuenga Boulevard
Hollywood, Ca. 90068
(213) 851-4135
  Tangent Group is a counseling and information center on homosexuality. They offer assistance in legal aid and with the draft. They publish, occasionally, *Tangents* magazine, and have a large library on homosexuality that is open for public use, and publish a *Bibliography on Homosexuality* for 25c.

COUNCIL ON RELIGION AND THE HOMOSEXUAL
330 Ellis Street
San Francisco, Ca. 94102
(415) 771-6300
  Part of the Glide Foundation, the Council on Religion and the Homosexual "works to promote dialogue between members of the religious community and homosexuals, in order to bring about new and deeper understandings of sexuality, morality, and ethical behavior. They also work with professionals in the mental health and counseling fields, to broaden their approach to sexuality."

  They have several publications available:
  The Church and the Homosexual, by Donald Kuhn. $1
  Homosexuality: A Contemporary View of the Biblical Perspective, by Rev. Robert L. Treese. 60c
  What It's Like to be a Teen-Age Homosexual, by Charles Thorpe. $1
  Homosexuality and the Sickness Theory, by Louis Crompton. 50c

GAY LIBERATION CENTERS:
See also, Gay Revolutionary Video Project; National Gay Student Center.

GROWTH CENTERS

GESTALT INSTITUTE OF CANADA
Box 779
Chemainus, British Columbia
Canada
(604) 246-3540

The Gestalt Institute of Canada is a community of people living at one end of Kuper Island (Indians live at the other end) and offering three kinds of programs.

Residential training programs: "Three months of communal living and working on our 100-acre farm centre for a limited number of residents and the staff. In this program we hope for more integration between therapy and day-to-day living. We would like people who have had experience in therapy and who have something to give as well as gain from this program. To apply send us a letter about yourself—your background, skills, fantasies of this program—and anything else that will help us to get a sense of you." Cost is $1500, including a nonrefundable deposit of $100; "children can come for the cost of food plus a small equipment fee."

Month-long workshops: "...a variety of experiences, participation in all aspects of community-Gestalt work.... We encourage families to participate together." Cost is $600 per person, same arrangement for children as above. "To apply, send a letter about yourself and a $100 non-refundable deposit."

College House program: "An on-going program for college-age people which combines Gestalt experience with community living. The program includes Gestalt groups, yoga, music, and organic gardening.

"Cost is $125 per month plus cost of food; the program accommodates about 15 people on a space-available basis."

COLD MOUNTAIN

Manson's Landing
Cortes Island, British Columbia
Canada
(605) 935-6317
Also: Box 2884
    Vancouver 3, B.C.
    Canada
    (604) 288-5922

Cold Mountain is "devoted to the exploration and development of human potential." To this end, they offer week-long workshops in such areas as yoga, bioenergetics, self awareness, and experiential living, utilizing both Eastern and Western philosophies and methods. There are also shorter workshops (one to three days) on similar topics.

In addition to programs on Cortes Island and in Vancouver, Cold Mountain provides workshops and consulting services for organizations and schools. A description of the Resident Fellow program:

"The program is planned for ten Resident Fellows who will pay to live, work and learn in the setting of the Cold Mountain community. They will attend workshops listed in the regular schedule and will have available to them the time and experience of the staff and associates-in-residence.

"Areas of the resident fellow program include
— personal growth activities pursued through encounter, gestalt, body awareness and movement, bio-energetics, T'ai Chi Chuan, dance and ritual
— creative endeavors such as crafts, art, music, writing and construction
— sustenance activities as experienced in organic gardening, vegetarian cookery and other life support and survival technniques
— reading and discussion of commentaries related to human growth processes and philosophy. . . .

"Applicants will be accepted without regard to age, sex, or educational background; however, some prior group workshop experience would be helpful. Letters of inquiry and request for application forms should be directed to Jean Weaver, Program Director, at the Cortes Island address."

Workshops require an advance deposit. Prices for week-long workshops are usually $150 and up, though some are lower. Short workshops are much less. Some scholarships are available, primarily for weekend workshops. Participants are also expected to cooperate in such activities as gardening and kitchen work.

centre for gestalt learning

auchinachie road

duncan, b.c., canada

(614) 748-1603
The Centre for Gestalt Learning is located on a converted farm at the base of Prevost Mountain, and conducts seminars and workshops on Gestalt therapy, learning, and awareness. The farm house and outbuildings provide living spaces, and the huge barn is being converted into art studios, a meeting place/ theatre, sauna/bath house, darkroom, graphics area, and bio-analysis laboratory.

"In addition to the Gestalt workshops, the Centre operates as a non-profit society which is devoted to the development of varied innovative programs in cultural, educational, and scientific fields. It is currently constructing the world's first working prototype of a Children's Musical Playground, and plans to offer a summer program incorporating Gestalt and the arts."

The Centre conducts workshops around the U.S. and Canada upon invitation. Length (weekend or longer) and emphasis can be negotiated.

BRIDGE MOUNTAIN FOUNDATION
11780 Alba Road
Ben Lomond, Ca. 95005
(408) 336-5787
Bridge Mountain is located northwest of Santa Cruz in redwood-forested mountains. They offer weekend programs throughout the year, covering every-

thing from the void, doing nothing, wilderness tripping, and self-hypnosis to Gestalt, psychosynthesis, breathing, dance, and encounter. There are also five-day encounter workshops available, and a month-long residence program which includes a bit of everything—Gestalt, hatha yoga, art, wilderness camping, individual sessions.

Weekend workshops go for $30-70. Five-day workshops are $150, and the residence program is a whopping $700. The facilities (including the art facilities) without the programs are available at $12 a day, which covers food and lodging. Participants are expected to help out with household chores at the lodge.

NEW ENGLAND CENTER
Box 575
Amherst, Mass. 01002
(413) 584-0240
The New England Center runs encounter and human potential workshops in many areas, including "Massage Workshops," "Discovering Your Creative Potential," "Being a Woman," "How to be Happily Unmarried," "Sufi Training," and "Being Human in Professional Roles." In an effort to help humanize the nation's schools, they have conducted workshops in affective education all over the country, in the areas of emotional education, self-concept development, value-clarification, education of the self, creativity, and gestalt awareness. The Center's latest developments are a publication series, a gestalt training program, and a Fall, 1972 comprehensive guide to resources for humanizing education.

Rates are $30-$65 for weekend workshops, $5-10 for one-nighters. Scholarships and barter agreements can be arranged.

GROWTH CENTERS:
See also, Adventure Trails Survival School; Bio-Meditation Society; Cultural Integration Fellowship, Inc.; The Life Center.

MEDIA CENTERS

Holography

SCHOOL OF HOLOGRAPHY
454 Shotwell
San Francisco, Ca. 94110
c/o Gerry Cross or Gerry Pethick
(415) 282-6611

Holography is a relatively recent development in optics and media. It is "the first optical process to reconstruct visual reality without stereo-illusion or other optical tricks. A hologram records, stores, and replays a visual scene by high resolution photography of laser beam interference patterns. . . . Whereas a photograph represents an image in a flat, two dimensional space, a hologram presents an object in depth, as it would appear if you were looking at it through a window. . . ."

The School of Holography in San Francisco is the only such place that we know of where anyone can learn about holograms without being a "qualified" research scientist or technician. It was set up in the fall of 1971, "to make information about holography available to the general public and to develop holography as a visual medium. The major activities of the school in the coming year will be the offering of basic and advanced classes in holography, workshops, and a Journal of Holography. Initial facilities of the School include four complete holographic studios and associated equipment, including lasers, optics, viewing areas and darkroom facilities, as well as a permanent exhibit of current work in holography. "Also available are information booklets, notes and bibliography on the subject of holography."

Fees for the basic holography course are $85, which includes a registration fee as well as tuition for six sessions; advanced course in holography costs $100, which includes all chemicals, model shop materials, and a box of 12 test plates.

Class sessions are for four hours over an eight-week period, with classes limited to twelve people.

Photography and Film

THE NEW THING ART AND ARCHITECTURE CENTER
1811 Columbia Road, N.W.
Washington, D.C. 20009
(202) 332-4500

The New Thing offers free community workshops for children and adults on filmmaking, photography, creative writing and graphics. They're a non-profit organization serving the black community in Washington, D.C. as a cultural center and gathering place.

COMMUNITY FILM WORKSHOP
441 North Clark Street
Chicago, Ill. 60610
c/o Jim Taylor
(212) 527-4065

One of several community film and video workshops around the country, the Community Film Workshop offers a rigorous 10-week course in videotape, editing, filmmaking, writing, and technical aspects of media.

Classes are usually kept small, 6 to 8 at a time, and follow a carefully planned program of involvement and learning. Originally set up under an OEO grant, the Workshop now offers access to media to people who otherwise would never be able, for any one of several reasons, "to get their hands on media equipment."

"By the time a student emerges from this 10-week, total immersion in film, he has made both a two-minute black and white, voice-over film and a five-minute, color, synchronized sound one. In the process, he has learned every phase of film production from loading the camera to editing."

Workshop students pay no tuition, admission being determined by a self-eliminating process . . . the only requirement is that learners be present at eight Wednesday evening screening sessions of film history and esthetics.

CENTER FOR PHOTOGRAPHIC STUDIES
131 West Main Street
Louisville, Ky. 40202
(502) 583-5170

A learning center for full-time or part-time photography students, the Center for Photographic Studies describes itself as being "established in the belief that a great many more people should be introduced to the photographic medium, its functions, and how it affects their daily lives."

Their program is offered as a supplement to or an alternative to college study. "A student may enroll in the program for one or more semesters. The curriculum is individually structured for each student depending upon his goals and level of competence. . . . The Center offers no degree nor gives any grade as a matter of basic educational philosophy. Tuition for one semester is $500. Some tuition remission may be possible in exchange for work.

They also offer community workshops in beginning through advanced photography, color photography, workshops for high school students, photo silkscreen, and alternatives to the silver print. Fees range from $25 to $150.

APPALSHOP
Box 743
Whitesburg, Ky. 41858
(606) 663-5708

Appalshop is a group of Appalachian young people who published *Appal Seed*, an Appalachian newspaper that acts as a network/communications tie between groups in Appalachia working for social change, and who offer film courses on a one-to-one basis between those who have made a film and those who want to make one. "We supply the film and equipment, and the student is responsible for gathering whatever he needs to create his film." Priority seems to go to people from Appalachian states, but that's probably not a rigid rule.

Appalshop people also work in videotape, still photography, recording, and media distribution.

"We have completed eight films (about our own area, culture, and heritage) so far, with five more soon to be released—all of which are available for sale or rental. Write to us for *Appalbrochure*, with more information on the workshop, and with list and description of films available." Write c/o Marty Newell, co-ordinator of the shop.

APEIRON WORKSHOPS IN PHOTOGRAPHY
Box 551
Millertown, N.Y. 12456

Apeiron offers nine-day workshops running May through November. Nine days with the "name" photographer of your choice: Les Krims, Danny Lyon, Bruce Davidson, Paul Caponigro, Duane Michals, Emmet Gowin, Linda Conner, Mike Bishop, Frederick Sommer, Jerry Uelsmann, George Tice, Gary Winogrand, and Lee Friedlander. The workshops are held in the foothills of the Berkshire Mountains on a 91-acre farm. The 150-year old barn has been converted into six single-position darkrooms, two film developing rooms, loading closets, wet and dry finishing areas, a print viewing area/classroom, and an exhibition area.

Students live in a new six-bedroom, two-bath dormitory (two to a room) and meals are included in the tuition price. Vegetables for meals are organically grown at Apeiron.

Each workshop is limited to twelve students; admissions will be on a "rolling" or continuous basis. Fees for the nine-day workshops, including darkroom access, living space, meals, bed linens, blankets, and basic photographic materials, are $340. Scholarships are available, based on "cases where creative merit is combined with extraordinary need."

COUNTRY PHOTOGRAPHY WORKSHOP
Woodman, Wisconsin 53827 608-988-5492

c/o Peter Gold

"Country Photography Workshop is a year-round project for teaching photography to those who want to learn it. We approach photography as a language which depends on what you *feel* for its content and expression. We are on a 160-acre farm in southwest Wisconsin's hills, four hours' drive from Chicago.

"Six-day workshops are $150. Weekend sessions are $50. We provide instruction, darkroom facilities, equipment and chemicals, meals, and a place to sleep. "You bring a good attitude, camera, meter, film and paper and personal needs for the week." Instruction at Country Photography Workshop includes "Basic Seeing Workshop" for people "who have been working a little while. We also have Intermediate and Advanced workshops. . . . Our six-day and weekend workshops are very intensive and concentrated. Classes begin at sunrise." They also offer workshops and special rates for school groups.

"The backbone of our teaching is helping you connect with your intuition. Once you make this connection you will find your pictures inside yourself. Our goal is helping you become your own photographer."

Press and Publishing

631 State Street
Santa Barbara, Ca. 93101
c/o Noel Young
(805) 966-4590

Capra
press

A small press that publishes approximately 10 new titles yearly, Capra Press offers apprenticeships. These are very scarce and usually it will be an opening in the bindery part of the press. This is a chance to learn binding by small press methods, not the large machines that bind a book in a wink of an eye.

Capra Press people say, "We like to do things that come through our lives naturally." They print fiction from area authors, as well as some history and culture of the area. They are perhaps best known for their *EST: The Steersman Handbook*.

Write or call before you try to land one of these rare apprenticeships.

TOOLKIT   50c donation
c/o *EdCentric*
Center for Educational Reform
2115 "S" Street, N.W.
Washington, D.C. 20008

EdCentric Magazine describes *Toolkit* in these words: "A tabloid for the media freak-to-be (printed media in this case). Presents in rapid succession 'The Case for an Alternative Press, advice on photography—developing, printing, half-toning and special effects—a rap on the pros and cons of mimeographing versus offset printing, a cartoon lesson on layout, a skeleton for a disorientation catalogue, including information on how to research the power structure of your school or community, and a Help Directory—four pages of national resources in categories such as Appalachia, crafts, legal aid, women, G.I.'S, peace, media, high schools and publications. . . . Helpful production hints are scattered throughout the 20 pages. Wondering about why or how you should do a paper? *Toolkit* should help."

THE GREAT SPECKLED BIRD
Box 7847, Station C
Atlanta, Ga. 30309
(404) 874-1658

The staff of the *Great Speckled Bird*, a weekly radical underground paper, invites Southerners and others interested in learning how to put out an underground paper, to get in touch with them.

"The best way to learn," they say, "is to come and work with us for a while. Training guaranteed in all aspects: business, advertising, circulation, production, layout, and editorial. People can make a sparse living selling the *Bird* (we have no money for salaries).

"If you're interested, write us a letter; after an exchange, we'll know better if we're suited for each other."

RED STAR PRESS
1657 North Halsted
Chicago, Ill. 60614
(312) 642-9284
From time to time this small movement print shop offers workshops in photography and printing. Contact them for dates and places for future workshops.

NEW ENGLAND FREE PRESS
791 Tremont Street
Boston, Mass. 02118
The New England Free Press, a major printer and publisher of Movement literature in the Northeast, has an apprenticeship program for people who are planning to set up movement presses. They ask that you send them a detailed letter explaining why you want to do movement printing and what ideas you have for setting up or working with a movement press. They are accepting people for late fall and winter.

RPM PRINTERS
1355 Williamson Street
Madison, Wisc. 53703
(608) 257-3059
A movement print shop serving the Madison area with all kinds of printing: comix, leaflets, posters, you name it. *Source Catalog* describes them as a "small and busy shop; RPM people try their best to share printing skills with any who are interested."

LIST OF PUBLICATIONS
In addition to the above places that will teach printing, how to run newspapers and movement presses, the following publications may be helpful.
Starting a Community Newspaper   50c
by David Ranson
from: Vocations for Social Change
Canyon, Ca. 94516

How to Put Out Community News   25c
from: Southern Conference Education Fund
3210 West Broadway
Louisville, Ky. 40211

See also, Gay Women's News Service; Organizers Training Program.

Radio

KTAO-FM
5 University Ave.
Los Gatos, Ca. 95030
c/o Lorenzo Milam
(408) 354-6622
If you're interested in setting up a radio station, it can be quite a hassle.

(Have you seen the application for a license?)

However, there is a station that is willing to help new stations set up. They're mentioned in the *Source Catalog* and the *Whole Earth Catalog* as being very willing to help out. They've also put out a book called *Sex and Broadcasting*, which lays out some details on how to set up a station, or how to take over existing ones. Price is $2, plus 15c postage.

"HOW TO BE A ONE-MAN RADIO NEWS NETWORK" $1.35
Mother Earth News (No. 9)
Box 38
Madison, Ohio 44057

Mother Earth News ran a nice article on how to set up your own one-man radio news network. Starting with a good cassette tape recorder, and an induction coil for taping [legally] from telephones, Chuck Crouse turned himself into a stringer for several radio stations. The pay isn't anything to get excited about, but it is adequate to keep you alive.

Crouse's article in *Mother Earth* tells how to set yourself up, where to make contacts, who to sell your service to, and just about everything you need to know.

Some of the advice he offers is sound: Don't be tempted to goof off just because there's no boss; don't take sides in either political or personality disputes; be prepared to be treated as a secondclass newsman for a while; and so forth.

AQUARIAN RESEARCH FOUNDATION
5640 Morton
Philadelphia, Pa. 19144
(215) 849-3237

The Aquarian Research Foundation encourages the development of "block radio stations." Basically, block radio is a local station that operates without an FCC license (legally) within a given area, using carrier current to get the signal out. The equipment is commercially available at reasonable rates.

The idea is to get neighbors, kids, parents listening to one another. It provides everyone in the community a chance to put their programs on the air without the "approved" viewpoint that is broadcast on commercial radio.

Contact Aquarian Research Foundation for information on equipment needed, and for details on how to do it.

Recording

ASSOCIATED RECORDING STUDIOS
723 Seventh Avenue
New York, N.Y. 10019
(212) CI 5-7640

A forty-hour course on "contemporary record production techniques" is offered by Associated Recording Studios in New York City.

For a fee of $250 Associated teaches a complete course in professional record production, covering both technical and creative procedures. They describe their course as offering "a fundamental knowledge of the tools of the trade . . . Until now, such information has been obtainable only in round-about ways, such as watching others or through costly and time-consuming 'trial and error' methods. . . . This course provides a practical alternative. . . . The objective of each twenty-session class will be to produce, from start to finish two stereophonic master recordings, or the equivalent of the 'A' and 'B' sides of a 45 rpm single. Whenever possible, original material and performers will be selected from members of the class, providing students with experience on both sides of the glass." Classes will be limited to a maximum of 20 students.

Video

COMMUNITY ACCESS/VIDEO $3
by H. Allen Fredricksen
695 30th Avenue
Apt. E
Santa Cruz, Ca. 95060

This is one of the key resources for video in the community. In five chapters, beginning with video hardware and how to use it, through how to distribute your information, to forming a non-profit video corporation, Fredricksen leads the beginner as well as the "pro" through some of the intricacies of "media by the people" and standard commercial pablum media. A *Whole Earth Catalog* format size, the $3 is well spent for this publication.

Areas of information covered include: video hardware techniques and format; editing; sources of begging, borrowing or buying video equipment; cable television; closed circuit systems; video-to-film transfer; tape exchanges and network broadcast; free your local cable for alternate programming; city council and cable franchises; forming your own non-profit corporation for $20; economic survival with video; video porn for fun and profit; Santa Cruz community service tv project; and more, more, more.

GAY REVOLUTIONARY VIDEO PROJECT
Box 410, Old Chelsea Station
New York, N.Y. 10011
(212) 237-1049

From *Vocations for Social Change* (now *WorkForce*): "The Project is presently a group of gay males in NYC exploring gayness through video; open to gay women interested in working with or separate from us. We are involved in making tapes that can be shown to other people in the gay community, and to accompany gay liberation speakers going to colleges and other speaking engagements. Future plans include organizing a gay revolutionary speakers bureau, and a group to prepare and distribute printed material and graphics relevant to gay struggle. We are non-profit, tax-exempt."

MEDIA CENTERS:
See also, Aquarius Project.

MISCELLANEOUS CENTERS

WILLIAM BUTLER YEATS SUMMER SCHOOL
c/o Yeats Society
Sligo, Ireland
c/o Mrs. Kathleen Moran, Secretary
　　The Yeats Summer School, in its fourteenth year, is "a living memorial to William Butler Yeats. It provides lectures, seminars and discussions of Anglo-Irish literature, emphasizing the work of Yeats but also dealing with other Irish writers, past and present. Performances of Yeat's plays, as well as excursions and visits to the places of interest in the Yeats Country are arranged, and there are formal and informal poetry readings."
　　Lectures and seminars are held in the morning and in the evenings. Tuition is $55, and some of the planned excursions and entertainments are extra, with the highest priced one in their catalog being £1.20. Housing is available in Sligo at prices ranging from $38 a week in a hotel, to rooms in guest houses at approximately $3.50 per day including breakfast, to private homes with breakfast for approximately $3 a day.

cuauhnahuac

Avenida Morelos Sur 712
Apartado 140
Cuernavaca, Morelos
Mexico

instituto colectivo de lengua y cultura

　　A language and Latin American studies center, Cuauhnahuac was founded in 1972 for the purpose of Spanish language instruction and the "exploration of cultural and political problems in Mexico and Latin America."
　　Founded by 15 language instructors who were "refugees" from another language school in Cuernavaca and from CIDOC, Cuauhnahuac is set up as a collective and is "dedicated to work with the Mexican community in a form of mutual cooperation and aid. . . . We are constantly endeavoring to augment our regular program of Spanish instruction with activities, discussions, and programs" with the Mexican community in Cuernavaca, and to enable the student to see the "social ambiguities" which permeate Cuernavaca, a large cosmopolitan city with a large foreign population and with a great contrast between the socio-economic classes and the ways in which they live.
　　"In Cuauhnahuac, you can study Spanish intensively, five hours daily, five days a week, Monday through Friday. Programs are designed for all levels—beginning, intermediate, and advanced, with specially constructed programs available. Classes are composed of no more than four students." Tuition is $112. Classes are offered year-round.
　　Cuauhnahuac offers a limited number of scholarships for persons of Latin-American descent. The Institute can help arrange housing in Cuernavaca, either with a Mexican family or in an apartment or bungalow. (*See also*, Centro Intercultural de Documentacion).

CALIFORNIA INSTITUTE OF ASIAN STUDIES
3494 21st Street
San Francisco, Cal. 94110
c/o P. Ghose, Registrar
(415) 648-1489

At the Institute of Asian Studies, Asian scholars teach and conduct research under three broad headings: area studies (including Far and Middle East, and South Asia); comparative studies (East and West); and integral philosophy and psychology, emphasizing the integral fullness of man.

"Course offerings include various Asian languages such as Sanskrit, Chinese, Japanese, Arabic, Bengali, Hindi, Punjabi; Zen, various yoga systems, meditation workshop, Tibetan mysticism, research in the Psychophysiology of Peak Experiences relating to Kundalini, authentic Self, Being, etc."

Degree programs (M.A. and Ph.D. are the only degrees offered) are supervised by Dr. Haridas Chaudhuri, professor of comparative philosophy and president of the Institute, and author of *Integral Yoga, Philosophy of Integralism*, and other books. Persons with special interest in Asian studies are welcomed, as well as students working on advanced degrees. Tuition for full-time students (14-16 units) is $300 a quarter; part-time students, $22.50 per unit. Students not working for advanced degrees are welcome as auditors at a 10% discount. *(See also,* Cultural Integration Fellowship, Inc.)

THE MACDOWELL COLONY

Peterborough, N.H. 03458
c/o Conrad Spohnholz
(603) 924-3886, 924-3563

This is a colony/retreat for painters, writers, sculptors, and composers in the "wilds" of New Hampshire. "To give painters, sculptors, and other artists an opportunity to pursue their projects under working conditions far better than they would normally find elsewhere is the simple function of the McDowell Colony.

"Established artists with projects requiring concentrated attention for one to four months will, in general, find acceptance whenever vacancies allow. Young artists who have done enough work to achieve reputations in a discriminating if limited circle are equally eligible. There is no 'community life' at the McDowell Colony beyond what an individual wishes to create for himself. Painters and sculptors may, if they wish, have breakfast and dinner in the central dining room with other artists; they are free not to. The midday meal is sent to the studios."

The Colony takes thirty painters, sculptors, writers, and composers during the summer and half this number at other times. Their fee is $35 per week, which covers room, studio, and meals. Some fellowships are available.

There are no accommodations for families at the Colony. Applications for the summer months have a February 15 deadline. An application at least 90 days in advance is required for other seasons. Each person accepted by the Colony has his own studio, a room in one of the residences, and in some cases he may be given a separate cottage equipped both as a residence and studio. Each artist has exclusive use of his studio while at the Colony.

SIGHT POINT INSTITUTE
Box 1156
Reed College
Portland, Ore. 97202
c/o Alan Walworth

Sight Point Institute is an "experimental summer community of scholars . . . intended as a realization of Einstein's dream of an 'island for those who are wise and of good will.'"

The Institute is located in tents and cabins on the Coast of Nova Scotia in Canada, and activities include conversation, seminars, informal seminars, or formal classes designed by the participants.

"Rapport among the participants is facilitated by the small size and communal lifestyle of the Institute." Previous summer groups have undertaken projects and studies in areas such as psychology, creative writing, philosophy, and Russian language instruction. "When not studying, participants took advantage of the opportunity provided by the locale to engage in such activities as observing schools of small whales at close range. . . , examining tidal life, fishing and gardening." The focus of any given moment is what the group or members of the community decide that they want to undertake, whether it be study or conversation or work.

Costs are $180 for the full ten weeks; those who bring their own tent (one large enough to live and study in for a summer) get a discount. The general fee covers the cost of food; it does not cover such things as clothing costs, medical insurance, etc. It is strongly advised that each member of the summer Institute bring approximately $100 in addition to the $180 fee. Write to Alan Walworth for complete details. (*See also*, Mountain Institute for Man)

NEW-LEARNING CENTERS

Ontario College of Art

100 McCAUL STREET, TORONTO 2B, ONTARIO, CANADA

(416) 366-4977

"A number of concerned people here at Ontario College of Art are embarking on a living-learning probe called 'Life, Institute for Environmental Forces and Alternate Structures.' Several experiments have been going on this year from our school; building our own structures and participating in survival and basic living experiences from rural Ontario to Andros Island, Bahamas. This probe will be one of researching information through mobile units all over the world from groups already experimenting with alternate structures and life forces. . . ."

"Our terms of reference are: free schools, housing, food, education, communication, science, ecology, world thinking, philosophy, awareness, systems and modes, design, growth."

VOYAGE OF THE WET ORCHID
Ontario College of Art
100 McCaul Street
Toronto 2B, Ontario
Canada
c/o Frank Ogden
(416) 920-1670

"A 'learning adventure experience' held aboard a 60' sailing yacht cruising the Caribbean.

"Groups of ten students at a time will be making six-week Trans-Cultural Probes into 25 countries in and surrounding the Caribbean attempting to utilize 'cultural shock' as an immunization process against 'future shock.' Five such expeditions will be carried out between the Fall of 1972 and the Summer of 1973. While under sail students will in effect 'man the ship', standing sea watches, learning navigation, seamanship, meteorology, oceanography, etc. Also while aboard, language instruction in the tongue of the next culture to be visited will be carried out on a 'total immersion' basis, i.e., only the language of that culture will be spoken aboard ship. While ashore, participation in local cultures in art, social, economic, technological and cultural spheres will be carried out. Scuba diving, underwater photography and videotaping will also be utilized in 'under water classrooms' where advantageous. (Example: Andros Island barrier reef.)

"Cost of 'scholarships' per student for each six-week period will be $1150, including room and board aboard ship. Students also provide their own method of getting to the varying embarkation points. Passports, visas, full innoculations, etc. have to be provided by all participants. Age limit: 18 up. (U.S. citizens may anticipate some hassle on trips destined for Cuba and some other locations). Contact Frank Ogden for scholarship information.

NORDENFJORD WORLD UNIVERSITY
Admissions Office
Skyum Bierge
7752 Snedsted
Thy, Denmark
Tel (07-935111) Koldby 234

Nordenfjord World University is a cluster of experimental learning centers located on the peninsula of Jutland. New Experimental College, the oldest, was established in 1962, and the others have grown/are growing up since. All the centers are small (about 25 students), in farm or rural settings.

A curriculum evolves for each term through the interests of the participating students and teachers (who also pay to participate). "Every aspect of life is utilized as a vehicle for learning including independent studies, community responsibilities, seminars, 'Ting' meetings called by student/faculty and regular weekly presentations to the community."

A book on the first seven years of New Experimental College, written by its founder, is recommended, for anyone interested in attending:

Lust for Learning, by Aage Rosendal Nielsen $5
NEC Press   7752 Snedsted
Skyum   Denmark

Sketches of the centers are presented below.

Asgard
Ydby
7760 Hurup
Thy, Nordenfjord
Denmark
"The name means 'home of the gods' in old Nordic terms, and the place is an arts and crafts center which 'stresses the philosophy of freedom and informality in teaching and learning' through the media of ceramics, textiles, weaving, leathercraft, woodworking, plastic and fiberglass construction and metalwork."

New Experimental College
Skyum Bjerge
7752 Snedsted
Thy, Nordenfjord
Denmark   .
"The three-fold situation at NEC of creating one's education, evolving an idea and a practice of community, and becoming an institution for oneself generates a process of examination and unfolding. When ventured, it places 'demand' in the air—a demand for mutual efforts in our lives and which gives us confidence in our ability to make of the world what we want it to be."

NEC has a "desire to communicate with people who are ready to make a commitment both to a consistent and continuing pursuit of their studies and to the development of a community in which the mutuality of such an approach to life-work is nurtured. Everyone else, all those who are looking for what is *offered* at different places, we need to discourage, for their sake and ours."

Nordenfjord Højskole
Gaerup
7752 Snedsted
Thy, Nordenfjord
Denmark
A Danish Folkehøjskole (High school) was also started in conjunction with Nordenfjord World University. The language in usage at the højskole, however, is Danish, and therefore only Danish-speaking persons are encouraged to join in this program on a full-time basis.

Praestegaard
Kettrup
9690 Fjerritslev
Han Nerred, Nordenfjord
Denmark

Praestegaard is a 200-year-old "priest's farm" where director David J. Nelson lives with his wife, two sons, a new daughter, two golden retrievers, and a black cat named Sarah. It is also "an educational community of both students and teachers whose interest and work in film and photography provide the common ground for our coming together, to learn the craft, to discover the vision, to put it together, and see it relate to the life and living that we dare to pursue. Each semester we are an average of ten people to make up the basic working group which includes both beginners and working professionals. . . .

"Our working facilities include two fully equipped photographic laboratories, shooting studio, lighting equipment and work rooms. Technical facilities are such as to encourage work in large format photography as well as 35mm. . . . Our film facilities include 16mm camera and sound equipment. General production facilities at Praestegaard are limited and it is necessary to go outside for sound editing facilities. . . . It is hoped that part of the focus of creative filmmaking will include concentration on creating new possibilities and methods which can overcome the economical limitations which have given us a great many 'students' of film, but proportionately few film makers."

Fees at Praestegaard are $960 per semester, which cover room, board, and tuition as well as health insurance which is effective seven weeks after your arrival. The summer fee is cheaper: $520. The calendar of semesters at Praestegaard starts with a fall semester in September, a spring semester in February, and the summer semester begins in July.

Writing Farm
14 B Hundborg
7700 Thisted
Thy
Denmark

Another unit of Nordenfjord World University, the Writing Farm does all its work in English, with a little Danish thrown in. There is a core of five adults and one baby who compose the Writing Farm, and they describe themselves like this:

"We live in Denmark in a house in the country where you can see a long way, where it is usually peaceful. . . . We are in the process of saying what we mean. We are students of literature. We like to write: poems, stories, journals, plays, letters, novels, each in our own style, well. We are all creative. We are not to be defined. We paint. We play music. We talk. We attempt to share our work. We speak some Danish. We learn. We are open. We fall down. We feel as artists we are living the challenging life.

"If you come to live, we would like you to have work to do in writing or the study of literature, to feel that you are capable of doing your own work for yourself, to share yourself communally, to like being alone sometimes, to be able to see yourself and your work inspired, enhanced or given meaning through living in a house with ten other writers, to have not stopped asking questions about yourself, to affect our lives and take responsibility for the quality of your work, your life, during the time spent with us.

"We don't know you at all. If you come, we would like you to send us a portfolio of your writing. It will cost you $150 a month for room, board, and tuition. If you come, we shall expect you to stay at least two months. The longer you stay, the less it will cost per month."

Other centers at Nordenfjord are:
Susan Herman   (Yoga)
Skyum
7752 Snedsted
Thy, Nordenfjord
Denmark

Herb Rosenbaum   (Physics)
Englholm
Visby
7760 Hurup
Thy, Nordenfjord
Denmark

Ronald Manheimer   (Philosophy)
Overlund
Gaerup
7752 Snedsted
Thy, Nordenfjord
Denmark

"Exchanges between centers are possible within the semester with the agreement of the centers concerned. Moreover Nordenfjord also utilizes other farms in the vicinity, and some associated groups and individuals welcome student/faculty into their projects.

"An ecologically oriented magazine with poetry, writings, and items of interest is also a source of information about Nordenfjord. Write:
   Physiognomy $10/year
   c/o New Experimental College

THE WILDERNESS SCHOOL
6996 Mission Street
Daly City, Ca. 94014
c/o Bill Curran or Reno Taini
   "The Wilderness School is a public school alternative for high school kids in Daly City and a model-in-development of deschooled environmental education for kids everywhere. We use nature—rugged wilderness areas all over California—to learn about responsibility, decision-making and commitment; and the city—supermarkets, door-to-door, city hall—to put our lessons to work. Our kids are working class, white, black, and brown. Our environment is a sprawling, decaying mess ridiculed everywhere as a 'ticky-tacky dump.'
   "Our basic philosophy is doing. We are not a free school; there is structure, pushing, and many decisions are made by our staff. Our projects and goals are real. We try to stop billboard construction, overdevelopment, and pollution; we work at making city hall and developers more responsible; we inform ordinary citizens of environmental threats; we run a three-acre organic farm, and work closely with other Bay Area ecology groups.
   "Our program is staffed by six people—three credentialed teachers, two paraprofessionals just out of high school, and a media specialist. We take 20 kids

out of traditional school full time for a semester, returning 15 and keeping 5 on to help the next group. We are presently funded by grants from the Office of Environmental Education and the Gerbode Foundation. Next year we intend to expand our operation and run a teacher training program, with kids, for an entire district so they can set up their own wilderness schools.''

Deganawidah-Quetzalcoatl University

Post Office Box 409
Davis, California   95616
916-758-0470

A university dedicated to the progress of the Native American and Chicano people, DQU "is a new institution of higher education, established in 1970 (on the site of a former Army base/648-acre campus) . . . Indians and Chicanos have considered the wisdom of initiating higher education programs designed to meet the needs of the people. DQU is a direct outgrowth of that concern.

"Any student who is eighteen years of age or older or who is no longer required to attend public school is eligible for admission to DQU . . . students will be admitted to the school on the first Monday of each month during the regular school year. . . . Only pass and superior will be entered in the student's record. DQU will not record any other grade or mark." Tuition fees are $20 per unit for full-time and part-time students.

Medical services, living accommodations, cafeteria and library services are available at DQU.

Course offerings include all the things you would expect to find in a university, plus courses that reflect and meet the needs of Native Americans and Chicanos: introductory Navajo, agricultural marketing, farm organization, Native American art workshop, Indians and literature, Native American music and dance, Southwest religion and philosophy, introduction to Chicano history, Chicano political thought, Chicano literature, the education of Chicano children, and the Chicano in social institutions. And more. The University is on its way to becoming accredited, and work done at DQU will transfer to other universities. They have a catalog of information and course listings.

SYMBAS
One
1380 Howard Street
San Francisco, Ca. 94103

"Symbas exists primarily for individuals 14 to 18 who want to assume major responsibility for their own learning.

"Symbas is housed in ONE, a recycled warehouse containing everything from computer technicians to rock musicians. People of ONE share skills and information with Symbas, and during the past year offered instruction, training, and sometimes employment in such diverse areas as: printing, carpentry, batik, French and Spanish, physics, holography, Elizabethan drama, wiring, music, encounter groups, environmental studies, dance and massage. At noon each

Monday the school meets to determine policy and schedule curricula. Outside ONE, we have the Bay Area for coursework at Sonoma State College, walking the streets of the city, working with the New Shakespeare Company and backpacking at Point Reyes National Forest.

"Symbas is open all year long; individuals may join at any time. There are no requirements for admission beyond an expression of interest." Symbas offers a high school diploma; a monthly tuition of ten dollars or more is suggested.

ADVENTURE TRAILS SURVIVAL SCHOOL
Laughing Coyote Mountain
Black Hawk, Colo. 80422
c/o T.D. Lingo

T.D. Lingo describes his program at the Adventure Trails Survival School as: "A teacher training center for those interested in starting their own Homestead Schools. Teaching neural cybernetics: brain self control. Forward searching to discover the most efficient ways of circuiting into dormant frontal lobes. Basic physics and chemistry of neurology extrapolated into demonstrable measurable/predictable increase of primary creative production.

"Quite simply, the word psyche is out; the word brain is in. From now on the objective scientific method of inquiry is irrevocably harmonized with the science of subjective experiencing."

The name comes from T.D. Lingo's statement: "The Trail is Life. The Survival is the moral imperative: know thyself. Nature in the mountains is merely the most effective catalyst to help the still-curious individual reduce himself to his first principles."

Tuitions vary "all the way from nothing to much," depending on the ability to pay. "Those that are genuinely bold and visionary will write and get our secondary and tertiary mimeo sheets—which will either scare them off or bring them in."*(See also*, Bio-Meditation Society)

WINDSOR LEARNING COMMUNITY
309 S.E. 7th Street
Gainesville, Fla. 32601
(904) 378-8486

Windsor Learning Community is just that: not a school, but a group of people who choose to come together to pursue their own individual learning interests. A participant is expected to set his own learning priorities as soon as possible, with other group members as resource people, and to commit as much energy, time, money, and other resources as he chooses. The life of the community is expected to develop organically, without "frozen" curricula or statements of expectation.

There are no age boundaries, but at this point the core group prefers not to be bound by the needs of caring for many small (5-9) children. Families with young children may, however, work out ways to be related to the community.

Learning environments will include natural surroundings as well as buildings, and the Windsor community is working out exchange programs with other
learning communities and apprenticeships within the Gainesville community.

FT. WAYNE FOLK SCHOOL
Box 681
Fort Wayne, Ind. 46801
c/o Terry Doran
(219) 742-1241

The Fort Wayne Folk School is modeled after the 19th century Danish folk
schools, and is set up both as an alternative high school and community learning
opportunity open to anyone, regardless of age. The Danish Folk Schools had
three basic principles adhered to by the Ft. Wayne people. The Schools are:
open to anyone; governed from within by the exercise of willing consent; and
not authoritarian diploma-granting. Fees for classes are based on the student's
ability to pay, and courses "among the 33 offered include art, daydreaming
workshop, life style for survival, math, Spanish, chemistry, astrology, music,
outdoor thinking, occult sciences, history, etc., etc." They also offer speakers
and workshops and conduct weekly discussion programs called Theatre for
Ideas featuring speakers on many topics. All teachers at the Folk School are
volunteers.

They also publish a newsletter and a magazine, *Return to Learning*. Single
copies are 50c.

THE UNIVERSITY FOR MAN
615 Fairchild Terrace
Manhattan, Ks. 66502
(913) 532-6442

This is the free university for the Manhattan area. It's been around for quite
a few years and is a stable, healthily happy place to be. Some of the people
running it have come from other parts of the country to help with it. (They even
got written up in the *New Yorker*.)

Courses offered are, of course, free, and there are no grades, and the
prerequisites are simply that you make the effort to participate. No age limits.
Topics listed in their latest catalog include everything from decoupage to dog
obedience, to theatre workshops to the art of jello making to gay consciousness
to basic guitar to organic farming, to God the father, to international folk dancing . . . and so much more.

Write for a catalog. (Send a donation to cover mailing.) It's fun to read even
if you're not in the area. It's also a good model.

CFC Campus-Free College
466 Commonwealth Ave. Boston MA 02215

Campus-Free College is an on-the-way-to-being-accredited liberal arts college with a unique and radical structure. Without campus or buildings, CFC
consists of a home-base group of administrators and 180 Program Advisors in
about 100 cities and towns in the U.S. and Canada. A student works on a one-

to-one basis with an advisor who is accessible to him (usually living nearby, but not necessarily) to work out the kind of educational program in which he's interested, using the resources at hand (institutions, people, apprenticeships, etc.). At the end of the course of study, the work is evaluated by the student, his teacher or evaluator, advisor, and the CFC Academic Council.

The student pays $250 to $750 a year (or $260 on a quarterly basis) to the college to pay for administration and advising services. He then contracts individually with other teachers/instructors/masters/trainers as necessary. The college may grant its own degree and/or affiliate with accredited institutions. Dual enrollment for high school students who wish to get college credit for CFC work may be arranged on an individual basis. A letter to the college address will get you information on how to get in touch with a Program Advisor, and the latest news of what's going on.

P.S. Graduate studies may be possible soon.

RAVEN INSTITUTE
21 Eighth Avenue
New York, N.Y. 10014

"Raven was started . . . by a group of people who had run a hostel for runaways at Judson Church. At present Raven includes half a dozen students, a full-time teacher in the city and a full-time teacher in the country (in a school-run cabin in Woodstock), a psychiatrist, a director, and many part-time tutors. We are open five days a week from 11-4.

"Each student makes his own program from resources in four general areas: academic tutoring, crafts and artwork, the country, and facilities and people located near the school. For instance, one student's program includes an apprenticeship to a veterinarian, classes outside the school in baking and macrobiotic cooking, classes in the school of English, biology and the occult, and a part-time babysitting job.

"Many of our students have had trouble with their families and their schools. Some were living dangerously. We are aware of this, and we are not interested in supporting crazy behavior. We are not a hospital, a drug program, or a therapeutic community. We are a group of people who are a part of the school reform movement and who want very much to give high school kids a chance to learn what they are interested in, in their own way."

pendle hill WALLINGFORD PENNSYLVANIA
338 Plush Mill Road
(215) 566-4507   19086

"Pendle Hill has been called an adult school, a folk school, an enlarged family, a Quaker type of monastery, an ashram, an intentional community, a watch tower, an energizing center, a haven of rest, a school of the prophets, a laboratory of ideas, a fellowship of cooperation. . . . Pendle Hill gives no grades, or examinations, offers no degrees nor is the element of competition present at any point."

Named after an actual hill in the north of England which was notorious for its witches, it is also the hill upon which a young English shoemaker and shepherd climbed in 1652. George Fox, the "founder" of Quakerism, had a vision of a great company of people waiting on that hilltop.

Pendle Hill offers seminars year-round for resident guests, courses for non-resident guests, and free public lectures, among their other programs. The actual "plant" of Pendle Hill is a large, high-ceilinged, stone Pennsylvania country house.

Courses and seminars at Pendle Hill, which have been going on since the 1930's, include topics such as illness and healing, leisure, contemplation and involvement, creative dance workshops, techniques of centering, mysticism east and west, crafts, Quakerism past and present, poetry, tales of the Hasidim, life styles, art of India, China and Japan, love, and many, many more.

Costs are from $850 to $2,200, including room, board, and tuition for each 11 weeks. Considering the quality of the seminars, the warm supporting environment of Pendle Hill, and the marvelous people one meets here, the price is very reasonable.

A QUAKER CENTER FOR STUDY AND CONTEMPLATION

NETHERS COMMUNITY SCHOOL
Box 41
Woodville, Va. 22749
(703) 987-9011

Nethers Community School is located on a 27-acre spread in the Blue Ridge Mountains, where community members farm (organically), learn, and are slowly building their own facilities. They are a "magical blend" of community and school, where students "are free to decide how to spend their time, whether to work on a community project, study, go to a class or a tutorial, do programmed materials, or apprentice themselves to a community member who has enough self discipline to be striving towards excellence in his own thing—be it learning Yoga, carpentry, poetry, music or dance." Room, board, and tuition are $2500 for the year, $1600 for one semester, for students between 11 and 18. Admission is by personal interview.

In addition, some community members live at Nethers year-round. "For community members we want people who have skills to offer, preferably a combination of teaching and practical skills. Some of the skills we need right now are piano, dance, math, science, voice, and history teachers, auto mechanics, construction, electrical work, organic gardening, and a business manager. People who wish to join should first come and visit, and then there is a three month probationary period. We ask $180 for the first three months. . . .

"We also want people who will work with us toward Future Village, a social experiment in which a thousand poor people will step out of poverty, and demonstrate the potential in our society of abundance for the traditional link between work and income to be separated. Arrangements to visit must be made in advance. People are asked to stay a week, either as hard working guests ($17.50 per week) or vacation guests ($50 per week)."

SUNRISE HILL FREE SCHOOL
Route 3, Box 70
Davenport, Wa. 99122

"Sunrise Hill Free School is an attempt to make learning a foremost activity for people of any age in a rural, anarchistic, intentional community. The community, founded in 1963, is called Tolstoy Farm. It comprises 200 acres located in a beautiful rugged canyon in Eastern Washington, and it is in the midst of the multi-leveled Columbia River Basin, a region of hot summers and cold winters. Last year about 20 adults and 20 children were involved with school projects. . . . riding, gardening, yoga instruction, block printing on textiles, wild food gathering, auto mechanics, etc.; construction projects; and curriculum planning for the coming year, mathematics, art, science, social studies, literature, creative writing, and many other subjects. . . .

"It is up to the individual teachers and students to decide what and how they will teach and learn. School policies are decided by consensus rather than by majority, in open meetings of the people involved. Here, an abundance of disagreement provides an appreciation for the difficulties and for the dynamics of social intercourse. One thing we are definitely learning is an awareness of the diverse nature of individuals."

There is room for a few boarding students, who live in the homes of Tolstoy Farm families. One source of income for the Farm is from the sale of leathercrafts, from sandals to Sioux Indian saddles, available through the *Community Market Catalog.*

NEW-LEARNING CENTERS:

See Also, Aegina Arts Centre; Centro Intercultural de Documentacion; Community Improvement Through Youth; Creative Arts School of Shasta at Artaud; The Free Learning Projects; *Free University Catalog;* Greenerfields Unlimited; Innisfree; Institute Mountain West; LEARNING EXCHANGES; Liberation School for Women; The Life Center; Los Llanos; New Thing Art and Architecture Center; Next Step; North American Student Co-operative Organization; Pacific Studies Center; Roots, Inc.; South Shore Community High School; Third World Awareness Workshops; Urbanzai Multi-Versity.

OUTDOORS CENTERS

Horsing Around

ESCUELA ECUESTRE, S.M.A.
Apartado y 185
San Miguel de Allende
Guanajuato, Mexico
    This riding school, located in one of Mexico's most fantastic small towns, offers intensive riding instruction under the supervision of Mexican cavalry officers. Instruction includes theory, dressage, cross country, and jumping. Classes are designed for beginners, intermediates, and professionals.
    Although one can live cheaply in Mexico (without Hiltons and American food), this place looks like it might be expensive. But it's probably no more than a similar course in the U. S. and if you are going to spend the money, why not spend it in Mexico?

North Texas Horse Clinic
Box 666
Mineral Wells, Texas 76067
(817) 325-5202
    A two-week clinic for horse owners and anyone working with horses. "The facts, as taught at the Clinic are not just some fine-spun theories; these are the result of practical knowledge gained in a lifetime study by a person . . . who is devoted to the most useful and beautiful creation in all Creation—the horse." The clinic concentrates on correcting faults of "problem horses", including: biting, shying, kicking, balking, hard to shoe, hard to mount, and hard to bridle; as well as how to throw a horse, how to use and rig a hackamore, and how to gain the confidence of the horse, etc.
    The clinic is held on the Seybold Ranch near Mineral Wells, Texas, and the all-inclusive fee of $400 covers room, all meals, lectures, use of all equipment, private conferences, use of horses, and privileges of future consulation at no cost. (*See also*, North Texas Farrier School)

NORTH TEXAS FARRIERS SCHOOL
Box 666
Mineral Wells, Texas 76067
(817) 325-5202
    The art of shoeing horses isn't dead as more and more people now own horses for leisure and recreation. The North Texas Farriers School offers a two-week course in the basics of shoeing. "This school was founded so that a sincerely interested person could learn the very best methods of correct horseshoeing in the least possible time consistent with perfect workmanship."

"After long years of experience teaching this course, we here at the School have found that if a student is conscientious and a hard worker, if he can use his hands and mind, he can become well-grounded in the farrier trade in the short space of two weeks. Long and more expensive courses are unnecessary. The two weeks period spent at the North Texas Farriers School is highly concentrated, streamlined, but the student must be willing to spend ten to twelve hours a day either in the classroom discussion periods, or in actual work at the forges or on the horses' feet.

"The North Texas Farriers School is held at the Seybold Ranch, near Mineral Wells, Texas. Accommodations are in comfortable rooms with bath overlooking the patio and pool. All meals are served in the main dining room.

"The all-inclusive fee of $400 a person covers all instruction, lectures, private conferences, forge work, use of all tools and equipment, room accommodation and all meals. There are no hidden charges."

Outdoor Living and Survival Training

MAN AND HIS ENVIRONMENT
Long Bay, Virgin Gorda,
British Virgin Islands
c/o Kenneth Webb

This is living/learning set-up like the world's greatest summer camp, specifically geared for people who would like to take a year out between high school and college, or during college. Participants live in a tropical setting which provides opportunities for challenging involvement with all aspects of the environment—hiking, organic farming, navigation, scuba diving, laying an underwater trail, building and construction, and interaction with the friendly natives.

A typical day is scheduled something like this: up at 5:30, heavy work, breakfast around 8, light work, swimming, siesta—relaxing, reading, etc.—water activities, supper, reading and informal self-organized learning activities or entertainment, to bed by 10. A schedule designed for physical, intellectual, spiritual, and social development.

It costs $1000, $50 of it with the application. Information is available from the above address, or from Kenneth B. Webb, Plymouth Union, Vt. 05057 (802) 422-3444.

AMERICAN RIVER TOURING ASSOCIATION
1016 Jackson
Oakland, Ca. 94607
(800) 227-0477 (toll-free)

The American River Touring Association is a nonprofit educational association which operates raft tours on several U.S. rivers, including the Colorado. Accomodations range from five-man oar-powered rafts to motor-powered 15-man carriers which make eight-day trips through the Grand Canyon. Tours include four or five hours a day on the raft, with the rest of the day spent ashore, hiking, sightseeing, etc. You sleep ashore, and either bring your own camping gear or rent it from the association. You can walk around the rapids if the going gets too rough.

Costs are $200 for a five-day oar-powered tour, going up to $350 for the eight-day Grand Canyon trip. Costs are reduced in the fall, near the end of the river season.

Other places with river touring information:

Canyonlands Expeditions	Utah Travel Council
P.O. Box 21021	Capitol Hill
Salt Lake City, Utah 84121	Salt Lake City, Utah 84114

(*See also*, Lute Jerstad Adventures; Outward Bound, Inc.)

INNISFREE

c/o Leinbach Educational Projects, Inc.
1039 Olivia
Ann Arbor, Mich. 48104
(313) 665-7179

Located in 200 acres of hills, fields and forests on a high bluff overlooking Lake Michigan on the Leelanau Peninsula in northern Michigan, Innisfree offers several options: for older teenagers, a family camp, a camp for girls, an ecology program, and a western wilderness trip for girls. They take their name from the poem *The Lake of Isle of Innisfree* by W. B. Yeats:

I will arise and go now, and go to Innisfree,
And I shall have some peace there, for peace comes dropping slow
. . . for always night and day
I hear lake water lapping with low sounds by the shore;
While I stand on the roadway, or on the pavements gray,
I hear it in the deep heart's core.

Innisfree "provides a place where people can be refreshed in spirit and learn to care more about themselves, others, and the land." A privately owned camp, Innisfree is available to families, individuals and rental groups from 10 to 100 in size. Meals are served at the main lodge, and living quarters are in frame, screened cabins with beds (you bring your own sleeping bag or linen).

Costs range from $15 per week for children 2 to 5, to $60 per week for adults in the family camp; other programs, including the ecology program, have different fee schedules.

LUTE JERSTAD ADVENTURES
9920 S. W. Terwilliger Boulevard
Portland, Ore. 97219

We found these folks in *The First New Earth Catalog*, and here's what they said: "A group of people who organize and guide outdoor expeditions. They have a heavy emphasis on climbing. A rock climbing seminar is offered at the Mount Hood School of Mountaineering, with ice climbing and rescue classes also offered.

"Their 'excursions' are offered in the Northwest and also in places like up Mt. Kilimanjaro (Africa) or trekking around in the Himalayas. For non-climbers they have a variety of canoeing and rafting trips, including some very heavy rapid shooting.

"Fees run from $30 a day for a one-day learning canoe trip to the Kilimanjaro thing at $1975 (including air fare). All in all the fees are reasonable and the whole thing is a good program."

OUTWARD BOUND, INC.
Reston, Va. 22070
(703) 437-5454

There are Outward Bound Schools worldwide, with seven in the U. S. They are based on the premise that man is part of nature and they push us civilized creatures far past our self-imposed limits in contests with the elements and with our own expectations and fears.

The Outward Bound program consists of 26-day sessions in rugged wilderness, learning survival techniques and culminating in a three-day "solo" confrontation with nature. Each of the schools listed below has its special focus, along the lines of mountaineering, rock climbing, open-sea survival, and white water canoeing.

Participants must be at least 16½ years old; there are no upper age limits. Some courses are for men, some for women, some co-ed, some for educators. Prices for the standard courses range from $425-550; shorter special courses are as little as $50. Scholarships are available. It's money well spent for a different kind of consciousness expansion.

Information is available from the address above or from the school of your choice:

Northwest Outward Bound School
3200 Judkins Road
Eugene, Ore. 97403
(503) 342-6044

Minnesota Outward Bound School
330 Walker Avenue South
Wayzata, Minn. 55391
(612) 473-5476

North Carolina Outward Bound School
P.O. Box 817
Morganton, N. C. 28655
(704) 437-6112

California Outward Bound School
780 Welch Road, Suite 203
Palo Alto, Ca. 94304
(415) 321-8084

Colorado Outward Bound School
P.O. Box 7247 Park Hill Station
Denver, Colo. 80207
(303) 287-3373

Dartmouth Outward Bound Center
P.O. Box 50
Hanover, N. H. 03755
(603) 646-3359

Hurricane Island Outward Bound School
P.O. Box 426
Concord, Mass. 01742
(617) 369-7474

NATIONAL OUTDOOR LEADERSHIP SCHOOL
Box AA
Lander, Wyo. 82520
(307) 332-4381
   NOLS believes that adventure is part of the growing up process, and encourages its incorporation in educational planning. Their courses are aimed towards, but by no means limited to, outdoor education leaders, and cover all phases of outdoor living and survival, plus practical conservation.
   The format is backpacking expeditions, usually at 8,000-12,000 foot elevations, for two to five weeks. Expeditions include mountaineering in Wyoming, spelunking in Tennessee, folboting in Alaska, two weeks of ski touring and winter mountaineering in Wyoming, and a two-week Baja Mexico desert and marine course. All of these are for participants from 16-50 years, with special programs for 13-15 year-olds and 21-50 year-olds. The NOLS people seek a diversity of background in applicants. Rugged outdoor experience is not a requirement, but some experience is recommended.
   The five-week courses cost about $550; winter mountaineering is $200, and the Baja expedition is $375, including transportation from the U. S. border. College credit can be arranged for some courses.

See also, Bridge Mountain Foundation; Hal Riegger Pottery Workshops; Jugtown Pottery; Mountain Institute for Man; Ontario College of Art; Questers Project; Sitka Center for Art and Ecology; Trout Fishing in America.

Sailing and Oceanography

TORONTO BRIGANTINE INC

Box 1035, Adelaide Street Post Office, Toronto 1

(416) 364-7851
   "The 60-foot brigantine Pathfinder is impressive sailing into Toronto's Harbor under 2,254 square feet of sail. . . . Pathfinder's crew has but one adult. All of the other hands are 14 to 18 years old who experience the beauty of sail through the help of a nonprofit organization called the Toronto Brigantine, Inc., which has been unlocking the beauty of sail and the sea to Canadian youngsters since 1963."
   This program places emphasis on sailing and sailing skills all year round. In the summer the group's two ships, the 60-foot Pathfinder and the 37-foot Trident II cutter set sail, and the winter activities revolve around Brigantine House in Toronto, where winter instruction in seamanship, navigation, and sail enables crew members to work up to "staff" if they so wish.
   All of Pathfinder's and Trident II's trips are on the Great Lakes. The program is a graduated one with a week's instruction on land in sail, navigation, etc. and successful completion of a week's training qualifies one for a second week aboard Pathfinder. Most of the programs are set up for boys 14 to 18, but there are girls' programs also.
   "To apply, a boy must be between 14 and 18 years of age and in good health. Previous sailing experience is not necessary. Write to Toronto Brigan-

tine, Inc., requesting an application form. These forms will be sent out after January 15, and the applicant will be awarded his berth in the order in which the application is received back by Toronto Brigantine, Inc. The courses are usually filled by the end of March so it is important applications be made early. The cost is $6 a day. However, a boy will not be denied a berth because of his inability to pay."

You may also want to make an inquiry of:

THE SAIL TRAINING ASSOCIATION
c/o The Secretary General   Sussex
Bosham, Chichester   England

COAST NAVIGATIONAL SCHOOL
418 East Canon Perdido
Santa Barbara, Ca. 93102

A crew registration service for boat owners who need hands or for people seeking work on boats has been set up by Coast Navigational School in Santa Barbara. Some boat owners ask crew hands to share expenses, others ask no money, and still others pay a salary. $5 is the charge for people wanting to sign on as crew. We imagine this is primarily for yachts and schooners, and not for ocean liners or freighters.

S·E·A

3 School Street
Boston, Mass. 02108
(617) 742-4246

SEA offers sailing apprenticeships on board a 100-foot topsail schooner, learning techniques in field oceanography, navigation, meteorology, survival techniques, marine engineering, and seamanship.

SEA operates its schooner with a full-time seasoned crew and 20 apprentices, 16 years and older. The *Westward* will be sailing around the Pacific and Southern Atlantic doing oceanographic research for various institutions on specific projects.

SEA describes *Westward*'s mission thusly: "*Westward* is engaged in oceanographic research and instruction. Her success is determined by how efficiently she collects and classifies oceanographic information and how effectively she instructs her apprentices in the knowledge and skills necessary for that task." High school and college credit is available if you want it. Costs of the sailing and oceanographic apprenticeships are $1000 and $2000 (money you might have spent on a school?), with limited scholarship help available. Apprentices are expected to be able to pay at least one-quarter of the total cost from their own earnings. *Westward* has two types of sailing trips available: a 4-week and an 8-week cruise.

SOCIAL AND POLITICAL CHANGE CENTERS

Community Organizing and Research

Along with all the other information about good places that we've received, we've gotten news from these sources which are dealing with community needs in various ways. They provide a wealth of information, from the nitty-gritty to some philosophical/conceptual considerations. We've made note of them here so you can get in touch with them, if you're trying to get something together in your community.

PACIFIC STUDIES CENTER
1963 University Avenue
East Palo Alto, Ca. 94303
From their literature: "The Pacific Studies Center is a radical research center which has been operating for two years out of a storefront in East Palo Alto, California. Members view PSC as an alternative educational form. Universities, such as Stanford—which many of us have attended—are structured to serve those in power. PSC serves those working for social change.

"PSC operates both as a research collective . . . and as resource center for students, teachers, journalists, and organizers."

The Center produces both documented, scholarly publications and mass distribution pieces. In addition to their own bi-monthly publication, *Pacific Research and World Empire Telegram*, which analyzes Pacific and local issues, they contribute to a wide variety of radical, underground, working class, and minority publications. The Center encourages collective work, but is open to new members, both experienced researchers and beginners. Minimal salaries are available for work on specific projects.

FINDING COMMUNITY: A GUIDE TO COMMUNITY
  RESEARCH AND ACTION $3.95
by W. Ron Jones
James E. Freel and Associates
577 College Avenue
Palo Alto, Ca. 94306
This is a book that tells you how to research what's happening in your community in terms of housing, food, consumer affairs, welfare, the draft, war industries, big business and ecology.

There are forms to follow to gather the data, and tips on how to go about gathering the information. A very good introduction to social research and a book that helps you begin from ground-zero to put the finger on any particular problem, its causes and its possible solutions.

ROOTS, INC.
109 Allyn Street
Hartford, Ct. 06103
(203) 525-1131
Roots is an alternative agency for reaching alienated youth and counseling them toward traditional community resources. Starting as a drop-in, call-in crisis intervention center, the original store-front has expanded to include group counseling and informal class facilities, with a crisis prevention emphasis.
Roots has published a "Survival Resources Guide" for the greater Hartford area. They also have a 12-page booklet outlining the history and financing of the project, which contains useful information on starting and staffing, some basic counter-culture agency philosophy, and a dazzling list of their financial supporters. The booklet was apparently created as a fund raising tool; it could probably help you approach the insurance companies and straight foundations in your area if you're trying to get a similar agency off the ground.

number nine

266 State Street
New Haven, Ct. 06511
(203) 787-2127
If you'd like training for working on a crisis line or community switchboard service, the people at Number Nine in New Haven, Connecticut, have an apprenticeship program to train you. They also offer training workshops in addition to the counseling apprenticeship. They have more details. Contact Sheila, Dennis, Ted or Barbara at the above address. They can help find a place to stay while you're training with them. *(See also, Contact)*

COMMUNITY IMPROVEMENT THROUGH YOUTH, INC.
1755 Church Street, N.W.
Washington, D.C. 20036
(202) 387-8794
"CITY is an organization working for higher education reform and social change in Washington, D.C. It operates (at three universities) a program of community-based learning experiences which serves as an alternative to traditional classroom instruction and provides opportunities for college students to engage in social change activities in their communities as part of their college experience.
"CITY is also a program of community education. It involves not only college students but also ourselves and the community people we work with in all our efforts. Together we are searching for alternatives and working for change—a process of self-education and of sharing information, skills, and resources . . .

"We wish to share the CITY concept with other individuals and communities. We have outlined two ways this can be done:
1. a university or group can send one or two individuals to CITY, to work with us for a period, and these individuals can then go back to their home area to start a program there;
2. two CITY staff members will travel to a college or group for short periods of time to work with students, faculty, administrators, and community people, and help them establish a college-community learning program. In both cases, fees for CITY's assistance would be worked out on an-ability-to-pay basis."

NEW JERSEY SANE
324 Bloomfield Avenue
Montclair, N.J. 07042
(201) 744-3263
    N.J. SANE publishes a manual on peace center operations which provides comprehensive information on all aspects of establishing and maintaining a community peace center. Topics covered include: developing a Board of Trustees, mailing lists and systems, office routines and financial accounting, telephone trees, staff, literature and circulating library, boutique items, fund raising, and other details you'd never think of. At some length, they discuss community involvement, draft counseling, programs (educational, fund-raising, interest-stimulating, etc.), and publicity (what will draw newspaper photographers, triple-spacing news releases, etc.).
    For a copy of the manual, write them at the above address. There is no cost; send a donation for a good cause.
    They have also conducted conference workshops on administration and operations, and community outreach and programs, covering all the above plus relating to school systems, politics and lobbying, etc. A summary report is available.

ORGANIZERS TRAINING PROGRAM
c/o War Resisters League
339 Lafayette Street
New York, N.Y. 10012
c/o David McReynolds

    In the summer of 1972, the War Resisters League, a group of pacifists dedicated to non-violent change in America, held a training workshop in New York City for people of high school and college age. The week-long program was for those who wanted to be more effective as local organizers, and will probably be repeated each summer. Write to check out the dates for 1973.
    "Topics covered included basic organizational techniques, mimeographing, layouts, writing leaflets and news releases, police contacts, and political, philosophical discussions and encounters. . . ." The week "will be a hard one, with ten and twelve hour days and little free time. It will amount to a cram course in movement training, ideas and techniques." Anyone can apply in the high school or college age bracket, with special preference given to those from smaller towns, minority groups and women.

||IGHLANDER RESEARCH AND EDUCATION CENTER

BOX 245A, R.F.D. 3
NEW MARKET, TENNESSEE 37820
PH. 615-933-3444

An old-timer (organized in the 1930's) in the people's rights movement, Highlander's educational philosophy has two radical fundamentals: working with poor people, and encouraging action based on their expressed needs. From farm and consumer co-ops, through collective bargaining groups and the civil rights movement, to work with Chicanos and Indians in the Southwest, these principles have been applied to "change society fundamentally by educating for a revolution which could basically alter economic and power relationships to the advantage of poor and powerless people."

While trying to tie its efforts into broadly based social movements, the school works with only a few small groups, hoping they will serve as effective pilot programs and inspiration for other grass-roots efforts. School representatives work with existing local groups in surrounding mountain communities, nurture the local organizations and bring a few community leaders to Highlander for resident workshops. Most participants and workers in the School's educational efforts are from the surrounding Appalachian region, though a multi-racial conference in 1970 included black and white Appalachians, American Indians, Chicanos, Filipinos, Puerto Ricans, and Black Panthers. Continuing projects are also underway in New Mexico.

See also, Cosanti Foundation Workshops; CSVA/Plowshares; The Life Center; Minnesota Experimental City; SOCIAL AND POLITICAL CHANGE CENTERS: Urban Crisis; SOCIAL AND POLITICAL CHANGE NETWORKS: Co-operatives, Rent Striking; Peace and Freedom Party; Questers Project; Third World Awareness Workshops.

Intentional Communities and Rural Living

THE QUESTERS PROJECT
Youth Resources, Inc.
978 Paseo de Anza
Palm Springs, Ca. 92262

The Questers Project is dedicated to the establishment of cooperative rural communities "whose over-all purpose would be the creation of an integral environment shaped by a 'human engineering' that considers the whole needs of a person and family." These would be large, stable (family-oriented, with individual members), developing small-communitytechnologies, and self-sustaining to as great a degree as possible. The organizational plan draws on the culture of the Hunza villages of Kashmir, with attention to American communal experiments and contemporary forms. The first scheduled co-op settlements were established in the Southwest in spring, 1972.

"To as great a degree as feasible TQP proposes co-op settlement development as follows: withdrawal from the big spenders economy; convert assets into productive facilities; cottage industries, organiculture and natural health practice; locate away from city congestion in clean atmospheric air; self-governing communities with emphasis on meritorious human values and work-learn education; research and development in the technology of small co-op settlements."

A New Community, by Paul Marks. $5 postpaid in U.S. This is the handbook for community development which provides a guide to the Questers plan. It includes an overview of mainstream cultural conditions (the rat-race etc.); the Questers proposal, including materials on youth and self-help education; and formats for implementation. There are also bibliographies on intentional communities and utopian colonies, education, health, "self-improvement," building, homesteading, and small business; and lists of intentional communities and related organizations and publications. Most of the books listed here can be ordered for you by the Questers.

BEAR TRIBE
c/o "Many Smokes"
P.O. Box 5895
Reno, Nevada 89503

In the tribe's own words: "The Bear Tribe is a group of traditional Indian and non-Indian people who are coming together and learning to place their dependencies upon the Earth Mother and each other. We began in November, 1970 and have grown in number from 5 to 150 since then. We have eighteen bases in California and are seeking to get people and land together throughout

the country. We have our own economy based on gardening, gathering, foraging and trading, which includes forty acres of land under cultivation for garden and 150 acres of orchards for harvest. . . .

"Our direction is toward the Earth Mother and each other. We are called together by Sun Bear, medicine person of the Chippewa tribe. . . . We seek to decrease our dependencies upon the society most of us have grown up in. . . . We have three laws necessary at this time: no hard drugs, no alcohol and no possessive trips, either of people, of things, or of land. . . . We have our 'school'—over fifty degrees and credentials among us to satisfy any 'state' requirements. We see ourselves as a tribe of teachers. Our children belong to the tribe as a whole—all the brothers and sisters tend the children. . . . We do not come bearing the tomahawk. We are looking for people interested in learning our way, and for land that we may use for tribal living. . . . We come offering the hand of friendship to our sisters and brothers across the land."

KOINONIA PARTNERS
Route 2
Americus, Ga. 31709

"A commune which might be regarded as a cultural link between the religious communities described by Charles Nordhoff and the numerous social experiments of the present is the one started in 1942 by Clarence Jordan and some friends near Americus, Ga. Jordan was a Christian theologian and a trained agriculturist.

"The purpose of Koinonia Farm was twofold: first, to live together in community and witness, especially to the Christian teachings on peace, sharing, and brotherhood, and second, to assist local farmers by introducing scientific farming methods." The members of Koinonia have organized Koinonia Partners, which offers portions of the 1400 acres of Koinonia Farm to families that want to work and live on the land. Financing is to become available through a fund to be used for loans (no-interest) to partnership participants.

"The members conceive the entire undertaking as an application of 'the radical ideas of the gospel message' of Christianity. A prime objective is to provide the dispossessed with an opportunity to reconstruct their own lives by their own labors in the community."

HEATHCOTE SCHOOL OF LIVING
Route 1
Box 129
Freeland, Md. 21053

The Heathcote School has been around for quite a while, dispensing useful information on farming, homesteading, and intentional communities. Heathcote runs seminars, and accepts some people as student-workers on their farm in rural Maryland. They publish the newspaper *Green Revolution*, one of the pioneers in the homesteading movement publications. Articles include detailed instructions on how to control contagious diseases in communities and communes, how to raise Christmas trees, the fine art of scouring trash dumps for usable materials, and articles on the wherefores and whys of homesteading.

Radicals and long hairs can be comfortable here. It's a good idea to let them know you're coming for a visit.

KIBBUTZ ALIYA DESK
Suite 1301
200 Park Avenue
New York, N.Y. 10003
c/o Shaul Peer
(212) GR 7-5663

KIBBUTZ

"A unique social experiment in cooperative living which strives for personal and community self-realization." Two programs are available: Kibbutz Ulpan, a six-month program of half a day's work on an Israeli communal farm and half a day's Hebrew studies; temporary workers, living and working on a kibbutz one month or more.

Age limits are 18 to 35. The only cost to you is transportation to and from Israel. All other expenses are covered by the kibbutzim. The program runs all year round. Permanent settlement, winter, summer, and teenage programs are also offered. For applications and information write to the above address.

The John C. Campbell Folk School
BRASSTOWN, NORTH CAROLINA 28902

(704) 837-2775

"Seeking a direct relationship with the land, with our past, and with each other, in building for the future," is the slogan of the Campbell Folk School. Founded over forty years ago and modeled on the Danish Folk School, John C. Campbell School offers a program called Internship for Rural Living. Basically, the program is community service and working the School's farms in rich, Smoky Mountain valleys.

Applications are accepted "from young people, 18-30 years of age, with varied backgrounds, both college and non-college. They enroll for different reasons. Young people eager to learn a trade suitable to rural living, have, as resources, opportunities for experience in the school dairy, farm, greenhouse, woodcarving, woodworking, weaving and other craft enterprises and, to a limited extent, through intern initiated irojects. Tri-County Technical Institute, located two miles from the school, ofners vocational training, college extension courses, and high school equivalency programs. Folk school interns may enroll in these programs.

"If you are interested in an Internship for Rural Living, write our Intern Coordinator for an application form, giving your reasons for wishing to apply." (See listing under ARTISAN CENTERS)

CHRISTIAN HOMESTEADING MOVEMENT
Oxford, N.Y. 13830

These fundamentalist folks mean business. And business means things like no cameras, no "gadgets" of any kind, no hard liquor or drugs, no cars, no machinery, and no "profanity" and no "vulgarity." So says Hal Smith writing in *Mother Earth News* (No. 8). Richard Fahey, of Christian Homesteading Movement, says, "We are a school. We teach and live Christian homesteading. . . . Some examples are harnessing a horse, knowing edible and medicinal plants, wild plants, story telling, natural childbirth, log cabin building, etc.

"We are Catholic (in the best sense of that word) Christians . . . we teach any sincere persons regardless of faith, in any of the three following ways:

1) Weekly Saturday morning classes, 9 to 12 a.m., open to the public.
2) Individual training weeks, based on what an individual wants and needs—and what we're doing at that season.
3) Homesteading weeks, held in the summer for many people. These are solid weeks of classes and work bees. An intensive week of fundamental homesteading skills.

"Refundable deposits for individual Training Weeks and Homesteading Weeks are necessary to secure reservations. Send two 8-cent stamps for details."

CHM was founded in 1961. All learning takes place on their own 68-acre farm in the rolling hills of south-central New York state.

Note: unannounced visitors must spend a day sawing wood, or you'll be asked to leave. So write or call first unless you're into wood in a serious way. (*See also*, Koinonia Partners)

within the cycles of life... of cycles... of energy...

the end is the beginning and the beginning is the end

"ON BUYING LAND"

The decision of what land to buy is usually based on information about the area and price. The following are some ways to obtain land/area information.

There is no substitute for personal experience in the area. The following are ways to be able to compare personal experience in one area with expected experience in a new area.

1) General "lay" of the land: obtain topographical maps of areas you are interested in and areas you are familiar with. Learn to read them so you can visualize land by looking at the maps.

2) Weather data: try to find data on two different places you have lived to establish what a stated difference in temperature, rainfall, snowfall, cloud cover, average solar energy, etc. means. Without this it is very hard to know in advance how hot a summer will be or how cold a winter.

3) If employment is important, get average income figures. Write the Chamber of Commerce, labor unions, anyone you can think of. Get the phone books for the area—especially Yellow Pages—and see what kind of business, manufacturing, supply houses exist. Write asking about job opportunities, prices, salaries, etc. The most information you can get will be a scant minimum. Contact a bank. Discuss your aims, plans, etc. with them—they *know* how things are. Shop around until you find a sympathetic one.

4) Subscribe to local newspapers. They will give you an idea of what goes on. Check classified ads. If used appliances are expensive, money is usually scarce.

5) Land prices: remember that real estate agents are in business to make money through commissions. They list and push the more expensive land first. By the time land and prices get listed by agencies, they are high in relation to face-to-face prices. The cheapest land usually changes hands either without advertising or by small private listing in the local paper. When approaching agents, *be honest* and realize they must make a living. Say you want cheap land (if you do) and request minimum service—no guided tours, etc.

Consider finding sympathetic private people to look for land for you—either paid or as friends. Maybe offer a flat fee to someone for finding you a place. Write up a "specification" to get clear what you want and what you will take.

Observe and respect the customs of the locals. Should you get branded undesirable while looking, all sources may dry ap and life become very unpleasant. Don't drop all your cash on land. Remember you need shelter, food, and other things just to live. If starting a business, farm, etc., it will probably take a minimum of a year before money starts coming in.

Check local regulations regarding housing minimums. You may be willing to live in a tent etc. but local authorities may not *let* you. Check with the local airport on existing and proposed air lanes. Could be next month 747's will be running in over your place.

Be aware that your land can be invaded by various interests "for the public good." Try not to be the access for lumber or mining roads, highway links, power lines, drainage canals, or potential park land. These are things you *may* be able to learn from local politicians and official surveyors, again mostly on a friendly basis.

If organic farming is your bag, try to get applications history on the land. The former owner may have it but if not try the local supplier of fertilizer and pesticides. But don't push things like "organic" which may threaten him into turning *you* off. Various labs can test for pesticide residue but it is expensive: about $35 for each test for each pesticide.

Same problems with water—look at the water shed to see where it comes from. If a heavy agrichemical area, beware.

Another good source of information is: The *Mother Earth News'* new magazine, *Lifestyle*, Box 38, Madison, Ohio 44057.

Most *tax sale agencies* are difficult to deal with. Land is described in area terms (i.e., concession 4 Lot 6) and unless you have direct, immediate access to county/province/town records, you can't even figure out where it is or how big it is.

General indexes:
U.S. Government Printing Office
Superintendent of Documents
Washington, D.C. 20402
Tell them what you want and they'll tell you where you can get it.

U.S. Department of the Interior
Geological Survey
1200 South Eads Street
Arlington, Va. 22202
U.S. topological maps. (They have other offices)

Information Canada
171 Scater Street
Ottawa, Ontario
Canada
They have or can tell you where to get all maps, books, weather data, industries, land use, etc. To list individual sources would take a couple of pages. Anyone wanting information can pick up the threads here.

General encouragement: good land is still available for $15 to $100 per acre.
from Glen Twombly
Theatre Systems, Inc.*
Old Route 202
Pomona, N.Y. 10970
*TSI consults on all kinds of systems, information, energy, etc.

See also, Aquarius Project; Cold Mountain Institute; Community Service, Inc.; Cowichan Centre for Gestalt Learning; Gestalt Institute of Canada; Japan Kibbutz Association; Karma Dzong; The Life Center; Mankind; Mountain Institute for Man; Nethers Community School; New Alchemy Institute; Nordenfjord World University (the Writing Farm, Praestegaard); Ontario College of Art; Pendle Hill; Planned Total Environment, Inc.; Sunrise Hill Free School; Survival and Community Farming; Zen Center of Annandale; Zen Mountain Center.

Resistance and Non-Violence

WORLD WITHOUT WAR COUNCIL
1730 Grove Street
Berkeley, Ca. 94709
c/o Office of the President
(415) 845-1992

From time to time, the World Without War Council has openings for peace interns. As described in *Vocations for Social Change* (now *WorkForce*): "The World Without War Council has openings in the peace intern program—a two-year program of academic and supervised field work assignments designed to prepare men and women for leadership positions in work for an end to war." The qualifications usually include 1) "persons with experience working in the religious community, and 2) persons interested in conscience and anti-war work who have administrative capacities or experience. . . . College graduates preferred, willing to make a two-year commitment to hard work at subsistence level pay."

 institute for the study of nonviolence
box 1001, palo alto, california 94302

(415) 321-8382

Believing that social change is "rooted in each person and grows to be significant in the process of collective work," the Institute for the Study of Non-Violence "is a group of people seeking to understand the subtle effects of our actions on other people, searching to understand how technology will serve human needs, building and exploring for peoplehood, exploring for alternatives, new forms, jobs that become ways to extend your individuality and creativity."

Workshops and seminars are offered throughout the year on topics that range through health care organizing, education and liberation. "Many of us have confused education with schools. When we've felt a need to break with old educational patterns, we've focused on reforming our existing school systems or creating free schools. But it is not a question of types of schools. More basic are the questions: how do we create that situation which nurtures the human imagination and fosters the feeling of power in our lives? How do we bring responsibility for our education/lives back from institutions to ourselves?"

Other seminar/workshop topics are "Resistance and meaning," "The military movement," "Political potency," "Imagination is not a commodity," "A high school session," "Doing non-violence," "On organization," "Doors of perception," and more.

Tuition for seminars, usually a week long, is $25, which includes housing. Food works out to about a dollar a day. There are no facilities for housing visitors except during sessions.

MANKIND OFFICE
833 Haight Street
San Francisco, Ca. 94117
(415) 431-8771

MANKIND FARM
P.O. Box 192
Legget, Ca.
c/o Oberraith
(707) 925-6327

Mankind is "a community and study center for non-violence," with an office in San Francisco and a 205-acre farm in northern California. At the farm they have seminars on nonviolence and resistance, and provide facilities for individuals and groups to have weekend retreats around these topics. In addition, the farm is "an experiment in self-sufficiency, learning to live as a community independent of outside sources of supply . . . constructing shelter in harmony with natural surroundings, finding interdependence with the earth around us as a step towards greater ecological sanity."

Weekend seminar participants are asked to arrive Friday night, sessions run all day Saturday and Sunday. Suggested tuition is $10, or $5 each for those in group retreats. Meal provisions and sleeping bags are the responsibility of seminar groups. (Mankind has a community dining room and a bunkhouse.) Reservations should include a $5 deposit. The farm also has a craft center, where visitors are welcome and encouraged to work.

In addition to activities at the farm, Mankind people work with people in the Bay Area non-violent community and will provide speakers and resource people elsewhere in the state.

Mankind seeks donations of any kind. They are also interested in expanding the community living at the farm.

PEACE AND FREEDOM PARTY
1727 West Washington Boulevard
Free Venice, Ca. 90291
(213) 821-5281 or 821-6101

WorkForce says: The Peace and Freedom Party is a broad-based left political party using the electoral process to promote radical change, political, social, and economic. They engage in community organizing, alternative institutions, demonstrations, and other non-electoral actions, as well as organizing through electoral politics. They are the only radical political party on the ballot in California, and are engaging in more activities, electoral and non-electoral, this year than ever before. Peace and Freedom Party and other radical third parties and groups have formed the nationwide coalition People's Party in order to have a radical third party on the ballot in every state for 1972 and beyond. The Peace and Freedom is run by its members on the basis of open meetings and one person, one vote. Its membership includes both those registered in the party and those denied by "law" their inalienable right to vote (minors, ex-felons, non-citizens, non-residents).

Write to them for information about local groups and meetings.

SHANTI CENTER
1407 North Van Ness
Fresno, Ca. 93728
(209) 485-7485

Shanti Center (formerly Shanti Community Co-Op Bookshop) is an umbrella for several movement groups: Green Tree Press, Fresno War Tax Resistance, Joyous Struggle NRG, San Joaquin Valley Vocations for Social Change, Fresno Chapter Peace and Freedom Party/People's Party and The Happy Cow natural foods restaurant, among others.

The Center has literature available on subjects of "social relevance" and is compiling a "living-learning-survival manual directed towards City College and State College here in Fresno. The main emphasis will be local, but we plan to include many national organizations."

In the past they have had film and tape programs and discussion and study group sessions.

INSTITUTE MOUNTAIN WEST
2096 Emerson Street
Denver, Colo. 80205
(303) 573-6394

Describing themselves as a "community for living revolution," Institute Mountain West members "live and work together believing that fundamental social change is necessary and possible in this country. This means struggling with personal liberation as well as confronting the power structure and experimenting with alternatives. Who we are is best communicated by what we do and the services we offer.

"We see most people in this country living fragmented lives. . . . We would like to see people have the responsibility for their own houses and land, as one step toward re-integration of their lives. We believe that consensus decision by the people who share their responsibility, though less efficient in use of time than decisions made by a professional manager, are far more meaningful to the people involved. We affirm the value of meaning over efficiency."

IMW operates a library, holds classes in sexism and non-coercive schools, and hosts pot-luck suppers on Thursday nights and discussions on non-violence as an active, living force to bring about social change.

Membership is open to people who share their concerns. Often they have room in the house for more people to come and live with them. Everyone shares in the work and laughter. Rent is $25 a month and food is 90c a day. Aside from this, people who come are free to structure their time with Institute activities or wherever their interests take them.

"If you are interested, write and tell us when you want to come and for how long. We'll let you know if we have room."

THIRD WORLD AWARENESS WORKSHOPS
Third World Team
1500 Farragut Street, N.W.
Washington, D.C. 20011
c/o Bob Kochtitzky
(202) 723-8273

The Third World Awareness Workshop Team is "an ecumenical group initiated in December, 1970 with seed money from the United Methodist Board of Missions for the purpose of raising the consciousness of church members in the U.S. to the struggle of the world's poor and powerless for dignity, justice, and self-determination.''

Workshops are usually held on weekends, beginning Friday and running through Sunday at a conference center. The team uses the educational methods of Paulo Freire, the "goal of which is 'conscientization' or the liberation of people to shape their own destiny. . . .

". . . The Workshops . . . are a microcosm of group self-determination in contrast to the traditional hierarchial teacher-student relationship. Thus, *process* becomes important rather than content. There are no experts telling people what to believe or what to do, only people with different experiences." Workshops usually include "Third World resource persons making their testimony, role play and simulation games, movies, dialogues, liberation theology, problem-solving exercises."

Costs vary with each workshop, depending on resource people and location. An "average figure for the cost of a four-person Team, not including travel and accommodations is $600." Write Bob Kochtitzky at the above address for information on setting up a workshop in your area.

NON-VIOLENT TRAINING AND ACTION CENTER
542 South Dearborn
Chicago, Ill. 60605
(312) 922-8234

The Non-Violent Center in Chicago offers workshops built around the theme/idea of "training for social change through non-violent direct action."

One of several non-violent training centers around the country, they say this of themselves: Our "training goals: 1) basic understanding of the philosophy and practice of non-violence, 2) increase competence and confidence when participating in non-violent direct action, 3) provide significant opportunities for exploring conflict and violence, and for discovering creative responses."

In the workshop programs, "groups will learn about the following: picketing, civil disobedience, role playing, strategy games, street speaking, guerrilla theatre, negotiating, sitting-in, planning and marshalling a demonstration, leafletting and situation analysis.

"We also conduct weekends on special projects: women's liberation, war tax resistance, alternative life styles, non-violent philosophy, Catholic radicalism, non-violent revolution, guerrilla theatre and civil disobedience."

emmaus

241 E. 116 St.   ●   New York 10029   ●   (212) 348-5622

"Emmaus is an experimental Christian community and center for nonviolent alternatives. Toward that end, it has fused educational and research programs with efforts of resistance to injustice as well as the creation of new possibilities in community, vocation, religious forms and lifestyle.

"Seeking to stimulate ourselves and others to shape life in a new way, Emmaus encourages not so much an accumulation of facts but a process of heightened awareness, deepened involvement and commitment. Together we become fellow searchers, 'as one beggar who tells the other beggar where to find bread.' The result, hopefully, is a certain transformation of our lives, the church and society we live in."

Emmaus sponsors three kinds of programs: workshops, "Sunday evenings," and weekend retreats.

Weekly workshops and seminars cover topics like radical theater (guerilla and street theater as tools of nonviolent action), beginning and intermediate Spanish (they're located in Spanish Harlem), women's and gay men's consciousness-raising, alternatives in education, nonviolence (history, philosophy, theology), charismatic prayer, and gourmet cooking on next to nothing.

Weekends focus on faith, resistance, and practical nonviolence. They are in a retreat format and cost about $15. Emmaus Sunday evenings feature speakers such as William Kunstler, Anthony and Mary Scoblick of the Harrisburg Eight, Third World groups, and New York City authors, churchmen, and artists.

Nearly all Emmaus activities are free and they depend on contributions. Workshops begin in January, but other activities go on year-round. Write for more information.

Emmaus also serves as a Vocations for Social Change center and has published a *People's Yellow Pages* for New York City. They welcome information-seekers and volunteer workers. (*See also, People's Yellow Pages* (N.Y. City); Vocations for Social Change)

there is no way to peace –
peace is
the way.

THE PEACE BUILDING
339 Lafayette Street
New York, N.Y. 10012
    Lots of people work in the Peace Building and that makes a lot of other people nervous. A New York daily newspaper printed the following answer to one such worried Mom: "The address is a few blocks uptown from New York's stately City Hall in an area notable only for its lack of skyscrapers. There are a few residential tenements, but mostly it is home for rows of small firms dealing in machinery and electronics. The building at 339 Lafayette is an undistinguished, three-story brick with small businesses on the street level. The tenants on the second and third, however, make up a catalog of causes. It is a Mecca for New York's young hippie crowd, who coined the name Peace Building. In its 5500 square feet of office space, the anti-war movement puts it all together. . . .
    The 'grand daddy' of the groups is no newcomer to the anti-war scene. The War Resisters League (WRL) is a pacifist group that dates back to 1923. Branching out from WRL and clinging closely to it (or just hanging around) is a clutter of other left-political groups such as the Catholic Peace Fellowship, the Jewish Peace Fellowship, *Liberation Magazine*, the G.I. Counseling Services, War Tax Resistance and, lately, a fledgling women's liberation magazine. . . . Not all the peace workers are young. Ralph DiGia, paid administrative secretary of WRL, has been at his job 14 years and is an old colleague of Bayard Rustin and the Rev. A. J. Muste. He served time for refusing the draft in World War II. He is the guiding spirit of the fledgling anti-war groups. . . . Part-time volunteers who are college students consider the regular workers at 339 Lafayette as terribly serious. Full-time 'movement' people most feel, know what they're doing. Their families, it appears, have little to worry about as far as safety is concerned. They get little money and work very hard, but they are doing something they believe in at 339 Lafayette."

THE LIFE CENTER
1006 South 46th Street
Philadelphia, Pa. 19143
(215) EV 6-1371
    The Life Center is an intentional community of Quakers and non-Quakers experimenting with non-violent action, working for radical social change. A handful of collectives and communes have been established in the Philadelphia area. The interests of the several groups include the development of macro-non-violence; another is concerned with community justice administration; another is a movement building collective with the task of spreading the idea of non-violent

movement for fundamental social change; a training collective is a large group involved in a program for training organizers for non-violent change; and the latest commune is a farm in Chester County.

Workshops are offered in all the areas of concern, and last 9 to 12 months with full time devoted to training, with one or two days working for bread money. Participants live in communal groups when possible, and emphasis is on personal involvement in non-violent projects.

Areas of study also include skills and techniques of organizing, contemporary American power, surviving and thriving in community, building alternative institutions, building alternative societies, alternative theories of social change, non-violent conflict resolution, and building a disciplined life (which includes exploration of ways of worship, meditation, yoga, the arts, and the self in society).

The Life Center is part of the Movement for a New Society, which is beginning to spread throughout the country—small action communities of six to twelve persons called Non-violent Revolutionary Groups. A brochure and details available from George Willoughby at the Life Center.

Additional groups and individuals around the country have expressed an interest in the Nonviolent Revolutionary Group idea that grew out of the Life Center and its work.

Some of these are:

Shanti (see listing)
c/o Larry Sheeky
1407 Van Ness
Fresno, Ca. 93728

War Resisters Tribe
1631 Indus
Santa Ana, Ca. 92707

Charles and Leslie Gray
1059 Hilyard
Eugene, Ore. 97401

Another Peace Group
2429 N.E. Thompson
Portland, Ore. 97212

George Carns
4721 North 2nd Street
Milwaukee, Wis. 53212

See also, CSVA/Plowshares; Koinonia Partners; New Jersey Sane; Organizers Training Program; Pendle Hill.

. . . I fell in with a teacher who turned me on to the intellectual world. He said, "Here, read this." It was 1984, when I was 11 or 12. And all of a sudden it was a whole new—that was like when I was turning on, so to speak, or became aware of a whole other world that was other than the thing you got in school, that you got in the movies and all that; something very different. And so right away I was really a long way from school at that point. . . .

—JERRY GARCIA
of the Grateful Dead

Urban Crisis

The Action Training Center Coalition publishes a yearly directory to all their member organizations and you can get a copy free on request from:
Commit
817 West 34th Street
Los Angeles, Ca. 90007
Some of the descriptions in this section were taken verbatim from the directory.

The Coalition describes itself as being made up of members who "are primarily but not exclusively rooted in the Judeo-Christian tradition, and are devoted to training for social change . . . The fundamental training done by ATC member agencies is called action training, or action reflection training. This training is direct engagement in social problems, with inter-disciplinary reflection and skill development in the context of this engagement. Other methodologies most often used by ATC member agencies include exposure, confrontation groups, labs, lectures, and simulation games."

CANADIAN URBAN TRAINING PROJECT
875 Queen Street East
Toronto 8, Ontario
Canada
c/o Dr. Edward File, Exec. Director
(416) 465-9177

"The major action training program offered consists of a six-week live-in program followed by a six to nine month back-home engagement and project, ending with a two-week recall and strategy session. This program is primarily for church professionals and community leaders who are involved in social change.

"The summer student training program involves students from all disciplines in a training action program."

THE URBAN TRAINING CENTER
21 East Van Buren
Chicago, Ill. 60605
(312) 939-2762

The Urban Training Center runs an incredible number of training and discussion workshops on everything from housing and education to urban health care. They say:

"The training focus is the development of ministry in the context of community development. Special attention [is given] to analysis of major societal issues and the peculiar role and responsibility of institutions of the private sector for exercising initiatives (through pilot projects and experiments) and putting their own working definitions into the public sphere."

Urban Training Center recruits nationally for: three to four-week orientation courses in urban ministry and issue analysis; one-week intensive project workshops (in housing, education, etc.); nine-month research and development programs; and specially designed one to three-day institutes.

The various activities of Urban Training Center have centered around public housing, alternatives to school, and inner city health care.

Write to George Younger, director, for details about their workshops and programs, and ask for a copy of their publications list, which is very impressive in its scope and thoroughness.

METROPOLITAN URBAN SERVICE TRAINING, INC.
110 East 125th Street
New York, N.Y. 10035
(212) 876-7006

"MUST works with laity and clergy from religious groups and institutions, and with staff, leaders, and members of community organizations, business, and government. The stress is on action training to meet objectives worked out with each training group. Special emphasis at MUST is on: planning, community organization; institutional racism; researching power; power analysis; strategy development; leadership skills; evaluation; theological analysis; and training of trainers.

"Other services available from MUST include: research and documentation, proposal writing, and evaluation."

CENTER FOR URBAN ENCOUNTER
0245 S.W. Bancroft
Portland, Ore. 97201
(503) 224-1144
"The Center for Urban Encounter has three broad objectives: training laymen and clergy for community service through urban encounter; research into the causes of urban problems and strategising their solutions; and experimentation in the arts, liturgy, and communication. In the difficult struggle to make the city more liveable and more human, CUE seeks to provide a responsive and responsible resource for individuals, parishes, clusters of parishes, and various ecumenical groups. Staffed by leaders qualified both by competence and conscience, CUE functions within a framework which is serious theologically and sociologically."

URBANZAI EXCHANGE MULTI-VERSITY
1255 Orcutt Road, B-33
San Luis Obispo, Ca. 93401
We discovered these people in *The First New Earth Catalog*. They are a group of students (some ex-) of urban planning, interested in being joined by/communicating with all groups and individuals working on urban crises.
"We don't like being labeled as having a specific orientation but if forced into one we would say we are working on solutions to urban problems with our emphasis placed on and around the social-cultural-economic-political-psychological-anthropological-ecological-etc. design determinants involved in urban problems."
They welcome people interested in urban problems and solutions who are able to direct their own learning/investigation programs.

See also, Cosanti Foundation Workshops; Questers Project; Third World Awareness Workshops.

SOCIAL AND POLITICAL CHANGE CENTERS:
See also, ALTERNATIVE FUTURES CENTERS; ALTERNATIVE FUTURES NETWORKS; ALTERNATIVE VOCATIONS NETWORKS; Cultural Integration Fellowship, Inc.; Nethers Community School; North American Student Co-Operative Organization.

SPIRITUAL CENTERS

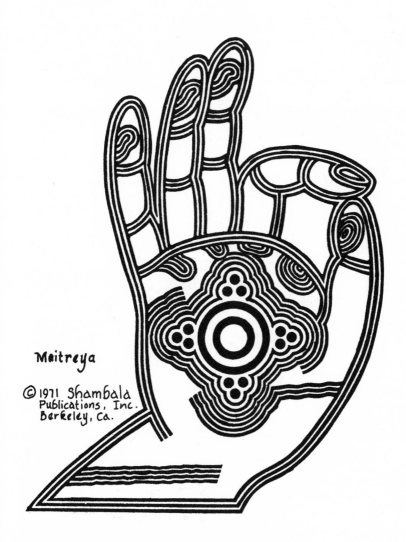

Maitreya

© 1971 Shambala
Publications, Inc.
Berkeley, Ca.

BROCKWOOD PARK KRISHNAMURTI FOUNDATION
EDUCATIONAL CENTER
Bramdean
Arlesford, Hantshire
England
"The main purpose of the school is for a group of adults and students to explore together the implications, in practice, of Krishnamurti's teachings, while at the same time following academic courses of their choice leading to G.C.E. exams. We started in September, 1969 with a small group of teachers and students, and this September we expect to have about 20 students, boys and girls, from a number of different countries, aged between 14 and 18. Krishnamurti himself lives here for several months each year, and at those times takes a very active part in the school. . . . Brockwood Park is a fine house on 40 acres of ground—fields, woods, gardens, swimming pool, tennis courts—in a lovely part of the country. We are gradually adapting parts of the premises for use as science labs, art and theatre workshops, etc."

CULTURAL INTEGRATION FELLOWSHIP, INC.
2650 Fulton Street
San Francisco, Ca. 94118
(415) 648-1489
"Founded in San Francisco in 1951, Cultural Integration Fellowship is dedicated to the ideals of universal religion, intercultural understanding between America and Asia, and practical application of essential spiritual principles with a view to integral self-actualization. Every Sunday morning there are nonsectarian religious services, every Tuesday evening there is meditation workshop and discussion of Eastern self discipline, and other days instruction is given in the practice of various yoga disciplines and Tai Chi Cheun.
"At different times Seminars are held on the essential unity of all religions and the various techniques of meditation and self-realization under the guidance of the president, Dr. Haridas Chaudhuri." (*See also*, California Institute of Asian Studies)

We have included Buddhist centers with our listings in the *Catalog* because we feel that Buddhism offers a fundamental alternative: not just a different way of doing, but a different way of *being*. Although serious practice requires a discipline which is best followed in a withdrawn, sometimes monastic setting, this is only preparation for the reintegration of the student into daily life.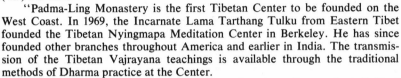

Tibetan Buddhism

PADMA-LING MONASTERY
c/o Tibetan Nyingmapa Meditation Center
2425 Hillside Avenue
Berkeley, Ca. 94704
(415) 549-1618

"Padma-Ling Monastery is the first Tibetan Center to be founded on the West Coast. In 1969, the Incarnate Lama Tarthang Tulku from Eastern Tibet founded the Tibetan Nyingmapa Meditation Center in Berkeley. He has since founded other branches throughout America and earlier in India. The transmission of the Tibetan Vajrayana teachings is available through the traditional methods of Dharma practice at the Center.

"Students can be either extensive or intensive, depending on the individual circumstances and Karmic vibrations. At present there are 100 students partaking in full practices and another eighty in basic practices. Seminars are held quarterly."

TIBETAN NYINGMAPA MEDITATION CENTER
2522 Webster Street
Berkeley, Ca. 94705

Directed by Lama Tarthang Tulku, the Center is dedicated to "continuing the transmission to disciples of the West, of the timeless truths of Buddhism; the analysis and solution of the problem of human suffering." Forty-five students are presently receiving instruction in Buddhist theory and practice.

KARMA DZONG
Meditation Center
1111 Pearl Street
Boulder, Colorado 80302
303-444-0202

Karma Dzong is one of several new centers established in the U.S. for the study of Tibetan Buddhism. (See also Tail of the Tiger in Vermont. Both centers are meditation community centers offering intensive meditation practice, private instruction, occasional seminars and lectures, and retreat facilities.) A number of people from Karma Dzong have moved to a site in the mountains near Fort Collins, Colorado, to build a third meditation community, the Rocky Mountain Dharma Center.

The purposes of the communities are to publish the original works and translations of Chogyam Trungpa Rinpoche, their founder; to bring Tibetan scholars and translators to the U.S.; to prepare students for study in Asia; to support Asian Buddhist communities dispersed by the Communist invasion of Tibet; and to preserve and transmit the heritage of Tibetan Buddhism.

Income for the centers is from fees for seminars and guest lodgings, plus contributions. A donation and inquiry to Karma Dzong will bring you newsletters, *Garuda*, a regular publication of teachings and information, and details on instruction or seminars available. Rinpoche lectures nationally.

In addition, 10-day seminars ("Meditation in Daily Life," *Tibetan Book of the Dead*, study of the process of mind, etc.) are held in the vicinity of both centers, fees are $40 and up for lectures, room, and board.

TAIL OF THE TIGER
Star Route
Barnet, Vt. 05821
(802) 633-9389

Tail of the Tiger is the older of two Tibetan Buddhist centers established in the U.S. by Chogyam Trungpa Rinpoche and followers from Scotland.

In addition to the instruction and seminars described under Karma Dzong (Colorado), Tail of the Tiger operates a month-long children's camp to introduce meditation and Buddhism to children 8-15. It costs $250.

A craft center is underway and improvements on the community's farm will provide expanded facilities for seminar participants and winter retreats.

Zen Buddhism

VANCOUVER ZEN CENTRE
139 Water Street
Vancouver 3, British Columbia
Canada

The Vancouver Zen Centre is of the Rinzai Sect and is affiliated with the Cimarron Zen center and the Mount Baldy Zen Center in California. The Centre holds public zazen Tuesday and Thursday evenings and Saturday mornings; after attending a few of these instruction and discussion periods people can join daily morning sittings. No monthly pledges are required to participate in the Centre, but donations are asked for rent, supplies, and expenses.

Seven-day sesshin are held in spring and fall, usually for $25. Dai-sesshin may be held, where participants live at the Centre for the week, at a cost of $40.

A newsletter brings information on Zen and the Centre. A donation is requested. (They may be moving soon; write ahead if you want to visit.)

ZEN MOUNTAIN CENTER
Tassajara Springs
Carmel Valley, Ca. 93924
call Salinas Toll Station Operator,
ask for Tassajara Springs Number 1
    Zen Mountain Center was founded in 1967 in order to establish the practice of the Middle Way in the U.S. In addition to spiritual development and practice, students do all food growing and preparation, care for the facilities, and raise funds for operation. Work "integrates meditation and everyday life."
    "A center for spiritual practice like Zen Mountain Center affects not only the students who practice there, it also increases the spiritual—hence human and cultural—possibilities for the surrounding society. These possibilities, even if one has not realized them, become part of the definition of what is possible for human beings—alternatives which have to be considered. Also those who do practice at Tassajara return to the city or country, not to propagate Buddhism, but just to live and work with others and in that way increase the possibilities for those with whom they come into contact."
    Students must have practiced regularly for at least six months at the San Francisco Zen Center, one of its affiliates, or with a recognized meditation group before application. Zen Mountain Center is closed to all visitors during intensive six-month training periods.
    Guest facilities are available in late spring and summer for individuals or families who wish to enjoy the mountain seclusion (20 miles down a dirt road, in National Forest land), hot springs, and wilderness beauty of the site. Guests are expected to support the spirit of the community and may participate to some extent in the study program. Accomodations range from $12-18 a day for members, $14-21 for non-members, with reductions for groups and children. $1.50 pays for a towel, dip in the pool, and use of the picnic area.

CIMARRON ZEN CENTER
2505 Cimarron Street
Los Angeles, Ca. 90018
Joshu Sasaki, Roshi
(213) 732-2263
    Cimarron Zen Center is a branch of Rinzai-ji, Inc., one of four affiliated centers in California and British Columbia. (See also Vancouver Zen Centre.) Regular zazen and sanzen are held, with beginners' classes on Saturday morning. A beginner may come to regular sittings and be instructed privately.
    Membership is $10/month minimum. In addition, there are usually monthly dai-sesshin (week-long meetings of intensive zazen and sanzen) for $40 at Cimarron or $60 at Mt. Baldy. Students half price. Information is also available from:
Mt. Baldy Zen Center
P.O. Box 526
Mt. Baldy, Ca. 91759
(714) 985-6410

Redondo Beach Zen Center
2305 Harriman Lane
Redondo Beach, Ca. 90278

ZEN CENTER OF LOS ANGELES
927 South Normandie Avenue
Los Angeles, Ca. 90006
(213) 384-8996
    Zen Center of Los Angeles is affiliated with the Soto Sect and includes a
Zendo and residence house for students.
    ZCLA has daily zazen and offers free instruction to beginners on the first,
second, and fourth Saturday of each month. Three-day sesshin is held monthly
for a fee of $15 for members, $35 for others.
    The quarterly *ZCLA Journal* carries articles and lectures on Zen, plus news
of the Center. It's free, but a donation marked for publication expenses would
help.

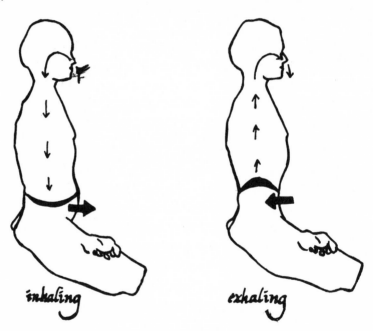

inhaling   *exhaling*

ZEN CENTER
(Maha-Bodhisattva Zendo)
300 Page Street
San Francisco, Ca. 94102
(415) 863-3136
    Full-time students at the Maha-Bodhisattva Zendo follow a daily schedule
of several periods of zazen (Zen meditation), group meals in silence, and work.
The Center welcomes visitors and new students to San Francisco or any of its
affiliates (see below); visitors and students alike are requested to stay a week,
however, and participate in the activities of the zendo.

Temporary housing is available for $3 a day, which covers room, meals, and teaching fee. A personal visit (preferably) or letter in advance are requested, discussing personal background, interest in/experience in Zen or other religious practice, and reasons for wanting to stay at the Center.

Students who have practiced with the Center for three months may apply for membership, pledging $90 a month; after six months students may apply for a practice period at Zen Mountain Center. (See listing)

In addition to daily practice, sesshin, a five-day extended meditation period, is held the first week of each month, and there are weekly lectures on Buddhism.

Zen Center publishes *Wind Bell* for a suggested subscription price of $3/year. The Fall-Winter 1970-71 issue carries extensive interviews with students, both those who live at Zen Center and those who live outside and practice at the Center. It reflects the difficulties of Zen practice in an urban environment, the conflicts of adjustment of Zen living and teachings, and the transformations possible through faithful practice.

Affiliates of the San Francisco Zen Center, offering zazen, lectures, and sometimes sesshin:

1670 Dwight Way
Berkeley, Ca. 94703
c/o Mel Weitsman
(415) 845-2403

Dolores Street, near 7th,
above P.G. & E. office, Apt. 4
Carmel, Ca. 93921
c/o Jean Ross
(408) 624-6808

745 University Avenue
Los Altos, Ca. 94022
c/o Les Kaye
(415) 948-5020

Almonte Improvement Club
Almonte at Jody's Junction
Mill Valley, Ca. 94941
c/o Bill Kwong
(415) 388-5835

114 Swift Street
Santa Cruz, Ca. 95060
c/o Ruth O'Neal
(408) 426-9092

MAUI ZENDO OF THE DIAMOND SANGHA, INC.
R.R. 1, Box 220
Haiku, Hi. 96708
(808) 572-8163

The Maui Zendo is a community of twelve who work and meditate together, and provide counseling and referrals of various kinds (draft, drugs, dilemmas). Interested students are invited to attend evening and Sunday sittings.

Living in the Zendo and participation in zazen are both open only on a space-available basis (they were full, with no vacancies anticipated when we heard from them), so write ahead before you just show up there. Residents should expect to pay about $12.50 a week, though other arrangements may be made for "earnest students." A discipline of religious practice, diet, and appropriate silence is followed.

An inquiry to the Maui Zendo will bring you a very attractive brochure. This one contains "Hints for Meditation" for the beginner.

ZEN CENTER OF ANNANDALE
c/o Richard Clarke
Bard College
Annandale-on-Hudson, N.Y. 12504
   People at the Zen Center of Annandale have been practising together for
three years and are now forming a residential center. Their purposes are to
"carry on the teaching and practice of Zen Buddhism, especially according to
Philip Kapleau Roshi and his historic line of Zen teachers; to develop, apply,
and further the understanding of the principles and practice of Zen Buddhism in
the contemporary American context; to help serious-minded men and women to
apply Zen Buddhist teachings to their daily lives; and to provide a place where
members and others seriously intent on Self-Realization may carry on meditation, study, and other forms of practice.
   "There will be daily formal supervised zazen, lectures, seminars, hatha
yoga, manual work, and individual counseling as the program for those accepted
to be part of the community. A financial contribution must be made by all
participants also to help with the expenses of the house, etc."
   The Center is in a rural setting across the Catskill Mountains, and is not
connected with Bard College.

NEW YORK ZENDO
紐 育　　禪 堂

SHOBO JI
正 法 寺

The Zen Studies Society, Inc.
223 East 67th Street
New York, N.Y. 10021
(212) 628-9652

   The New York Zendo holds regular zazen and monthly retreats for
students; however, space limits student practice to regular members. People
interested in joining the practice are invited to public meetings on Thursday
evenings from 7 to 9; after at least 20 of these meetings applicants may be
considered for the student waiting list.
   Residents of New York who are students pay $20 monthly dues; those who
live out of town and attend irregularly pay $20 quarterly.
   The Zendo has a quarterly publication, *Dharma Seasons*, and will send you
an annotated bibliography on request. They exist on contributions, so you might
send them one with your request.

THE FIRST ZEN INSTITUTE OF AMERICA, INC.
113 East 30th Street
New York, N.Y. 10016
(212) MU 4-9487
The First Zen Institute holds zazen practice weekday mornings for members, and monthly sesshins, usually during the first weekend of the month. Longer sesshins may be scheduled.
Three membership categories are available: associate, $5 per year; sustaining, $60 per year, and zazenkai, for sustaining members wishing to take part in zazen practice. A three-month trial period is required for zazenkai, with instruction and meditation available.
The Institute has library facilities and offers discounts on books to members. There is open house on Wednesday evenings, for information and instruction. Groups welcome by appointment.

SPIRITUAL CENTERS:
See also, California Institute of Asian Studies; Center for Urban Encounter; Christian Homesteading Movement; Cultural Integration Fellowship; Emmaus House; Koinonia Partners; The Life Center; Metropolitan Urban Service Training, Inc.; Pendle Hill; Third World Awareness Workshops.

WOMEN'S CENTERS

WOMEN'S HISTORY RESEARCH CENTER
2325 Oak
Berkeley, Ca. 94708
(415) 524-7772
Women's History Research Center "is the only International Women's history archive in the world. Among the services they provide are: an index of tapes available at the library; an index of women's films; the Women's Song-

our history has been stolen from us

book; *Herstory Synopsis*, a list of women in world history; List of Women's Studies' Course Syllabi, and Bibliographies; List of Women's Research Projects." They are in the process of cross-indexing an enormous archive of material about and by black women. They need volunteers to index the material for microfilming.

"Please call before you visit, and when sending requests, send a self-addressed stamped envelope; all donations appreciated, and tax deductible."

BREAKAWAY
434 66th Street
Oakland, Ca. 94609
"Where can a woman go if she wants to study auto mechanics, talk about feminism and politics, or learn karate?" Now starting into its second year, Breakaway offers two basic types of courses for women: consciousness raising small groups and "content courses."

Debbie Majteles of Alternative Features Service describes Breakaway: "Like many other institutions that sprung directly from people's needs, Breakaway is organized very simply with almost no bureaucracy."

The most popular courses thus far, according to Ruth, one of the original organizers, have been movement and body courses, karate, massage, and dance. Auto mechanics and consciousness raising groups are next in popularity. A catalog of courses, schedules, and fees is available.

LIBERATION SCHOOL FOR WOMEN
852 West Belmont
Chicago, Ill. 60657
(312) 348-2011
There aren't many institutions set up to directly help women to overcome the weight of oppression, but the Liberation School is one of them. Their motto is "What we don't know, we must learn. What we do know, we should teach each other."

The Liberation School offers "introductory courses which help women understand how we are oppressed and what liberation could mean." The School also offers several kinds of skills courses, including self-defense, legal skills, prepared childbirth, and repairing such things as home appliances and automobiles. "There are also study groups in such areas as health, economics, education and psychology. These courses help women develop a unified and radical understanding of how American society operates. They give us confidence in our ability to think and act for ourselves."

Each class of the Liberation School meets once a week for six to eight weeks. Classes are open to any woman who registers and who pays $4.00 per class, if possible, in order to keep the school running.

GREENERFIELDS UNLIMITED
318 Happ Road
Northfield, Ill. 60093
(312) 446-0525

Greenerfields is a continuing education center for women offering daytime, non-credit courses "designed to help women examine their life style, assess their abilities and accomplishments, and determine future goals" as well as study creative writing, the arts, philosophy, current events, literature, yoga, and special series.

Courses are held on a semester basis, with such juicy titles as "Creative Art and Gestalt: Using various media to transform the unconscious into visual form;" "A Woman's Place: Alternative ways of being a woman and human being;" etc. Courses cost $25-45, $115 for "Potential I," which includes individual counseling and testing. Write for brochure and information on current offerings.

WOMEN'S CENTERS:
See also, CSVA/Plowshares; Emmaus House; *The Eupsychian Network*; Gay Women's News Service; Human Rights for Women; Non-Violent Training and Action Center.

As we come marching, marching, we bring the greater days. The rising of the woman means the rising of the race. No more the drudge and idler·· ten that toil where one reposes, But a sharing of life's glories: Bread and roses! Bread and roses!

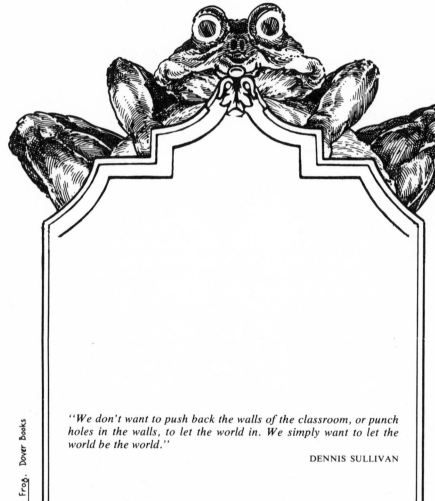

"We don't want to push back the walls of the classroom, or punch holes in the walls, to let the world in. We simply want to let the world be the world."

DENNIS SULLIVAN

Part II

NETWORKS

Resources for learning and how to find them.

ALTERNATIVE FUTURES NETWORKS

contracultura ⊖

C. C. C. 1332 - CAPITAL - ARGENTINA

Miguel Grinberg publishes (irregularly) a journal entitled *Contracultura*, a newsletter called *Eco Contemporaneo*, and a series of minihandbooks on such subjects as communes and ecology. He also contributes to *2001* (see above) and states "We are working as the Latin American branch of the Underground Press Syndicate."

2001
Enrique Loiacono, Editor
Av. Cordoba 1367
Piso 13°
Buenos Aires, Argentina
This is "the only regular futures oriented publication" in Argentina, in Spanish.

ROBERT THEOBALD
The Old School House
Box 1531
Wickenburg, Ariz. 85358
(602) 684-2173
Robert Theobald is "working to create an information service which will provide people with the information they need to find their way into the future. For the moment, this consists of a bi-monthly service containing key documents, bibliographies, lists which provide information about the world as it moves out of the industrial era into the communication era. It is hoped eventually to personalize this service, so that each person can be given the list of materials which will be most helpful to him/her. The cost of this service is $30. If you cannot afford it write about the possibilities of obtaining it at a reduced cost."

The information service is also initiating a monthly trendletter, *Futures Conditional*, which is "based on the belief that America and the world are involved in a massive social transformation. ... We are moving out of the industrial era into the cooperative, communications era ... The dislocations we can expect will be as severe as in the previous transition—yet we have far less time to make the present transition successfully.

"*Futures Conditional* will examine why a transformation is essential, how the transformation is to be achieved and the results which will follow it. Existing publications deal with changes in policy: we, on the contrary, shall show how our fundamental perceptions are altering. ... The media today report events which have already occurred and which we are powerless to affect. We shall, on the contrary, examine the trends and patterns which are developing today and which you can yourself help to shape. There will be opportunities for feedback within the trendletter, for contact with the contributors and between those subscribers who wish to meet each other." Other futures works by Theobald include:

An Alternative Future for America II. Chicago: Swallow Press, 1971. $2.
"We have a socioeconomic system which forces the dehumanization of man. I believe that our first task, therefore, is to begin the restructuring of the socioeconomic system to create a human order."

Economizing Abundance. Chicago: Swallow Press, 1972. $2.95
This book shows that the discipline of economics, as presently studied, flies in the face of our growing knowledge of systems.

The Dialogue Series. Indianapolis: Bobbs-Merrill. $1.25 each.
Separate volumes on *Poverty, Education, Technology, Science, Women*, and *Violence*. These are good starting points for those who have not previously studied these issues.

Futures Conditional. Indianapolis: Bobbs-Merrill, 1972. $2.95.
Presents three views of the future, and provides methods for discovering which view *you* hold.

Habit and Habitat. Englewood Cliffs, N.J.: Prentice-Hall, 1972. $8.95.
An examination of the environmental/ecological issue showing that there is no hope of significant progress in dealing with these issues until we recognize the need for massive, systemic change.

Teg's 1994. Chicago: Swallow Press, 1971. $2.50
The "autobiography" of a girl who is awarded an Orwell fellowship in 1994. She travels round the world trying to discover the process by which the world avoided disaster in the years 1969-1994. A participation book, the reader discovers what he presently believes rather than being fed the biases of the authors. (With J.M. Scott)

MANAS

Box 32112, El Sereno Station
Los Angeles, Ca. 90032
"MANAS is a journal of independent inquiry, concerned with study of the principles which move world society on its present course, and with search for contrasting principles—that may be capable of supporting intelligent idealism under the conditions of life in the twentieth century. MANAS is concerned, therefore, with philosophy and with practical psychology, in as direct and simple a manner as its editors and contributors can write."

An indispensable weekly journal for keeping up with all sorts of philosophical and psychological trends, book reviews, and so forth. Samples of MANAS can be had free by writing and asking for them. Subscription rates are $5 a year, $8 for two years, and $12 for three years.

INTERNATIONAL COOPERATION COUNCIL
17819 Roscoe Boulevard
Northridge, Ca. 91324
(213) 345-8325
"The International Cooperation Council (ICC) is a coordinating body for more than 90 educational, scientific, cultural, and religious organizations which aim to 'foster the emergence of a new universal man and civilization based upon unity in diversity among all peoples.' It was formed to continue the ideals and activities undertaken by a few of these organizations during International Cooperation Year, 1965. ICC believes in utilizing the methods and discoveries of modern science coupled with the deepest insights of religion, philosophy, and the arts.

"The Council has a number of activities:

1) an annual International Cooperation Directory, which contains statements about the purposes and activities of the member organizations plus about 125 additional listings of groups whose purposes are related to those of ICC.

2) 'The Cooperator,' designed to get individuals and organizations in communication with each other in relation to the many dimensions of ICC work.

3) an annual International Cooperation Festival, at which all organizations can gather for inspirational and educational sessions, present displays of their materials, and conduct interest groups related to their work.

5) the Universal Development Center, where experiential worship, growth groups, and workshops are held for the purpose of stimulating individual growth and consciousness expansion.

6) a weekly radio show in Southern California, which will be made available to other stations across the country.

7) the New Consciousness Institute, which is being developed in order to expand the educational program into classes, inter-group exploration sessions, and workshops.

8) the Mankind Center, which has been in existence for two years in downtown Los Angeles, as a service coordination center for ICC and other inter-group action.

"The Council has a regular mailing list and invites participation in any part of the world."

THE FUTURES GROUP
c/o Wayne I. Boucher
124 Heburn Avenue
Glastonbury, Ct. 06033
Wayne Boucher is preparing a 200-entry *Bibliography of Futures Bibliographies*.

THE WORLD FUTURE SOCIETY
P.O. Box 30369
Bethesda Station
Washington, D.C. 20014

Subtitled "An Association for the Study of Alternative Futures," WFS has about 10,000 members and 20 chapters in major cities. Their headquarters, at 4916 St. Elmo Avenue (Bethesda), Washington, D.C. 20014 includes a member's lounge and the only bookstore in the world which specializes in books dealing with the future.

WFS publishes the leading journal on general trends and activities in futures research, *The Futurist*, and supplements this with a monthly *WFS Bulletin*. Membership fee of $7.50 per year provides a subscription to *The Futurist* and a 10% discount on major publications dealing with the future.

THE ALTERNATIVE FUTURES PROJECT
c/o Stuart Umpleby/Valerie Lamont
252 Engineering Research Lab.
Urbana, Ill. 61801

"The Alternative Futures Project is a group of graduate and undergraduate students who have been working on a variety of projects stemming from their interest in futures research and the impact of new communications technologies on society. Their work at the University of Illinois has dealt with the following:

1. How to involve a larger proportion of the public in the planning process.
2. The advantages and disadvantages of public involvement in planning.
3. The application of information theory to understanding economic systems.
4. The teaching computer as a mediator among groups with different viewpoints.
5. How information can best be presented on a computer-based communications medium.
6. The idea of an electronic world university.
7. Developing computer models and scientific theories of social systems which include the impact of technology on society.

Papers dealing with these topics are available for a small fee to cover mailing and handling."

FUTURISTICS CURRICULUM PROJECT
Billy Rojas, Director
Alice Lloyd College
Pippa Passes, Ky. 41844

While developing a futures curriculum at Alice Lloyd College, Billy Rojas continues his general research on futures curricula begun at the University of Massachusetts, where he founded The Program for the Study of the Future in Education. He publishes a periodically updated guide to "Who's Who in Educational Futuristics," listing individuals who teach futuristics or who utilize futures research for educational administration.

"The Meaning of Futuristics," *World Order*, Fall, 1970.

A general overview of futures; description, and definition of futures research and education.

CONSORTIUM FOR FUTURES IN EDUCATION
Jerry Glenn, Director
Program for the Study of the Future In Education
School of Education
University of Massachusetts
Amherst, Mass. 01002

Jerry Glenn has gathered together teachers, administrators, and graduate students from Connecticut, New Hampshire, Massachusetts, and Vermont who are future oriented in their approach to education. The purpose of the Consortium is to survey, compile, *create, test,* and disseminate future oriented teaching processes from the day care center to the doctoral level in education. Rather than simply create and promote futures courses, the Consortium is working to *futurize understanding* by future-orienting all instruction, i.e., future-orient art, science, history, etc.

Anyone may join the Consortium who is willing to help fulfill the Consortium's purpose and contribute to the information interchange.

Futures Information Interchange. $2 a year.
A monthly newsletter containing papers explaining the participants' ideas, their results in the classroom, and reasons as to why.

Future in Curricula. $1.
A paper explaining the nuts and bolts of future-orienting any curriculum.

CENTER FOR INTEGRATIVE STUDIES
c/o John McHale
State University of New York
Binghampton, N.Y. 13901

This Center examines the long-range social and cultural implications of scientific and technological developments:

1. to analyse the large-scale "future" consequences of ongoing social, political, economic, and technological trends; to function as a "sensing" unit concerned with the effect of such trends on the forward quality of the human environment.
2. to integrate the analysis, interpretation, and synthesis of information on the above trends from a great variety of sources.
3. to bring this trans-disciplinary and "social consequences" emphasis into overall educational planning, and to provide a focus for graduate education and research.
4. to link activities in these areas with that of various international centers, institutions, and agencies with whom it exchanges information, and in whose activities it participates.

The Center issues series of working papers and reports derived from its ongoing studies.

"A Survey of Futures Research in the United States," *The Futurist,* December 1970.
A brief overview of surveys on who is doing what type of futures. To be updated.

Typological Survey of Futures Research in the U.S. Washington: National Institute of Mental Health, Center for Studies of Metropolitan Problems, June 1970.
The major survey itself.
The Future of the Future. New York: Ballantine, 1971. $1.50.

WORLD LAW FUND
c/o Michael Washburn
11 West 42nd Street
New York, N.Y. 10036
"The Fund seeks the introduction of the subject of world order into the curricula of all major educational systems of the world—on the graduate, under-graduate, and secondary school levels. We have been working for a decade with scholars in this country and in eight other regions of the world to develop this future-oriented, value-centered, global approach to international relations and world affairs. World order materials are now being published by the major publishers, and the Fund's services and materials have been used by hundreds of American educational institutions. The Fund's program of research, publica-tion, consultancy, and teacher training is entirely supported by contributions from private sources—individuals and small foundations."

MICHAEL MARIEN
Educational Policy Research Center
Syracuse University Research Corporation
1206 Harrison Street
Syracuse, N.Y. 13210
Michael Marien is coordinating a "Futures Information Network" that lists several dozen compilers of futures materials. Write him for further information. He is also an indefatigable documentor of futures literature, with particular emphasis on education. He has been very helpful to us in the development of this section of the *Catalog.*
Alternative Futures for Learning: An Annotated Bibliography of Trends, Forecasts, and Proposals. Syracuse: EPRC, May, 1971. $5.
936 items, mostly annotated; about 80% books or book-length documents from governments and research centers; extensive categorization; indexed by author, organization, and selected subject; special list of bibliographies.

Essential Reading for the Future of Education: A Selected and Critically Annotated Bibliography. Syracuse: EPRC, Revised Edition, February 1971. $1.50.
200 items, virtually all of which are in the above work. Up-to-date editions are being prepared.

LIST OF PUBLICATIONS
 The principal formal sources of current information on futuristics in general are:
 Futures: The Journal of Forecasting and Planning, from IPC (AMERICA) INC., 300 East 42nd Street, New York, N.Y. 10017.

The Futurist, published by the World Future Society, P.O. Box 19285, 20th Street Station, Washington, D.C. 20036

Notes on the Future of Education, published by Educational Policy Research Corporation, 1206 Harrison Street, Syracuse, N.Y. 13210

Social and Human Forecasting Newsletter, published by the Instituto Richerche Applicate Documentasione e Studi, 6, Via Paisiello, 00198 Roma, Italy

ALTERNATIVE FUTURES NETWORKS:
See also, Dennis Livingston; The Life Center; Minnesota Experimental City.

ALTERNATIVE VOCATIONS NETWORKS

What kind of work would you do if you could do anything you wanted? Is there a way to make a living without separating work from life? How can a livelihood be derived from doing what you'd rather be doing instead of whatever it is you're doing and hating doing?

Peg Decious, at Sacramento State College in California, has done a lot of work in encouraging people to think in categories other than a "job." She says that most of the alternative "jobs" that she knows about were created by the people doing them.

"There are no jobs outside the mainstream waiting for likely candidates. The idea that there are jobs is a misconception that all of us hold at one time or another. But there are opportunities to create things to do. . . . Realize that life isn't a series of 'wait untils' (I get out of school, get married, have the baby, get the kids out of school) but more a series of 'right nows.' The person who can repair cars, plant a garden, cook, write, do carpentry, and so forth is more independent. He is free to tell a boring job to get lost. He doesn't have to spend so much money for services. He is able to value freedom and to enjoy change. Our world is changing so rapidly that it makes no sense for someone to decide at 18 to be a biologist, get married at 24, have three kids and live in San Francisco. Instead, he's going to have to take things as they come, trying to avoid unnecessary commitments that tie him down (like spending money for things he doesn't need). . . . Learn to take some of the pressure off by becoming skilled at many jobs, rearranging family patterns (why couldn't a couple both work half-time or live communally or let her work and him stay home, etc.).

"In other words, turn it upside down, inside out and try it another way."

COMMITTEE ON CHRISTIAN VOCATION
Canadian Council of Churches
40 St. Clair Avenue
Toronto 7, Ontario
Canada
    The committee puts out *Jobs Worth Doing*, a directory of service opportunities, summer, one-year, and longer, available through churches, government, and voluntary agencies in Canada and overseas. It covers and provides addresses of sponsoring agencies.

vocations for social change,

Box 13
(415) 376-7743

CANYON, CA 94516

Vocations for Social Change asks the question: "How can people lead meaningful lives in an oppressive society? Answer: By working with others to build alternatives to institutionalized forces that oppress us all.... We exist because many people, young and old, feel alienated from traditional life styles and feel repulsed by careers that reinforce racism, sexism, and exploitation.... Traditional counseling does not show people ways to use their skills to change this society—it only channels people into existing institutions.

"VSC is a living/working collective dedicated to worker/community control of basic institutions, community reconstruction, and the strength of the same as a political force. We publish *WorkForce* (called *Vocations for Social Change* prior to Spring, 1972), a bi-monthly magazine which lists job openings, resource people, and information sources on various aspects of the movement. Sample copies of *WorkForce* are free on request. We ask if you can to please send $5 for receiving the magazine for six months. We exist entirely on donations."

In addition to subscribing to *WorkForce*, you can help VSC by keeping them up to date on activities in your community, and by letting other people know they exist. They need articles about local projects, how they started, why, and how they work.

The following is a regional and local listing of VSC-connected counselors and programs:

Local Counselors:

AR	Fayetteville:	Joe Neal, UA Box 1635, 72701
CA	Davis:	Isao Fujimoto, Dept of Behavioral Sciences, UCD, 95616
	Pasadena:	AFSC, 980 N Fair Oaks, 91103, (213) 791-1978
	Redding:	Pete Rand, Shasta Community Action Project, 2704 N Market, 96001, (916) 241-7631
	San Diego:	Ray Schwartz, 1507 Tarbox, 92114, (714) 262-5360
CO	Boulder:	Marcie Rothberg, Community Free School, 1030 13th St, 80302, (303) 447-8733
		Jacky Richards, c/o Peter Pan Liberation Academy, 1602 Grove, 80302, (303) 442-8938 or 443-2301
CT	New Haven:	Number Nine, 266 State St, 06511, (203) 787-2127
	Storrs:	Mary Maher, Box 366, Storrs, 06268, (203) 742-9611
DC	Washington:	SAJA Collective, 1830 Conn. Ave, 20009, (202) 483-0622
		Mike Koblentz, Washington VSC, Box 231, AU Station, 20044, (202) 244-1075
IN	Terre Haute:	Chuck Norman, 806 N 6th St, 47809, (812) 232-9968
MD	Columbia:	Ric Moore, 5361 Brookway No. 3, 21043, (301) 739-0690
MA	Cambridge:	Margaret Partridge, Education for Action, Radcliffe College, 02138, (617) 495-8604
	Worcester:	Worcester VSC, Box 1260, Clark U., 01110
NB	Omaha:	Gary Giombi, 135 N 32nd Ave, 68131, (402) 346-6711
		Roger Duncan, 3624 Hawthorne, 68131, (402) 553-3623

NH	Portsmouth:	Susie Papeman, 26 Profile Ave, 03801
NC	Charlotte:	Dave Blevins, 2901 Danlow Pl, 28208, (704) 399-0885
NY	Rochester:	Elaine Greene, 32 Sanford St, 14620, (716) 271-6753
OH	Oberlin:	OPGC, Peters Hall, Oberlin College, 44074
RI	Providence:	Beverly Edwards, Chaplain's Office, Brown U, 02913, (401) 863-2344
TN	Sequatchie:	George Brosi, Star Route, 37374, (615) 942-3565
UT	Salt Lake City:	John Wade, Campus Christian Center, 232 University, 84102, (801) 364-4357
WI	Madison:	Whole Earth Co-op, 817 Johnson, 53703, (608) 256-8828
WY	Laramie:	Dick Putney, UCM, 1215 Grand Ave, 82070, (307) 742-3791

Local programs:
CALIFORNIA
Fresno

Center for Change
1407 N Van Ness, 93728
(209) 485-7485

a bookstore/contact center for the central valley—they do drop-in counseling and share energies with a printing collective, food conspiracy and other community projects.

Los Angeles

Creating VSC
c/o Lance Perlman
3224 Sunset Blvd. 90012
(213) 660-2400

involved in group and individual counseling; attempting to initiate new projects by getting people with similar interests together; hope to set up permanent resource center; have several drop-in centers in area; working on yellow pages and publish a newsletter.

San Francisco

New Vocations/AFSC
2160 Lake St., 94121
(415) 752-7766

drop-in counseling and resource center for Bay Area they've pioneered techniques for group job raps; published *Working Loose*, a guide to personal liberation; *Seed People*, about those who've made basic changes in life/work; travel in resource bus throughout California, spreading literature and ideas.

MASSACHUSETTS
Cambridge

Boston VSC
353 Broadway, 02193
(617) 661-1571

storefront counseling and resource center for activities in greater Boston; also extensive library with literature from around country; act as organizing center to connect people with ideas and groups—also spread information about antiwar actions; publish a yellow pages.

MICHIGAN
East Lansing

Alternatives Resource Center
458 Evergreen St., 48823
(517) 351-8760

counseling center and resource library; they've published a directory of alternatives for Michigan and are planning a multi-media display on creating alternative life vocations.

NEW YORK
New York

Emmaus House
241 E 116 St., 10029
(212) 348-5622

resource center for many movement activities in area; much involvement in anti-war organizing; do a lot of phone counseling; have good library for research and general information.

Flushing

Queens VSC
Victoria Catz
153-11 61 Rd., 11367

emerging as a center for social change activities in Queens; publish newsletter and setting up resource library; do drop-in counseling focal point for anti-war organizing in area.

Ithaca

Center for Ithaca Alternatives
412 Linn St., 14850
(607) 539-7359

informational/contact center; trying to initiate new alternatives in area; publish a newsletter and willing to travel in region as resource people, especially into alternative economics; setting up a community of communes with self-supporting cottage industries.

NORTH CAROLINA
Durham

OPT
Box 6487 Duke Sta., 28208
(919) 684-2618

presently operating as a drop-in center at the Y; for job raps and job matchups, have published a community directory and planning a resource library as part of development into an information/community center.

OREGON
Eugene

Black Bart Brigade
1948 Olive St., 97405
(503) 344-1093

publishes a magazine devoted to the idea of leaving the system and finding new ways of living and working aimed at the middle-aged, middle class; also has set up small, personalized support groups on the theme of finding ways out of the system.

WASHINGTON
Bellingham

VSC Program
Fairhaven College, 98225
(206) 676-3679

a new local effort; much one-to-one job counseling; involved in community cooperatives (food and garage), researching power structures and organizing workers around such local issues as pollution by paper companies; will be publishing Puget Sound Alternatives directory in conjunction with Cascade.

Vancouver

Cascade
OKAY Community Center
308 W 15 St., 98660
(206) 694-4440

NW regional VSC, do drop-in counseling; attempt to hook up people and groups to generate new alternatives and ideas; have published their first regional directory on alternatives along the Oregon Coast and in the Willamette Valley and plan five others for the Pacific NW area.

WISCONSIN
Milwaukee

VSC
2415 Oakland Av., 53211
(414) 332-3508

a budding, local project; opened an office in August-involved at present in alternative job counseling and placement; in process of printing an alternatives directory for region.

CANYON COLLECTIVE   25c
Box 77
Canyon, Ca. 94576

The Canyon Collective, the people who help put out *WorkForce* (formerly *Vocations for Social Change*), say "To change the world completely is all we want. And it isn't that hard. The emergence of living situations that play with this world as they create a new one. People taking their own power into their own hands: This is possible all the time—everywhere.

"If you're into social change and want to set up an underground paper, draft counseling center, free school, food buying co-op, movement coffee house, switchboard, child care center, clearing-house, free clinic or whatever, this special 24-page tabloid can be a real help. Single copies of *Canyon Collective* are 25c and bulk rates are available to community centers, liberation schools, peoples' book stores, and street salesmen."

NEW LIFE VOCATIONS NEWSLETTER
Placement Center
Sacramento State College
Sacramento, Ca. 95819
c/o Peg Decious
(916) 454-6231

Ms. Decious publishes a very fine newsletter on new life vocations. Aimed primarily at people counseling in colleges and college placement offices, but with many valuable leads and ideas. Subscription is $5 a year, sample copies 25c donation.

Peg Decious has let us reprint a partial list of her subscribers and the list makes a very nice network/guide to people in many states, in and out of colleges, who are at least sympathetic to counseling and information sharing around the idea of alternative vocations. We suspect that some of these people will probably insist that you be an enrolled student at their institution before they will share their information with you. One way to get around that might be to get to see them during slack times in their schedules, i.e. when they're not busy talking with students, or when, maybe, the school is on vacation and these people have to be in their offices anyway.

Mrs. Bettie S. Harrop
Career Planning & Placement
University of Alaska
College, Alaska 99701

Robert A. Hale
Educational Placement
University Placement Service
University of Arizona
Tuscon, Ariz. 95721

Mrs. Nansi Corson, Manager
Mrs. Suzanne Koehn, Placement
    Interviewer
Student & Alumni Placement Center
University of California
Berkeley, Ca. 94720

Valley Free School Switchboard
1362 N Street
Fresno, Ca. 93721

Gary Sweatt
American Friends Service Committee
2160 Lake Street
San Francisco, Ca. 94121

Maris Charnow, Placement Interviewer
Isaac Reams, Job Developer
Placement Center
San Francisco State College
1600 Holloway Avenue
San Francisco, Ca. 94132

Gene L. Nelson, Placement Director
University Placement Center
Stadium Building, Entrance 10
University of Colorado
Boulder, Colo. 80302

Douglas Daring, Director
Placement & Career Planning
University of Connecticut
Storrs, Conn. 06268

Mrs. Gertrude McSurely
Student Career Service
The George Washington University
Washington, D.C. 20006

Samuel M. Hall, Jr., Director
Office of Placement & Career Planning
Howard University
Washington, D.C. 20001

Mrs. Anita Sandke, Director &
    Assistant Dean of Students
Career Counseling & Placement
University of Chicago
5706 University Avenue
Chicago, Ill. 60636

Mrs. Janet R. Davis, Placement
    Officer
Placement & Credentials Services
University of Maryland
College Park, Maryland 20740

Johanna Halbeisen
Vocations for Social Change
c/o AFSC
48 Inman Street
Cambridge, Mass. 02139

Dr. Spencer Potter
Career Planning & Placement
Clark University
Worcester, Mass. 01610

Miss Leith Shackel, Director of
Placement
Carleton College
Northfield, Minn. 55057

Miss Beverly J. Schrader, Assistant to
the Director
University Placement Office
University of Missouri, St. Louis
3001 Natural Bridge Road
St. Louis, Mo. 63121

Edward J. Doherty, Director of
Placement
Placement Service
University of New Hampshire
Durham, N.H. 03824

Jack Wilson, Career Counselor
Rutgers University
New Brunswick, N.J. 08903

Sonya M. Weil
University Placement & Career
Services
Columbia University
607 Dodge
New York, N.Y. 10027

Richard F. Delmonte, Director
Central Placement Services
Rochester Institute of Technology
Rochester, N.Y. 14623

Lucie W. Barber
Counselors for Peace and Social
Change
Union College
Character Research Project
10 Nott Terrace
Schenectady, N.Y. 12808

Mrs. Josephine P. Schaeffer,
Placement Director
Placement Office
University of North Carolina
Greensboro, N.C. 27412

Dorothy M. Smith, Director of
Placement & Graduate Counseling
Oberlin College
Oberlin, Ohio 44074

Eugene W. Dils, Director
University Placement Service
University of Oregon
Eugene, Ore. 97403

Mary Lee Hassall, Counselor
Career Services
Temple University
1819 North Broad Street
Philadelphia, Pa. 19122

John F. Jenkins, Director of Placement
Portland State University
Portland, Ore. 97207

Zachary R. Hodges, Placement
Assistant
East Texas State University
East Texas Station
Commerce, Tex. 95428

Blair Hale, Director of Placement
Utah State University
Logan, Utah 84321

Mrs. Arthur S. Bates, Director of
Vocational Guidance
Sweet Briar College
Sweet Briar, Va. 24595

B. Dean Owens, Placement Director
College Placement Service
Central Washington State
Ellensburg, Wa. 98926

Scott Glascock, Placement Counselor
Career Planning & Placement
University of Washington
301 Loew Hall
Seattle, Wa. 98105

Miss Cornelia Ladwig, Placement
Director
Frank Carney, Placement Assistant
West Virginia University
Morgantown, W. Va. 26506

ALTERNATIVE EMPLOYMENT
Project One
1380 Howard Street
San Francisco, Ca. 94103
(415) 626-1917
   This outfit was set up by a "businessman-turned-freak." He made the transition to a more humane and liveable lifestyle and is sincerely interested in helping others create their own space. He knows a lot about the ins and outs of the various systems within the System. Call to check the hours.

ECOS
Project One
10th and Howard
San Francisco, Ca. 94103
(415) 626-0267
   The People's Yellow Pages of San Francisco describes ECOS in these words: "Organized to assist groups and individuals with realizing an alternative living and working style in warehouses south of Market, to provide any assistance people require in actualizing this kind of alternative—technical assistance, design, engineering, building codes, legal questions, and human inter-action problems."

next step

1240 Fourteenth Avenue
San Francisco, Ca. 94122
(415) 664-2421
   Next Step is a non-profit organization set up to deal with people in transition, started in 1968 with a program to help former clergymen and Religious make the transition to lay life. Their emphasis is on vocational redevelopment. Since then they have expanded their program to include a wide range of personal and professional transitions including released prisoners, school teachers, and people in divorce situations. They conduct six-week career forums, and have open house every Friday at 8:30 p.m. There is a nominal fee, but the first interview is without obligation.
   "They also offer on an occasional basis courses in group leadership, photography, lithographic skills, painting, etc., and publish a bi-monthly newsletter announcing these. One year's free subscription to the newsletter simply by writing for it."

INVEST YOURSELF
475 Riverside Drive, #665
New York, N.Y. 10027
   Mother Earth News says about *Invest Yourself*, and we basically agree, that "this catalogue of service opportunities is one of the handiest little directories we've seen to work camps, apprenticeships, seminars, community action projects, caravans and other learn-while-you-work programs. "If you're young or old, idealistic, looking for meaningful work that needs to be done (in this country or abroad) . . . and can be happy with room, board and—in rare cases—a meager salary, invest $1 in *Invest Yourself*." ($1.25 by first class mail.)

THE MOONLIGHTER'S MANUAL   75c
By Jerry LeBlanc
Paperback Library
315 Park Avenue
New York, N.Y. 10010

The *Last Whole Earth Catalog* had this to say about Jerry LeBlanc's book: "Moonlighting means having a second job. Lots of people don't have a first job or want one. Birds of this feather flock economically together and pool resources for rent, food, dope, etc.—which still requires some modest income. Moonlight type work may be the answer. Most of the income sources in this book are part-time, or do-at-home, and involve low commitment of psyche (an advantage they have over stealing or dope peddling). The book includes a good list of technical training schools."

Some of the moonlighting jobs include crossing guards, running a clipping bureau from magazines and newspapers, waterproofing basements, notary public, typewriter repairs, home moving, laying tile, locksmithing, etc.

Black Bart

Brigade

1948 Olive
Eugene, Ore. 97405
(503) 344-1093

This magazine, published every 6 to 8 weeks, "contains a wide spectrum of personal-experience articles which should provide meaningful contributions to . . . planning for change. Also included is a resource guide and The Outlaw Register, a people communications device." (CFC *Journal*, No. 11)

". . . . The *Black Bart* philosophy opens the subject of revolution as a personal thing. In so doing, it makes a passing reference to the idea that it seems somehow improper in the middle age range to contemplate a radical restructuring of a life already half lived. This is a defense, albeit a reluctant one, for those who find themselves trapped midstream in life, looking longingly at those of lesser years who seem wise enough to avoid the traps before they are sprung. . . . So it is small wonder that the fearful among us hide our meekness behind our age. Independence has never been for the shallow of heart, and it is not today. But perhaps among these pages you will learn that you are not alone without resources. If we can help provide the spark which generates your own fire of confidence and determination, we shall consider the effort well justified."

By donation, $5 for half a year, $10 for a year.

ALTERNATIVE VOCATIONS NETWORKS:
See also, Emmaus House; PEOPLE'S YELLOW PAGES; Shanti Center; SOCIAL AND POLITICAL CHANGE NETWORKS: Radicals In The Professions.

ARTISAN AND SKILLS NETWORKS

There are so many strands to the crafts network that we've no doubt missed more than a few. What we've listed below is what we know as of now. Nearly every state and region has some form of craftsmen's guild or network of its own. There are some national organizations that cover specific types of crafts and the American Crafts Council in New York City takes most of those under its wing.

THE INTERSECTION NEWSLETTER
756 Union Street
San Francisco, Ca. 94133
    "The *Intersection Newsletter* is directed to artists and craftsmen, churchmen, organizations and the community. It appears every month or so. The *Newsletter* is a free service and should be freely passed around. Announcements, requests for inclusion on our mailing list, and communications of general or specific interest to the cultural life of the community . . ." are welcomed.
    Basically serving the San Francisco Bay area, *Intersection Newsletter* is published by Intersection: A Center for Religion and the Arts. It's a valuable guide to what's going on in arts and crafts in the S.F. area, and is very good guide to California crafts and arts networks. It lists events for the coming month, essays, exhibits, dance, theatre, film, music, and a category called Other Things which include just about everything else. Free.

AMERICAN CRAFTS COUNCIL
29 WEST 53RD STREET, NEW YORK, N. Y. 10019
    (212) CI 6-6840
    The American Crafts Council publishes two directories: one for craft centers and people in the U.S., and one for the rest of the world.
    Directory of Craft Courses $1.50. "A listing of universities, colleges, private workshops, museum schools and art centers which offer craft courses in their programs." However, some of the places they list aren't overly worried

about diplomas, degrees, or credentials. Crafts covered include stained glass, plastics, textiles, weaving, leather, bookbinding, ceramics, enameling, metals, silversmithing, jewelry, wood, furniture, and woodcarving. Summer programs are published separately, write for listings.

Short Guide to World Crafts $1.50. Brief but comprehensive information on crafts in 60 countries, including principal crafts, principal craft areas, contemporary craftsmen and designers in various fields, schools teaching crafts, museums and galleries exhibiting crafts, government organizations concerned with crafts, crafts associations or organizations with craftsmen members, crafts periodicals, folklorists, and exhibitions.

Three other publications from the American Crafts Council that are worth knowing about are:

Taxes and the Craftsman, by Sydney Prepau, $2.50. A guide to figuring taxes for the craftsman, much of whose work is seasonal, and whose income isn't always the same; how to deduct studio space, materials, time, etc.

Crafts for Retirement, ed. by Mary Lyon, $2.95. A guide book for students and teachers, providing basic descriptions of all the major crafts, including lists of suppliers, how to set up crafts centers (for any age group), and so forth.

Craft Shops/Galleries USA, $2.75. A national listing of craft outlets and galleries. Addresses, names of owners, telephone numbers, business hours, etc. A valuable guide to possible sales outlets for your work.

THE NEW MUSIC AND ARTS EXCHANGE $1
152 West 66th Street
New York, N.Y. 10023

"Art can articulate honestly what *is*, both the events of the human soul and the events on the stage of society; and it can give voice to what might *be*. We believe that many of the established art forms are no longer faithful to the task. New arts, both in style and content, are necessary. To participate in the process of humanization the new arts must speak to those who have been by-passed by the established arts—to the local churches of Harlem or Evanston, community centers, narcotic rehabilitation houses, neighborhood schools. . . .

"The New Music and Arts Exchange presents this catalog as the beginning of a central resource to facilitate the process of exchange of new materials between radical and experimental artists and other creative persons or groups. We have chosen these materials for two reasons: 1) their creative expression of the social revolutions of our times, and/or 2) their honest, serious experimentation with new forms, materials, technologies."

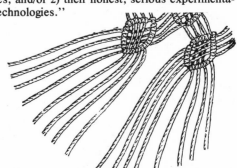

LIST OF NATIONAL CRAFTS ASSOCIATIONS

We asked the Southern Highland Handicraft Guild of Asheville, N.C., to compile a list of national crafts guilds and associations. The list below is based on theirs. Along with the American Craft Council materials, this covers the country pretty well, but we'd like to know of guilds, associations, or other networks in your region.

Society of Connecticut Craftsmen, Inc.
44 Audubon Street
New Haven, Ct. 06511

Handweavers Guild of America
339 North Steele Road
West Hartford, Ct. 06117

Georgia Arts Newsletter
University of Georgia
Visual Arts Building
Athens, Ga. 30601

Kentucky Guild of Artists and Craftsmen
Berea, Ky. 40403
c/o Garry Barker, Director

Maine Coast Craftsmen
82 Elm Street
Camden, Me. 04843
c/o Stell and Shevia

Potters Guild of Baltimore
201 Homeland Avenue
Baltimore, Md. 21212

Massachusetts Association of Craftsmen
18 Bowden Street
Newton Center
Boston, Mass. 02127
c/o Daisy Brand

League of New Hampshire Craftsmen
205 North Main Street
Concord, N.H. 03301
c/o L. G. Tackett

New Hampshire League of Craftsmen
13 Lebanon Street
Hanover, N.H. 03755

Southern Highland Handicraft Guild
Box 9145
Asheville, N.C. 28804

Carolina Designer Craftsmen
2707 Sevier Street
Durham, N.C. 27705
c/o Helen Pratt

Albermarle Craftsmen's Guild
c/o Chamber of Commerce
Elizabeth City, N.C. 27909

Madison County Crafts
Mars Hill College
Mars Hill, N.C. 28754
c/o Diane Brown

Piedmont Craftsmen
936 West Fourth Street
Winston-Salem, N.C. 27101
c/o Ann Bonitz, Executive Director
(919) 725-1516

Society of Vermont Craftsmen
Chelsea, Vt. 05038

West Virginia Guild of Artists & Crafts
Room 404
East State Capitol Building
Charleston, W. Va. 25305
c/o Don Page

LIST OF WEAVING RESOURCES

Weavers, like potters, are among the world's special people. Throughout history, weavers and potters have been the people who have fulfilled two of man's greatest needs: the need to create; and the need for beautiful, useful things. We've listed some weaving places and supply houses. All of the people and places below can give you more information on where to find weavers who will teach you all about warp and woof and the marvelous things you can do with them. Please let us know if you know of weaving teachers, as we'd like to list them.

Sheridan College of Applied Arts & Technology
School of Design
1460 South Sheridan Way
Port Credit, Ontario
Canada

Ida Grae Weaving Workshop
424 LaVerne
Mill Valley, Ca. 94941

The Yarn Depot, Inc.
545 Sutter Street
San Francisco, Ca. 94102

Brookfield Craft Center, Inc.
Brookfield, Ct. 06804

The Silver Shuttle
1301 35th Street, N.W.
Washington, D.C. 20007
(202) FE 8-3789

Indian Summer Fibercrafts
1703 E. 55th
Chicago, Ill. 60615
(312) 684-2197

North Shore Handweaving Shop
1807 Central Street
Evanston, Illinois 60201
(312) GR 5-4343

Worcester Craft Center
25 Sagamore Road
Worcester, Mass. 01605

Newark Museum Arts Workshop
43-49 Washington Street
Newark, N.J. 07101

Thousand Islands Museum Craft School
Clayton, N.Y. 13624

Woodstock Guild of Craftsmen
34 Tinker Street
Woodstock, N.Y. 12498

The Factory of Visual Arts
5040 9th Avenue N.E.
Seattle, Wa. 98105

LIST OF PUBLICATIONS
Specialized magazines provide good information about specific craft fields that is practically unobtainable anywhere else. We've listed a few of the magazines below that are useful for finding your way into the craft web.

The Craftsman $3.50
Box 1386
Ft. Worth, Tex. 76101

Craft Horizons $10
16 East 52nd Street
New York, N.Y. 10022

Ceramics Monthly $6
Box 4548
Columbus, Ohio 43212

Handweaver and Craftsman $8
220 Fifth Avenue
New York, N.Y. 10001

Journal of the Guilds of Weavers, Spinners and Dyers $1.20
c/o Mary Barker
1 Harrington Road
Brighton 1
England

GAY LIBERATION NETWORKS

When homosexuals come out of the closets and begin to publish and organize, it's more than a token effort. We started researching gay groups for this network section, and as with the women's section, decided that the best we could do was to list those national groups and publications that serve as clearinghouses and contact points between the various parts of the gay liberation movement.

There's a real need for someone to pull all this together into a central guide, for gays and for women, that is available from one source or from many sources, whichever is easiest and spreads the word. Someone out there must be doing it . . . who?

VOCATIONS FOR SOCIAL CHANGE
Box 13
Canyon, Ca. 94516
This isn't a gay organization, but the people at VSC put out a recent issue devoted entirely to "gay folk." It includes articles, bibliographies, autobiographies, and listings of homosexual groups around the country. Send them a 50c donation and ask for a copy of the January/February 1972 issue of *Vocations for Social Change* (now *WorkForce*).

GAY WOMEN'S NEWS SERVICE (GWNS)
Box 8507
Stanford, Ca. 94305
   VSC (now *WorkForce*) describes Gay Women's News Service: "The only news service communicating gay women's news to the world. They are willing to help lesbian or other women's groups with cheap, effective communications and public relations. They also publish *Mother*, a national publication covering lesbian news, features, interviews, and national coverage. All information mailed in plain envelopes. $3.50 a year, $5 a year by airmail."

NATIONAL GAY STUDENT CENTER
2115 "S" Street, N.W.
Washington, D.C. 20008
(202) 387-5100, ext. 77
   A project of the National Student Association, the National Gay Student Center is described in *EdCentric* as serving "the purpose of coordinating activities and communications among student gay groups throughout the country and offers a gay information and resource library, a reprint series, and development of regional and national gay student conferences.

MOTIVE $1 each
Vol. 32, No. 1 and 2, 1972
G.P.O. Box 1677
New York, N.Y. 10003
   After having been published by the United Methodist Church for over 20 years, *Motive* has left the church and come out. These last two issues are collections of articles, stories, poems, and art (No. 1 is the lesbian issue, No. 2 is the gay men's liberation issue). Both magazines carry extensive international lists of contacts and publications.

GAY LIBERATION NETWORKS:
See also, Council on Religion and the Homosexual; Emmaus House; Gay Revolutionary Video Project; The Tangent Group.

GROWTH NETWORKS

MODERN MAN IN SEARCH OF UTOPIA $3.95
Alternatives Foundation
P.O. Box 36604
Los Angeles, Ca. 90036
   The list below is a sample of the directory to growth centers in *Modern Man in Search of Utopia*. At the head of their list is the following admonition:
   CAUTION: Listing of these groups does not constitute endorsement by Alternatives Foundation. Some of them may be hazardous to your health. Check carefully before you experience.
   We agree, but the examples we have included in the Centers section will give you an example of what some of the good places are doing.

Florida

Center of Man, Micanopy 32667.   (904) 466-3459.

Han Institute, 855 So. Federal Hwy., Weir Plaza Bl

Heliotrope, Box 9041, Fort Lauderdale 33312.   (305

Maitreyan Foundation, 220 S.W. 2nd St., Boca Raton

Georgia

Adanta, 3379 Peachtree Rd. NE, #250, Atlanta 30326

Atlanta Workshop, 3167 Rilman Rd. NW, Atlanta 3032

Keystone Experience, West Ga. College, Psycho. Dep

Idaho

Western Ranch, Box 923. Hailey 83333.

THE EUPSYCHIAN NETWORK: A GUIDE TO THE HUMAN POTENTIAL MOVEMENT
John T. Canfield, Ed.
Center for Humanistic Education
University of Massachusetts
Amherst, Mass. 01002

This catalog/directory/bibliography is intended to serve as a comprehensive guide to all areas of what is currently being called "the human potential movement." Included in this category are encounter groups, sensory awareness, T-groups, Gestalt therapy, Psychosynthesis, Movement therapy, growth centers, humanistic psychology, bio-energetic analysis, affective and humanistic education, psychedelic experiences, Zen, Yoga, Sufi wisdom, T'ai Chi, ESP, meditation, Transpersonal psychology and many other forms of self-actualization.

The catalog will include descriptions of the major areas of the movement, lists of growth centers and similar places such as meditation centers and ashrams, a guide to leaders and teachers, a list of schools that are humanistically oriented, research centers, professional organizations, and a bibliography of books. Journals, magazines, newsletter, curricula, tapes, and films available.

TOWARD A GUIDE TO HUMANISTIC EDUCATION
By John T. Canfield
New England Center
Box 575
Amherst, Mass. 01002
(413) 549-0886

This book is to be a comprehensively annotated bibliography and guide to major resources in the area of humanistic and affective education. In addition to a listing of books in the fields of humanistic psychology and education, this guide will include Centers for Humanistic Education, a listing of major clearinghouses in the field, Affective Education Projects, resources in the area of creativity, growth centers concerned with humanistic education, a guide to people and consultants in the field, a guide to the alternative school movement, education in the communes, curriculum materials, associations, journals and newsletters, simulation materials, a guide to higher education, sources of classroom exercises, and a media guide to films, tapes, and instrumented programs.

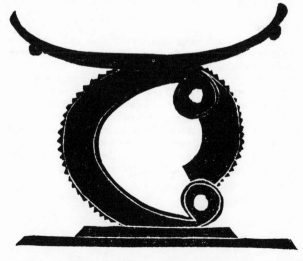

LEARNING EXCHANGES

Somebody finally made the connection between people in their hometown who knew something worth teaching and those who wanted to learn it.

Basically, a Learning Exchange works like this: someone with something to teach calls the Learning Exchange and offers to teach it to someone else, sometimes free, sometimes not. A person who wants to learn about something calls the Exchange and tells them what he's interested in. The Exchange then matches up teacher with learner and gives the learner the teacher's telephone number. If the Exchange has more than one person listed as a teacher or learner, then the caller gets them all, and decides which one is the one he'd most like to teach or learn from.

THE LEARNING EXCHANGE
P.O. Box 920
Evanston, Ill. 60204
(312) 864-4133

The Evanston Learning Exchange is modeled along the lines of Everett Reimer's and Ivan Illich's concept of learning networks. It is a free service through which persons who wish instruction in any of some 300 subjects are given names of persons offering instruction in the subject; usually the instruction is free of charge, though much of it is done on a barter basis: you teach her piano, she'll teach you Chinese cookery. The service gets its rent free, has no payroll and makes no outgoing phone calls; so its expenses are little more than the cost of its file cards.

Subjects available run almost from A to Z, specifically from African music to Yiddish. Matches are arranged also between people who wish to discuss a particular book or who share other common interests. None of the instruction is for credit. So far the Learning Exchange has matched several hundred students and teachers, aged 8 to 80.

COME TOGETHER
Box 27
Glenwood, Ill. 60425

This is the learning exchange that serves most of Chicago's far southern suburbs, and it is modeled after the one in Evanston, which serves Chicago's north side and northern suburbs.

". . . the medium used by Come Together is a postal box, rather than the telephone. Maybe someday, through growth, more can be done. To date, we're quite small. . . . a stamped and addressed envelope would be appreciated. Other than that, we will do what we can to match persons who delineate their interests.

"To complete the story, this is (as of today) a one-man operation. After having heard of the Learning Exchange [in Evanston], I searched and searched for almost any medium to join out here in the southern suburbs and found nothing. Now, we have Come Together, to bring people together to teach, to learn or to rap."

NEW LIFE EXCHANGE
912 South Henderson
Bloomington, Ind. 47401

New Life Exchange offers itself as a matching service "in helping you find the people you need to do your thing. Send us a description of your individual alternative, and we'll send you the names of others with compatible interests. Or if you need someone with special skills or assets, we'll try to help you find that person.

"Currently we're in contact with potential sponsors, skilled craftsmen and technicians, experienced real-life farmers, seasoned communards, dissatisfied school teachers, lost sheep, stray cats and others who are ready to start living again. And we're checking out all sorts of leads on established, embryo and visionary alternatives."

They invite contributions to help the cause, and have a bi-weekly newsletter ($2.00) "to help get people together with themselves and with each other."

KNOWLEDGE AND SKILLS EXCHANGE
c/o Action Studies Program
303 Jefferson Building
Iowa City, Ia.
(319) 353-3610

"To Learn-To Teach-To Learn" is a directory. "Its purpose is to promote a knowledge and skills exchange among individual members" of the Iowa City community.

The organizers of the Knowledge and Skills Exchange publish a directory of learners and teachers and topics that people want to learn about or teach. They started by direct solicitation of people on the street, posters (which they said were very ineffectual), setting up a card table on the sidewalk (which they said works well) and door-to-door campaigns (which they say are tiring but effective and good publicity, besides). And they depend entirely on volunteer workers.

Some of the learning-teaching topics include Aikido; abstract algebra; bagpipes; Chinese cooking; hunting; herbs; how to approach true intimacy with people; those incomprehensible things beyond human understanding; typesetting and printing; Swahili; and beginning waterpolo.

OPENINGS NETWORKS
613 Winans Way
Baltimore, Md. 21229
c/o John Ciekot
(301) 233-2621

"Openings Networks is a learning sources-exchange-switchboard-bank-reference-center-tool-field. ON is taking calls in the Baltimore area from people who are seeking to learn in a certain topic area and refers them to people who have called to make available learning in that same topic area. Where we have

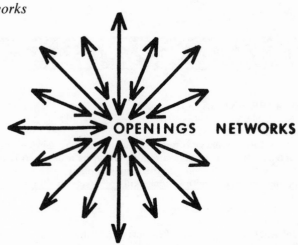

OPENINGS   NETWORKS

no one listed as a resource, we become detectives and try to find such a person (or situation).

"Looking for a resource gives ON an opportunity to open up one more segment of the ordinary daily activities of the 'adult world' so that the world might become the learning laboratory for the people. We want to see learners of all ages able to get at the learning they desire as that field of learning is actually put to practice in our culture.

"Money: Learning seekers and resource people make their own financial agreements, if any. For its services, ON requests contributions. If you want a copy of our model publication, please send a buck."

INGROUP
Public Learning Corporation
18 Brattle Street
Cambridge, Mass. 02138
(617) 868-0299

If you're living in a town or city that doesn't yet have its own learning exchange, and you're not up to organizing one, here's the next best thing. For a fee of $15 a year ($25 for two years), you tell Ingroup what you're interested in learning about. Ingroup finds six to ten people who share the same interests and sets up a meeting of the group, and for a few more dollars they'll find a resource person for the group, if the group decides it wants one. If that doesn't work, Ingroup will form another group or find a different resource person. They also plan a newsletter/catalog to keep people up to date on what they can offer for that $15.

Ingroup covers five broad areas: *situational groups*, which include back from Vietnam, changing careers, drug problems, buying land, culture shock, and new baby; *social groups*, which include playing music, foreign travel, mountain-climbing, playreading, wine tasting, rap sessions, and singing; *how-to groups* in ceramics, budgets, first aid, day care, film making, karate, and computer programming; *academic groups* to study Zen, ecology, aerospace, literature, and urban problems; and *self-study groups*, such as encounter groups, problem-solving, simulations, role-playing, couples groups, and self-directed change.

FRANKLIN COUNTY LEARNING EXCHANGE
c/o Greenfield Public Library
Greenfield, Mass. 01301
(413) 772-6305

An experiment of the Greenfield Public Library, the Learning Exchange operates during the hours the library is open. They use both the telephone and mail to match up learners and teachers. Anyone can register at the main checkout desk of the library.

(This is modeled after the Evanston Learning Exchange. Mark Cheren, who started the Greenfield Exchange, got a casette tape of questions and answers from the folks in Evanston.)

EDUCATION EXPLORATION CENTER
3104 16th Avenue South
Minneapolis, Minn. 55407
(612) 722-6613

The EEC runs a multi-service center that also includes a learning exchange. They have been around for awhile and know their territory pretty well.

They're interested in exploring the ideas of education with anyone at anytime.

would you believe ...

a whole city as a learning exchange?

MINNESOTA EXPERIMENTAL CITY (MXC)
7800 Metro Parkway
Minneapolis, Minn. 55420
c/o Ron Barnes

An experimental city is going to be built somewhere in Minnesota, on a site chosen in late 1972. Call it an information city. Or call it a communications city. Or call it a deschooled city. It will have many different kinds of centers, where people can learn particular skills and styles of life. It will have a computerized access system by which anybody in the city who wants to teach/learn anything can find all the other people in the city who want to teach/learn it.

"The experimental city envisioned for Minnesota goes a step beyond today's new towns. One of its aims is to be a living laboratory where innovative economic, social and environmental concepts will be tested. Harnessing all available technology and knowledge for the solution of urban problems, it will try to determine the efficiency of things hitherto untried and finally afford guidelines for the future rational development of the nation's existing cities and new towns still to be built.

"Planners intend to design a learning based alternative education system which has application in the new city *and* elsewhere. The city itself should become a learning center for its 250,000 residents and for people around the world. . . . a birth-to-death, regenerative system dedicated to exploring new ways of understanding change in a new age."

LEARNING RESOURCES EXCHANGE
4552 McPherson
St. Louis, Mo. 63108
(314) 367-4458

One of the granddaddies of the learning exchanges—they've been around for over 2 years, get their catalog printed by a leading St. Louis department store as a public service, and have a 30-minute radio slot on KDNA on Tuesdays at 5:30 p.m.

Learning Resources Exchange has people available to teach nearly anything: their catalog includes sections on life sciences, physical sciences, math, occupational skills, hobbies and sports, education, social sciences, language and communication, art, music, humanities, and general tutoring. Also listed are people who are willing to take responsibility, individually, for arranging the education of 3-16 year-old children on a regular daily basis in groups of approximately six to a dozen.

THE FREE LEARNING EXCHANGE
305 Riverside Drive, Apt. 7-E
New York, N.Y. 10025
c/o Paul Knatz
(212) UN5-9634

Operating throughout New York City in conjunction with several switchboards and alternative learning projects, "the Exchange invites all people to register both the skills or skill they would be willing to teach and the subjects they would like to learn. The Exchange will then do its best to match people according to their interests. Poetry, writing, two-stroke motorcycle engines, fluency in Mandarin or French. Maybe you've never thought of some of the things you do best as being 'subjects' or valuable and useful to somebody . . . how to scan a newspaper, buy and prepare fresh vegetables, buy a used car.

"It will be up to the individuals concerned to decide whether a particular pair or group is educationally compatible. . . .

"We are dedicated to educational freedom. And the service is free to anyone who cannot afford to make a contribution in money. We are, nevertheless, entirely dependent on donations, even for stationery and postage."

The Free Learning Exchange, used in conjunction with the *People's Yellow Pages* put out by Vocations for Social Change at Emmaus House, 241 East 116th Street, should just about cover New York City. (*See also*, Emmaus House; Vocations for Social Change; *People's Yellow Pages*-N.Y. City.)

THE LEARNING NETWORK
c/o The New School Movement
Earth Station 7
402 15th Avenue, East
Seattle, Wash. 98105

"In the interest of joyful, voluntary, non-institutional, cooperative, free learning, we are inviting you to join a learning network. This directory will help people who want to teach, to communicate with those who want to learn.

"There is a tremendous diversity of potential learning experiences—games, crafts, disciplines, discussions, encounter groups, slide shows, lectures, skills, workshops, trips, action groups, etc.

"Each member of the network describes learning experiences for which (s)he is teacher/facilitator. These descriptions, plus all other pertinent information, are listed in the directory. Members of the network arrange their own learning experiences by contacting the teacher/facilitator from whom they want to learn. No fees are charged. The initial session of each learning experience should be regarded as a time for teachers and learners to discover each other before making a commitment. Learners are free to terminate or continue their involvement after the initial exploratory session.

"We will not mail the directories out; they must be picked up at the office." We suspect that if you lived in Devil's Elbow, Mo., they'd mail you one, if you sent 50c to help cover printing and mailing costs.

THE LEARNING NET
c/o Whole Earth Co-Op
817 East Johnson
Madison, Wisc. 83703
(608) 256-8828

This new learning exchange is an outgrowth of the Madison Whole Earth community. They publish a newsletter/catalog with listings of people and skills, learners and teachers, and phone numbers.

To register in the newsletter/catalog, you call the Whole Earth Co-Op, or fill out a card at the store. They're open to any community people who want to help them with the learning exchange.

Topics and skills listed so far include yoga, dome building, knitting and crocheting, farm brigades to work on small farms that can't afford migrant labor, and leathercraft.

THE LEARNING EXCHANGE
East Side Community Center
911 East Ogden Avenue
Milwaukee, Wisc. 53202
(414) 273-1490

Bill Murtaugh has started a learning exchange modeled after the one in Evanston, Illinois. He says, "Structures in schools are mostly oriented like a Skinnerian box (with money as the prime force) toward that rat's bar of industry which designs for us our specialized livelihoods. . . . What is complicated is not that people want to learn and teach . . . but that we've been made to believe in ourselves as inferior beings by a system of positive and negative sanctions, success and failures which measures from A to F. However, a learning exchange is based on the premise that school is wherever you are, not determined by a thick wall or a flat professor."

MEDIA NETWORKS

Communications

SOURCE CATALOG $1.75
Vol. 1—Communications
Swallow Press
1139 South Wabash
Chicago, Ill. 60605
Or from: Source Collective
    Box 21066
    Washington, D.C. 20009

Planned as the Movement Encyclopedia to people and groups working for social change, *Source* "is designed to put people in touch with projects and resources and to encourage the building of creative new working relationships among people.

"This book is not a Sears catalog of emotionless products assembled by technicians, but a revolution in action." The first volume, with 1500 entries, is centered on Communications, with entries under mass media, periodicals, printing and publishing, language, libraries, community communications, music, art, theatre, video, radio, and tape. Additional volumes are being prepared on such things as health rights, environment, third world, etc. Swallow Press says, "If the *Whole Earth Catalog* is a wishbook for a mythical return-to-the land, *Source* is its action counterpart—a tool for initiating and spreading radical change in America's institutions. More than 400 books, periodicals, films and tapes—most of them focusing on how to get things done—are listed here. There are more than 500 print and media groups listed, as well as myriad film co-ops, community-controlled TV, political art, music, street theatre, and related community-based communications groups across the nation."

The *Source* people say, "The entire catalog will be a scenario of America as it is now—and what it could become."

See also, Minnesota Experimental City, Robert Theobald; *Source Catalog, Vol. II, Communities/Housing.*

Press and Publishing

ALTERNATIVE PRESS INDEX
c/o Alternative Press Centre
Bag Service 2500
Postal Station C
Toronto, Ontario
Canada

These people index approximately 118 publications that most commercial indexers don't even know exist, as well as many others that you *can* buy at any newsstand. Periodicals range from *The Catholic Worker* to *Chicago Journalism*

Review to *Los Angeles Free Press* to I. F. Stone's weekly to *This Magazine is About Schools.*

Publications indexed fall in the spectrum of women's publications, Chicanos, blacks, prison reform, education, underground newspapers, and more.

An indispensable tool for people wanting to research beyond the immediately apparent. $6 per year for individuals; $10 for movement groups; $15 for high schools; $30 for libraries and educational institutions; $60 for military and corporate institutions.

THIRD WORLD READER SERVICE

1500 Farragut Street, N.W.
Washington, D.C. 20011
(202) 723-8273

This is a reader's service for people who don't have the time to read all the periodicals they'd like to in order to keep truly informed. And for those who can't afford all those subscriptions, either.

Basically, Third World Reader Service reads dozens of magazines and newspapers regularly, selects the best articles dealing with various aspects of the Third World (those groups of people in the U.S. and elsewhere who have been traditionally exploited, poor and powerless . . .) reprints them, with permission, and mails them to subscribers throughout the year.

The Service offers "regular exposure to facts and viewpoints which balance the usual TV and local newspaper coverage, continuing education necessary for living responsibly today, an understanding of the struggles of the powerless and the poor, and an opportunity to stay aware of those ideas, events, and realities which affect the present and shape the future."

Individual subscriptions are $18 a year, for which you get five articles every month; institutional subscriptions are $75 for which you get 15 articles a month plus special arrangements for multiple copies of articles for conferences and study groups, etc. When you write for more details, send along $1 donation for a sample packet.

OMEGA GRAPHICS

711 South Dearborn
Chicago, Ill. 60605

Omega Graphics can help you get used printing equipment ranging from mimeographing machines to printing presses and camera equipment. The better mimeos are available from $45 for a hand-operated machine to $250 for the deluxe Rex Rotary electric. Printing presses range in price from $500-$800 for the Multilith model 80 or 81 to anywhere from $800-$1200 for the Multilith 1250 or AB Dick 350. They also have information on how to build your own copy camera, cheap. People from Omega may be available to come to a city and provide training. They charge some.

LIBERATION NEWS SERVICE PRINT SHOP

160 Claremont Avenue
New York, N.Y. 10027
(212) 749-2200

This is the print shop that prints news packets distributed to underground press papers, as well as other movement work.

ALTERNATIVES IN PRINT
Office of Educational Services
The Ohio State University Libraries
Columbus, Ohio 43210   3rd edition $4.00
    This is a thick paperback book that lists movement groups and publishers throughout the U.S., with their addresses, publications, and prices. Compiled by the Social Responsibilities Roundtable of the American Library Association, it is an incomplete "listing of some Movement publications reflecting today's social change activities."
    The Alternative Press Index is more complete, however, this book is very useful for surveying the field.

Radio

ALTERNATIVE RADIO EXCHANGE
Box 852
Felton, Ca. 95018
    A nifty newsletter from and for people who are interested in community radio, i.e. non commercial-broadcast-pablum. The newsletter has news of other community radio stations around the country, with all their ideas and hassles. A recent issue carried news of community radio efforts in Atlanta, Birmingham, Santa Cruz, Juneau, and Ft. Wayne. Subscriptions are $10 a year with free ad service, $5 for five months with no ad service. Canadian rates are $12.
    Also, the *Alternative Radio Exchange* carries job listings from time to time, for everything from engineers to station managers.

THE R.A. FESSENDEN MEMORIAL RADIO TIMES
KTAO-FM
5 University Avenue
Los Gatos, Ca. 95030
    This is, among other things, the program guide for KTAO-FM, "Radio Incomprehensible." A monthly guide to KTAO's programming, this has to be one of the liveliest program guides going. With none of the art and "fine taste" articles of many slick program guides, *Radio Times* costs $20 a year, which goes to support the station. Student rates are $1 a month, and for those in abject poverty, the rate is $6 for five months. A good source of news about alternative radio elsewhere, not just KTAO.

LIST OF ALTERNATIVE RADIO STATIONS
    "The reason I list these stations is that there is growing up a whole body of non-commercial, but non-educational-bull-shit type of radio station which is really in the business to serve the community, to give the disenfranchised and the unknown a voice to be heard—without all the fancy-dan equipment and *dis ease* creation devices that commercial broadcasters and non-commercial broadcasters seem to feel they need."
                                              —Lorenzo Milam
                                              KTAO-FM, Los Gatos, California

KUSP (new community station)
1025 Laurel Street
Santa Cruz, Ca. 95060

WRFG (new permittee for community-cooperative station)
227 Elizabeth N.E.
Atlanta, Ga. 30307

WYSO (college-cooperative station)
Antioch College
Yellow Springs, Ohio 45387

KBOO (community-cooperative station, on the air for four years)
3129 S.E. Belmont
Portland, Ore. 97214

KRAB (community-oriented station, on the air for ten years)
9029 Roosevelt Way Northeast
Seattle, Wash. 98115

John Buck
Radical Software

Video

RADICAL SOFTWARE
c/o Raindance
P.O. Box 543
Cooper Station
New York, N.Y. 10003
(212) 687-4210

This is the best single source of information about people, places, and developments in alternative video. *Radical Software* has just undergone an organizational change. Publishing is being done by Gordon and Breach, and subscriptions are available from *Radical Software*, Suite 1304, 440 Park Avenue South, New York, N.Y. 10016. Subscription price is $12.50 for nine issues per year; single issues are available for $1.95 at newsstands and bookstores.

The following list was excerpted from *RS* #5, Summer, 1972, and should help you get in touch with someone in your area.

ALGERIA

Black Panther Party—
International Section
B.P. 118 Grande Poste
78-21-05
A video tape program has been developed to be directed to the U.S. & Europe on a regular basis to cover the spectrum of the international anti-imperialist revolutionary movement. In the process of building up a tape library for information, research and distribution purposes.

AUSTRALIA

W.A.I.T. Media Workshop
Lyn Mincherton
Architecture Dept.
Western Austr.
Hayman Rd
Bently, Western Australia 6102
681931
Have Shibaden ½" & Ampex 1" equipment. Communicative medium in planning proposals—retaining old bldgs. information exchange between schools of architecture.

CANADA

University of Alberta
Students Union Art Gallery
Edmonton, Alberta
c/o Myra Davis
(403) 432-4191
Have access to Sony ½" & 1" equipment

make their own shows; helping to plan and establish VTR community facilities in interior B.C.

David Rimmer
New Era Social Club
358 Powell St.
Vancouver, British Columbia
(604) 681-9992
Use Sony ½" equipment. Interested in tape exchange, video environments, etc.

Andrew Selder
Laurel House
1896 West 15 Ave
Vancouver 9, British Columbia
(604) 723-9812
Have Sony portapak for use in instructional and treatment methods with young emotionally disturbed children (especially autistic).

Bell-Northern Research
Box 2511-Station C
Ottawa, Ontario
c/o Mike Mills
(613) 828-2761, ext. 538
Using Sony ½" portapaks as well as 1" editing equipment. Exploring all phases of video with emphasis on visual (2-way) interactions. Hope to explore new technologies while evaluating the behavior produced. Extreme interest in computer video hybrids.

Video Ensemble
515 Viger St.
Montreal, Quebec
(514) 842-5267/8
Has both Panasonic and Sony ½" equipment. Government grant from Secretary of State office for abstract and community projects.

Hyman Weisbord
880 Anvers Ave
Montreal 303, Quebec
(514) 277-7295
Has Sony ½" system. Self help through video playback—with the mentally retarded, video exchange re parental problems with retarded children.

ENGLAND

North Kensington Community
Television
Michael Hichie
837 A Fulham Rd
London SW 6
(01) 736-0533
Has Sony ½" system. Engaged in the setting up of a community television service in North Kensington, London.

through radio/TV dept. Involvement in this area actually only involves play-backs. Starting a tape collection which will be available to students on request. Also we work with groups who are doing tapes to give them exposure.

XTV
Martha Fiedler
9740 87 Ave
Edmonton, Alberta
(413) 433-1208
Have ½" and 2" equipment. Have VTR use; interest-universal.

Christos Dikeakos
2676 W. 13th Ave
Vancouver 8, British Columbia
(604) 732-5120
Have Sony ½" equipment. Street scan projects. "Art as a reflection of reality," gathering material to make ½ hr. precise programs.

Box Arnold
Winlaw, British Columbia
Has ½" equipment (portapak). Time lapse video, satellite video, video video, box video, international video exchange.

Richard Ward
715 Shakespeare St.
Trail, British Columbia
(604) 368-8114
Has Sony ½" equipment (2 portapaks). Documentary coverage suitable for ca-blecast; showing local people how to

Environmental Cinemas
730 Yonge St. Suite 27
Toronto, Ontario
(416) 927-6869
Have a videotape theatre, called "Vide-oteque 9" which was opened as a proto-type. Want to expand nation-wide. Inter-ested in product software and are presently using color video tape compat-ible with the IVC 900.

A Space
85 St. Nicolos St.
Toronto, Ontario
A non-profit corporation whose main concern is the organization and program-ming of a large gallery space. Sony ½" equipment.

Howie Arfin
7899 Wavell Rd.
Montreal, Quebec
(514) 482-1883
Have ½" production unit and 1" editing facility. Involved in community orienta-tion, animation turn-on to hardware, inspiration for software glow ... to-wards the general benefit.

Community Media
Dawson College
535 Viger St.
Montreal, Quebec
(514) 849-2351
Have Sony CV & AV ½" systems. In-volved in workshops, community ac-cess, community television, community cable.

FINLAND

Jo Mallander
Villagatan 12
Helsinki 15
Trying to get together a video group in Finland. Does not have American equip-ment.

GERMANY

Falk-Wang-Gabrie
Essen
Has European Std. Ampex 1" deck.

JAPAN

Takahiko Linavra
4-50-4 Yamato-Cho Nakano-Ku
Tokyo
(03) 312-2545
Have made 10 pieces in video tape ...: more than six hours but no place in Tokyo for showing. Using Sony ½" equipment; could be Japanese corre-spondent.

NETHERLANDS

Joe Pat
Rotterdanse Kunststichting
Rotterdam Arts Foundation
AFD. Tentonstellingen, Kruisplein
30-Rotterdam
Setting up a video News Service, con-tact for more information. Have ½" and 1" systems.

Tagiri Shinrich
Kasteel Scheres
Barre, Holland
(04707) 207
Has Sony ½" American standard 525 lines and is willing to help translate tapes into European 625 without charge. If there are any video freaks wandering around the south-east part of Holland, we're located on the Dutch-German border.

SWITZERLAND

Gandja Films Group
Circa and Jose-Maria Mondelo
5 Rue Pierre Fatio
1200 Geneva
A group of underground cinema people working with 8 & 16 mm. Studying the possibilities of creating an alternate television group in Geneva.

Stanislas Gard
Le Martinet
Bagnes, Valais
Will establish in Paris and possibly also in Geneva, a video center which comprises a video theatre, video-teque, a videomagazine and one or more production and research units.

sports dept., drama, small mad usage holds some hope. We are instituting a "class" which will generate information and get us into the TV studio.

Big Basin Ranch Art Institute
Susan Wilkinson
21200 Big Basin Way
Boulder Creek 95006
Opened a graphics workshop summer '72 and plan to offer video graphics experience. A group of them are in the process of building a small video camera. Contact them if you're in the area.

Peter J. de Blanc
Box 926
San Rafael 94902
(415) 453-5395
Has access to a tremendous amount of video equipment, ½", 1" and 2". He has complete facilities for cross dubbing all types of video tape.

Mafundi Institute
1827 E. 103rd St.
Los Angeles 90002
(213) 564-4496
Running a community video project called the Watts Community Communication Bureau. The program is attempting to train people in the use of video hardware, create community-related programming and get the CATV franchise for the S.L.A. area.

Video Free America
Arthur Ginsberg
1948 Fell St.
San Francisco 95018
(415) 362-0151
Have a lot of hardware to work with, (half-inch) including a sophisticated matrix (switcher) for multi-monitor presentations. They've done a lot of experiments with ½" video. Operate an ongoing theatre and production facility. Last summer presented a one-month video show in conjunction with the Berkeley Museum showing tapes from all over the country. They are working on a continuing video-tape called "The Adventures of Carol & Ferd."

COLORADO

Grass-Roots Network
Box 2006
Aspen 81611
c/o Eleanor Bingham
A freak video group working with ½" Sony portapak, Super 8 and 16mm film over an open channel on Cable TV.

CONNECTICUT

Phillip Bowles
3100 Yale Station
New Haven 06520
(203) 432-3100
Has access to Yale University equipment. Sony ½", 1" and 2" is available. Indicates that many people in the art and

ALASKA

Daniel A. Howard
General Delivery
Ester 99725
Has access to VTR equipment in conjunction with AV department at the University in College, Alaska. Doing a lot of work with social welfare agencies. Worked with prisoners inside the state jail. Presently working with Head Start pre-schoolers.

CALIFORNIA

Ant Farm
994 Union Street
San Francisco 94133
(415) 771-2368
A group of designers experimenting with new environmental forms. A lot of the tape they make has to do with the design forms they develop. Have done a lot of truckin' around the country in their media bus providing assistance in areas of electronic and plastic media and self-generating learning environments. Send us a tape and we'll send one back . . . no shit!

Art That Hurts
218 South Salinas
Santa Barbara 93103
Have small amount of ½" equipment and have access to more through the University of California. Video continues to be used in the usual unimaginative way by

Media Access Center
c/o Portola Institute
1115 Merrill St.
Menlo Park 94025
A video group that has been working out of the Portola Institute (home of the *Whole Earth Catalog*). This group has an expertise in many facets of the half-inch video medium. Have done a lot of work with setting up high school video programs.

Resolution
Jay and Tia Odell
818 Hayes
San Francisco 94117
Have Sony ½" equipment. Interested in the possibilities of alternate distribution in the community, colleges, cable, etc. Spent a year taping in Central America and are putting together a piece on the Guatemalan Indians.

Santa Cruz Community Service
Television
H. Allan Frederickson (Johnny Videotape)
695 30th Ave. #E
Santa Cruz 95060
These people are very much into using half-inch video equipment for intra-community communication with emphasis on approaches to liberating CATV for the people.

architecture depts. using portable video equipment.

DISTRICT OF COLUMBIA

Community Video Center
1411 "K" Street, N.W.
Washington 20005
(202) 628-5880
Working with a large supplement of Sony ½" equipment and a 1" editing deck they make tapes dealing with the Washington community. Interested in using video to facilitate information and turn people on to the potentials of CATV. Send for their tape catalogue.

Educational Video Service
Rainbow Video
2115 "S" Street, N.W.
Washington 20008
(202) 387-5100
Have Sony ½" portapak and access to Sony editing equipment. Work with National Student Association. Interested in student/college video network and Cable TV access in D.C.

Video Software Inc.
3515 Lowell Street, N.W.
Washington 20016
(202) EM 2-4918
Working with both Sony and Panasonic ½" equipment. They are developing helical scan VTR as communication medium in the areas of business, education and the arts.

136

FLORIDA

Stephen Westling
101 Elm Street
Pensacola 32506
(904) 455-1487
Has access to 1" IVC equipment, through the local CATV.

ILLINOIS

Tedwilliam Theodore
712 West Waveland
Chicago 60613
(312) 528-8618
Using ½" Panasonic (type one standard) and 1" Panasonic and Ampex equipment to facilitate community organization and social action, cable and tape as tool of non-profit, social action agency.

Video Free Chicago
8601 South Kilburn
Chicago 60652
Are you for real? People not intimidated by the above and wanting to evolve in a climate of life as art utilizing videotape as a means of expression. Contact: Dave.

IOWA

Howard J. Ehrlich
1157 East Court Street
Iowa City 52240
Has access to Shibaden ½" and Ampex 1" equipment through his University.

Earth Light
354 Broadway
Cambridge 02139
(617) 876-7807
A group originally with Comm-University. They are learning to fix equipment and willing to share the knowledge. Work with community groups on video to produce tapes and learn about cable.

Ghost Dance, Inc.
36 Bigelow Street
Cambridge 02139
(617) 661-1012
Have Sony ½" portapak and access to complete 1" and 2" studios. Work is largely concerned with what have been called "Special Effects", also with video image synthesis, computergraphics and the creation of meaningful abstract electronic patterns. Design information systems, have deep interest in 2-way CATV. Ghost Dance is developing tools and techniques to probe TV's impact on the brain. We build video environments.

MICHIGAN

Michigan State University
Center for Urban Affairs
East Lansing 48823
c/o Jason P. Lovette
(517) 353-9320
Using Sony ½" equipment and have access to Sony, Ampex and Shibaden 1" equipment.

MISSOURI

Oscar Acetate & Video Queen
6267 Delmar Boulevard
University City 63130
My experience with video has been to use closed-circuit units in environments contrasting, comparing, and juxtaposing it to basic elements, such as water. Just received a grant and are purchasing Sony ½" equipment.

NEBRASKA

Eric Somers
Creighton University
Omaha 68131
(402) 536-2817 (office)
(402) 348-1560 (home)
Somers is an instructor in communications at University. CCTV system, gives summer workshop in experimental video.

NEW JERSEY

Richard Lipach
Deepdale Drive Road #3
Dover 07801
(201) 895-2906 or 895-2927
Has access to lots of Sony CV and AV equipment. Is interested in working with others on VT projects (he must operate equipment).

KENTUCKY

University of Kentucky
College of Architecture
Pence Hall
Lexington 40506
A group of people have access to and are working with Sony ½" equipment. Contact Stewart Robertson or Louis Deluca.

MARYLAND

Antioch College
Baltimore Campus
805 North Charles Street
Baltimore 21202
(301) 752-3656
This institution may become the first video college. Primarily involved in social change methods—most of its programs have a video element. They have a good supply of Sony ½" video equipment and are experimenting with many facets of the "video experience". Contact Alan Kaplan or Tom Johnson.

MASSACHUSETTS

Audion Enterprises
W. Desmond
P.O. Box 93
MIT Branch Station
Cambridge 02139
(617) 868-9788
Working with Sony ½" equipment. They are producers of Broadside/Free Video Press . . . a quarterly 15-minute video taped magazine.

United Auto Workers
Family Education Center
Black Lake
Onaway 49765
c/o John Hunt
Currently teaching a workshop on the use of VTR for local unions. Using Sony ½" equipment.

MINNESOTA

Thomas Bender
1940 Sheridan Avenue South
Minneapolis 55405
(612) 374-1847
Has access to Sony ½" video equipment through local university.

Scott Helmes
606 8th Street S.E.
Minneapolis 55414
(612) 331-1211
Has access to Sony ½" video equipment as well as 2" decks. Working out tape exchange with universities.

Kailasa
1510 East 23rd Street
Minneapolis 55404
c/o Jon Shafer
Have introduced portable ½" equipment to free schools, a pre-school, and university programs as well as helping community groups (religious consortium, a street academy, model city project) to utilize ½" video.

NEW MEXICO

Ray Hemenez
517 Hillside Avenue
Santa Fe 87501

NEW YORK

Magus Vidicon
Louis M. Brill
155-05 71st Avenue
Flushing 11367
(212) 591-7699
Have access to ½" equipment to produce their tapes. They're a group of students of theatre and the occult (poets, magicians, psychics, alchemists and warlocks). Video is their common form of expression towards cosmic consciousness through the gate of the 2nd dimension.

Videofreex
Maple Tree Farm
Lanesville 12450
(914) 688-7084
Have extensive amount of Sony ½" equipment as well as a 1" editing deck. Working for a long time in New York City. Moved out of the city to set up a Mobile Video Bus which would go around to various New York communities in New York State. Some of their members are currently involved in projects outside the country. A technical video manual will be put out in early spring dealing with repair/modification procedures.

Alternate Media Project
144 Bleeker Street
New York 10003
c/o George Stoney/Red Burns
(212) 873-8640
Has planned and produced "events" to show people what can and is being done in video and cable. They travel, have a radio tape exchange with 400 hrs. of tapes and act as a clearinghouse for information.

Alternative Environmental Futures
316 West 88th Street
New York 10024
c/o Douglas White
(212) 724-7466
Have ½" production unit consisting of Sony portapaks and editing equipment. Programming related to the alternative culture.

Global Village
454 Broome Street
New York 10012
c/o Rudi Stern/John Reilly
(212) 966-1515
Have Sony ½" equipment. Involved in community work. Theatre presentations. Environments, consultation.

OKLAHOMA

LVO Cable, Inc.
P.O. Box 3423
Tulsa 74101
c/o Grep Liptak
(918) 587-1581
Have Sony ½" equipment and access to Sony, Ampex & IVC 1" equipment. Run a high school video workshop. Consult on cable/community programming. Work a great deal in free education.

OREGON

Terry Conrad
2750 Charnelton
Eugene 97405
(503) 345-6071
Has ½" portable equipment as well as 1" studio equipment. Instructions in research and expression, work study aesthetics and community documentation.

PENNSYLVANIA

Annenberg School of Communication
University of Pennsylvania
3620 Walnut Street
Philadelphia 19104
c/o Howard Goldblatt/Albert Rose
(215) 594-7053
Has complete access to IVC studio. Equipment is RAC & Ampex 2" also Sony & Craig ½", cameras and decks.

VERMONT

Robert Chappell
Goddard College
Plainfield 05667
(802) 454-9311
Has Sony ½" portapak and editing equipment. Trucking around with my portapak taping what I run across, letting everyone know what's going on everywhere else.

VIRGINIA

Eugene Productions
1239 Ingelside Avenue
McLean 22101
(703) 356-8406
Private, non-affiliate, SCS (single camera system) half-inch Panasonic 8100 series and standard (EIAJ). Interested in "in-being" vibe theatres, what they are doing and what they are showing.

WASHINGTON

Eyecon-Fourth World Cyber Systems
P.O. Box 276
Seattle 98111
(206) 524-8633 or 776-0695
A life/technology/media group producing video and audio tapes and photo and graphic copy. Make a lot of tapes in the Seattle area. Trying to set up information access and feedback systems with community agencies.

Space Videoarts
344 West 36th Street
New York 10018
c/o Frank Cavestani
(212) 947-4671
Have available Sony ½" equipment. Work with new performance groups in rehearsal and documentation of techniques, productions and research. Wish to establish tape exchange.

Video Community at Westbeth
463 West Street
New York 10014
c/o Ann Douglas/Al Katzman
(212) 243-2201
Own and have access to Sony ½" equipment. An artist housing complex which through a closed-circuit cable system is programming materials gathered from local New York groups as well as material organized at Westbeth itself to all residents within the complex.

OHIO

Bowling Green University
Bill Gubbens
WBGU TV-70
Bowling Green 43403
(419) 372-2676
Work at an ETV/public station in the university. Have access to Panasonic ½" equipment, Ampex 1" equipment and IVC 1" equipment. Interested in the formation of a company on the line of Videofreex.

PUERTO RICO

Nebula
Experimental Video
Edin Velen
797 31B Aevedo St.
Rio Piedras 00923
Group of Puerto Rican video and audio artists using a loft gallery in which they feature showings from different video artists in the U.S. and Europe as well as their own tapes. Station manager at a local Ed. TV station is into radicalizing programming and has been working on different types of programs. Interested in a tape exchange.

RHODE ISLAND

Rhode Island School of Design
(Performance) Don Monroe
Box 5BU R.I.S.D.
2 College Street
Providence 02903
New inputs into a video situation. A group working with behavior and other environments effecting changes, effecting habits.

TEXAS

Mosaic
Foto Gray Gang
1601 Pearl Street
Austin 78701
(512) 478-9049
Four people starting a video theatre, need programs.

WEST VIRGINIA

Community Focus
1222 Washington Street, E.
Charleston 25301
(304) 342-3411
They have two portapaks and have access to one-inch equipment through Capital Cablevision.

WISCONSIN

Lee Ann Mason
Box 151 Rt. #3
Ft. Atkinson 53538
(414) 563-4281
English teacher uses video for instruction. Access to equipment through the University Media Services.

140 *Networks*

UNET: UNION RESOURCE EXCHANGE NETWORK
Union for Experimenting Colleges and Universities
Antioch College
Yellow Springs, Ohio 45387
c/o Dinah LeHoven
(513) 767-7331, ext. 233

This is an attempt to get around some of the present difficulties involved in exchanging video information and video tapes across the country. Rick Newberger, director of UNet, says it "developed out of the frustrations of many institutionally based video people over the difficulty of exchanging information with other user/producers. . . . UNet is designed around a centralized catalog and direct user-producer procurement, with the suggested model being the user sends tape onto which the producer dubs his information."

The centralized catalog of UNet consists of three parts: 1) the obvious Catalog of Software, which includes all the tapes on hand at each affiliate; 2) the less obvious kind of catalog: each affiliate lists those kinds of events, experiences, processes, environments which are ongoing or extraordinary which could be taped and exchanged on request, and 3) the Catalog of Need in which anyone can list the kinds of information he needs, which isn't listed in the catalog.

At the present time, there are affiliated units in Chicago, New York, San Francisco, Baltimore, Yellow Springs, and Lexington, Kentucky.

There's a lot of media activity in New York that is set up so that people can get their hands on the equipment and "do media" instead of being a passive spectator. The "Film and Video" section of the New York *People's Yellow Pages* has a wide variety of media projects listed.

See also, Community Access/Video.

MEDIA NETWORKS:
See also, The Alternative Futures Project; Vocations for Social Change.

MISCELLANEOUS NETWORKS

NATIONAL HOME STUDY COUNCIL
1601 Eighteenth Street, N.W.
Washington, D.C. 20009

The National Home Study Council publishes a directory of over 100 correspondence schools throughout the U.S. Correspondence schools offer topics such as locksmithing, apartment house management, braille, slide rule, sign lettering, electronic organ servicing, to name a few. Below we've included some information from the *Last Whole Earth Catalog*, page 405, on correspondence schools.

"Although the National Home Study Council has set standards, it has no way to enforce them, thus leaving the question of quality up to the individual schools. Two schools which have maintained high standards are the Advanced Trade School and American School, both in Chicago and both offering a wide range of courses. . . . These two schools run credit checks on applicants, administer valid admissions tests, actually turning away those who fail, and pay their salesmen a salary rather than a commission based on how many people they sign up.

"Many schools don't have admissions tests, and those that do often make the tests ridiculously easy to pass. Many of the schools pay no attention to the results of their tests anyway. In other words, for many courses, if you can sign on the dotted line and make the down payment, you've met all the necessary requirements. . . .

"In many places, there are less expensive alternatives available to home study courses. Many universities, colleges, local government adult education programs, churches, YM and YWCA's, civic groups, etc., offer courses in a wide variety of subjects to the general public, usually for nominal fees and/or the cost of any materials. . . .

"Finally, should you sign up for a course and then find out that it isn't what it was advertised to be, send your letter of resignation by registered mail."

NEW-LEARNING NETWORKS

THIS MAGAZINE IS ABOUT SCHOOLS
56 Esplanade Street East
Suite 401
Toronto 1, Ontario
Canada

The foremost new schools magazine, next to *Outside the Net* and *New Schools Exchange Newsletter*. *This Magazine* has been around for a few years, and publishes consistently interesting and relevant materials on our young and what to teach them, and how to do it.

They've also published a book, out in paperback, called *This Book is About Schools* that is a collection of the best articles from the past few years.

For finding your way through the new schools movement in Canada, this is the place to start looking. Subscriptions are $4 a year in Canada, $4.50 in the U.S. Published quarterly.

NEW SCHOOLS NETWORK
3039 Deakin Street
Berkeley, Ca. 94705
(415) 843-8004

New Schools Network grew out of the community efforts of parents and friends in Berkeley. In their first ten months, the Network ran a campaign for school board elections, helped young teachers start new schools, and undertook an enormous load of information sharing. They now publish a newsletter that comes out monthly, and is available for a contribution of $2 or more. They publish a list of East Bay area alternatives to public schooling, and articles on California laws in public education, etc.

Nice people to know about.

NEW SCHOOLS EXCHANGE NEWSLETTER
Box 820
St. Paris, Ohio 43072
c/o Kat Marin

Another granddaddy listing, *The New Schools Exchange* people have been around for a while. It's the first publication that tried to be a link between free schools across the country. Published twice monthly, the *Newsletter* carries news of free schools that are just beginning, progress reports from already established free schools, and the classifieds: places seeking people, teachers seeking places, and kids seeking places. Another feature always worth checking out is the Good Things page. Listings of conferences, new pamphlets, books, interesting people, interesting places, etc. are in the category of Good Things.

Articles published in the past include ones on sexuality and kids, beyond free schools: community, alternatives to schools of all kinds, and on and on. A real goldmine of ideas, news, and good feelings.

Subscriptions are $10 for 12 months, or $5 for 5 months. Free with each subscription is a directory of free schools, periodic position papers, free ads in the newsletter, and "any other aid we can extend in the area of experimental education."

EDCENTRIC $5.00/year
c/o Center for Educational Reform
2115 "S" Street, N.W.
Washington, D.C. 20008
(202) 387-1145
   The Center for Educational Reform is concerned primarily with "higher" education, though not exclusively, and is interested in acting as a clearinghouse for people interested in educational and social change.

They publish *EdCentric*, a monthly magazine of educational change. "*Ed-Centric* does not exist in a void but links educational issues with other movements to change America." Along with *Outside the Net, This Magazine is About Schools*, and *New Schools Exchange Newsletter*, *EdCentric* is one of the most valuable educational change magazines.

Source Catalog was another project of CER and is "a descriptive directory of projects at all levels of social change . . . Other publications of the Center are announced each month in *EdCentric* and include studies of faculty evaluation at various colleges, how to organize on commuter campuses, etc. (*See also, Source Catalog, Vol. I., Communications; Source Catalog, Vol. II., Communities/Housing*)

NEW SCHOOL NEWS
407 South Dearborn Street
Chicago, Ill. 60605
c/o Bea Gillette
(312) HA 7-2533
   This is the major coordinating effort for new schools in the Chicago area, as well as most of the state of Illinois. They publish a newsletter with short articles about various schools and information centers that can help new ones. They also have gatherings at the American Friends Service Committee office in downtown Chicago for new-school teachers and friends to get together and swap information. This is one of the New-schools projects sponsored by the American Friends Service Committee.

TEACHER ORGANIZING PROJECT
New University Conference
622 West Diversey
Chicago, Ill. 60657
(312) 929-3070
   A project of the New University Conference for teachers in elementary and
secondary schools. Their primary efforts have thus far been directed at gathering
together people of shared interests in the Chicago area.
   They have published several pamphlets, including "Classes and Schools: A
Radical Definition for Teachers" and "Down the Up Staircase," that explore
questions about the nature of schools as they are presently structured in the
U.S. An entire series of pamphlets is planned and $3 will get you the pamphlets
that are already finished, as well as the remainder when they come out.

NEW SCHOOL SWITCHBOARD
319 East 25th Street
Baltimore, Md. 21218
(301) 366-7200
   "The American Friends Service Committee in Baltimore is sponsoring an
education project to encourage alternatives and innovations in education. One
part of this project is the *New School Switchboard*, a newsletter to keep people
informed about activities around Baltimore as well as across the country. The
Switchboard has listings of alternative schools in the area, articles, good things
to know about and people to contact.
   "The *Switchboard* encourages alternatives both inside and outside the
public school system, based on the belief that change can come wherever there
are people who are willing to relate to kids in a more humane way.
   "Subscriptions are $2 for 12 issues."

A GUIDEBOOK TO INNOVATIVE EDUCATIONAL PROGRAMS
by Thomas Linney
Center for Child and Family Mental Health
The National Institute of Mental Health, Bethesda, Md. 20014
c/o Ruth Falk
   This paper was prepared for the purpose of making available information
about colleges and universities which are attempting to meet the challenges of
the educational reform movement. Twenty-one colleges, innovative programs
within universities, and graduate programs are written up, plus mention of other
institutions with similar programs. The introduction to the paper is a rich and
personal musing on the progress and failings of experiments in higher education.
   Linney says, "Colleges today are learning places where if you know what
you want to learn and what you are willing to put up with to learn it, you can
learn literally anything you want. . . . but most colleges are not very well set up
to help you find yourself." The places he has written about are those where
hopefully institution and student can work together to accomplish both ends.

TEACHER DROP-OUT CENTER
Box 521
Amherst, Mass. 01002
   The Teacher Drop-Out Center seeks to discover schools at all levels, public

and private, that want the unusual teacher: the one who wants to make education relevant; the one who truly believes in letting students grow into individual, alive and aware humans; the one who breathes controversy and innovation. It also seeks to find these same unusual teachers, teachers who are finding it difficult to function freely as individuals with their own sense of style, teachers who see the classroom as a place for controversial ideas and innovations, teachers who want to be more than babysitters. The Center functions as a clearinghouse matching teachers and schools to their mutual advantage.

For $20 a year, a registrant receives school directories and monthly job mail-outs.

EDUCATION ACTION FUND
P.O. Box 27, Essex Station
Boston, Mass. 02112
"In the midst of a lot of abstraction and a lot of rhetoric on the subject of the Free Schools, there are a number of remarkable small schools—strong, passionate, stable and committed—which started up back in 1966 or 1967, set themselves the obligation of serving children of people who are poor and black, as well as children of the middle-class, and which have been fighting a very brave, realistic battle for the survival of their children.

"Most of these schools do not belong to the stereotype image of the "joyous" and "ecstatic" Free School for rich people, nestled in 200 acres in the country.... While others talk of handlooms, wheat germ and geodesic domes, these people talk of meat and milk and rent and doctors for sick children, heat in winter, money to hire lawyers to defend their kids before the courts.

"There are a number of exciting schools like these in several cities: among them Boston, Burlington, Providence, Chicago, Washington, New York, Milwaukee, St. Paul, Lansing, Albany, St. Louis and Santa Fe. Many, however, face the risk of closing down without much warning as the consequence of a sudden payroll-crisis, lack of heat or lack of cash to meet building code demands. The Education Action Fund exists in order to provide a back-up of advice and cash for emergencies like these. "There are many people who are interested in the Free School movement but who do not feel they can afford the time to work as partisans or activists within the schools. We are now inviting some of these same people to share in the survival struggle that the urban Free School faces. . . .

"In order to encourage small donations of this kind, we are hustling our own private mail-list (25-30 pages) of good leads and unsuspected contacts, money-raising tactics, teaching-schemes, curriculum-ideas, names of Free School boosters, allies-in-the-system, experts, organizers, friends. The mail-list is itself one type of hustle, since it is intended to raise money. We will send it free, however, to anybody who needs it and is broke.

Education Action Fund does not operate a fancy office; does not have a government grant; is not connected by IBM or Carnegie or EDC or any other corporation. The mail-address for those who would like to send some money or to get our mail-list is [above]."

Annette Holman
Jonathan Kozol
Jo Tackeff

YELLOW PAGES OF LEARNING RESOURCES $1.95
Edited by Richard S. Wurman
M.I.T. Press
Cambridge, Mass. 02138

This book, with all its good points, is an example of folks not wanting to give up their classrooms. The introduction tells where the book is at, in terms of schools versus the world as a teacher: "It is a classroom without walls, an open university for people of all ages . . . we will have created classrooms with endless windows on the world."

Yellow Pages of Learning Resources is a specific guide to how to utilize such things as candymakers, garbage men, junk yards, insurance salesmen, quarries, airports, courtrooms, anything in the city. It tells you how to get to the right person who can unlock these resources for you . . . unless you're one of those people who know already what the alderman *really does*. It is a guide to how to use everything in the city, any city, as a vast learning resource. It seems worth the money, if you don't mind the "classroom" idea of it all.

OUTSIDE THE NET
P.O. Box 184
Lansing, Mich. 48901

A quarterly newspaper of the new school and de-schooling movements. Articles, graphics, resource pages, anything you could need, all in a *Rolling Stone* format. Very readable, intelligent. Well worth the $2 for a year's subscription.

This is the newspaper that you should be reading, if you can only afford (like most of us) one or two of the new schools publications.

THE FREE LEARNING PROJECT
215 Middle Neck Road
Great Neck, N.Y. 11021
c/o Ron Gross

"The Free Learning Project is a collaborative inquiry based on the proposition that the problem of education consists of what we (adults) should, will, can, and must do about our *own* education. How, where, what, and why must *we* learn? What must we do, to ourselves and our society, to make it possible for us to learn what we most need to know—if we are to provide a world which is learnable, and worth knowing, for our children? How can we take command of our own lifelong and lifewide learning and growth?

"The Project is involved in such programs as the Free Learning Exchange in New York City; the New University in Washington, D.C., a national study of auto-didacts; and Action in the Classroom as Training, a self-education approach to professional growth for teachers. The Project operates through courses at New York University and elsewhere, an "invisible college" sharing information and ideas, and an Advisory Committee including John Holt, Harold Taylor, Robert Coles, Charles Silberman, Normon Solomon, and William Birenbaum.

"A packet including reprints, bibliography, and other background is available."

NEW NATION SEED FUND
Box 4026
Philadelphia, Pa. 19118

"Our struggle for a better world takes many forms, but none is more important than the rearing and educating of our children. We believe that children raised in wholeness and natural pride will not grow up to be slavish adults, nor agree to immoral politics and irresponsible technology. "Our present system of public education, coercive in its methods, is a symptom and major cause of our unsatisfactory way of life. . . . Perhaps this system can be changed from within. We hope so. But one thing is clear: it cannot be changed without working models of a better way, both as examples and as a competitive spur.

"Such models exist. They have been described in dozens of books and hundreds of periodicals. They are known as 'free schools', and are what is meant by the recurrent phrase 'alternative education'. . . .

"There are documented examples of brilliant success with these methods. Yet the libertarian schools have no friends in government, industry, or the foundations, and are always short of funds. There is special difficulty for the poor, whose children must be enrolled free of charge.

"The function of the New Nation Seed Fund is to help new schools get started, and existing ones stay alive. We have seen excellent schools founder for want of a small sum. We ask you to remember this fund by thinking of it on your own birthday, and we ask you to send it a gift at that time. Since it is easier to remember small gifts than large ones, we ask you to send one dollar. If you are a parent, and do agree with us, urge your own children and young people to ally themselves with other children by sending small presents on their birthdays, fifty cents, or a quarter. . . .

"The money will be used exclusively for children. It will be disbursed from the fund in consultation with reliable people in the field of education, including the sponsors named below. Priority will be given to schools enrolling significant numbers of the poor."

George Dennison
Paul Goodman (1912-1972)
Nat Hentoff
John Holt
Jonathan Kozol

Apprenticeships

Apprenticeships are an old idea, dating back to the crafts guilds of medieval and Renaissance Europe. An interested beginner apprentices himself to a master craftsman or artisan, and for subsistence wages learns the craft or trade well enough to go out on his own. Modern day apprenticeships (not the building trades unions apprenticeship programs) can include anything from fine printing, musical instrument making, and glass blowing to woodworking. Plus almost anything else you might want to learn.

We've listed, throughout the catalog, a few of the apprenticeship openings we know about, and here list some people who know even more about it than we could ever hope to know.

A FABLE FOR LEARNERS

One time the animals had a school. The curriculum consisted of running, climbing, flying, and swimming, and all the animals took all the subjects.

The Duck was good in swimming, better in fact than his instructor, and he made passing grades in flying, but he was practically hopeless in running. Because he was low in this subject he was made to stay in after school and drop his swimming class in order to practice running. He kept this up until he was only average in swimming. But average is acceptable, so nobody worried except the Duck.

The Rabbit started out at the top of the class in running but he had a nervous breakdown and had to drop out of school on account of so much makeup work in swimming.

The Squirrel led the climbing class, but his flying teacher made him start his flying lesson from the ground up instead of from the top of the tree down. He developed charley horses from over-exertion at the take-off, and began getting C's in climbing and D's in running.

The practical Prairie Dogs apprenticed their off-spring to a Badger when the school authorities refused to add digging to the curriculum. At the end of the year, an abnormal Eel, that could swim fairly well, climb, and fly a little, was made valedictorian.

12100 Skyline Blvd.
Los Gatos, Ca. 95030
(408) 867-2260

Carolyn Kaye, who founded ASP, says in a recent letter. "We want to help people from 14-18 years old find an alternative to learning in the conventional ways (schools). We want to help provide contact between apprentice and master, person and mentor, learner and teacher all over the country. When someone tells us what he/she would like to do, we will let them know if we know of any people who could help and/or try to find people. We will send the people we refer them to a copy of his/her letter of application. . . . It is up to the apprentice to get in touch with anyone we suggest if he thinks he would be interested in learning with any of them. . . . The arrangements are up to the two individuals.

". . . . We are primarily interested in situations where the apprentice can trade some work for learning, although in some cases the teacher may ask for a fee or money for supplies—or the student may be able to do enough work that he should be paid. These are all things that the two should work out before starting and keep evaluating if necessary as they work together. If people want to be enrolled in school and working toward a high school diploma while they are doing an apprenticeship(s) the cost is $200. Reductions are available. For those who do not want to be enrolled the cost is $5, if we are instrumental in helping you find someone to work with."

Get in touch with Sarah G. Bernhardt or Dianna H. Teague. They have contacts with teachers and people in 29 states and Canada, so far.

SOUTH SHORE COMMUNITY HIGH SCHOOL
Jack Spicer
1351 East Hyde Park Boulevard
Chicago, Ill. 60615
(312) 684-3308

An apprenticeship program for adolescents: "The major part of the program for each student is a 'field study.' This is a working relationship with an individual, group, or organization—a printer, architect, legal assistance clinic, nursery school, veterinarian, chef, carpenter, citizen's group, etc." Planned so that students can "see the uses to which qualified adults put various skills and knowledge, to learn under the close guidance of an adult, and to make use of what has been learned by assisting in the on-going activity itself.

"Counseling and parent consultations are provided; detailed records and evaluations are kept; and private lessons, tutorials, and academic classes at other schools are arranged."

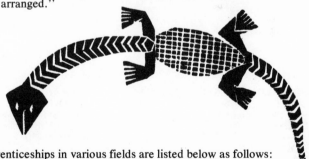

Specific apprenticeships in various fields are listed below as follows:
Boat Crew: see COAST NAVIGATIONAL SCHOOL
Cooking: see DUMAS PERE
Theater and Dance: see THE ENSEMBLE
Peace: see WORLD WITHOUT WAR COUNCIL
Pottery: see JUGTOWN POTTERY
Sailing and Oceanography: see AMERICAN SAILING EDUCATION
    ASSOCIATION
Switchboards: see NUMBER NINE

LIST OF FREE UNIVERSITIES

The following list, from *New Schools Exchange Newsletter*, was compiled by Jane Lichtman of the Free U Clearinghouse. We reproduce it here, with Kat Marin's permission and with special thanks to Jane Lichtman for her work in keeping track of this enormous network of learning places. For a similar but annotated list of 120 functioning free universities, order the *Free University Directory* for $1.50 from:
American Association for Higher Education
1 Dupont Circle, Room 780
Washington, D.C. 20036
"These are non-credit, low fee (less than $15 per semester), public learning centers. About 70% are funded by student governments of colleges and universities; the rest by these minimal tuition fees (actually donations) as well as outside donations. They are heavily 'skills oriented'—that is, many of the courses could be described as active, 'how-to' production-producing groups. . . . The other kinds of courses, in lesser frequencies, are those in individual and cosmic awareness (encounter/sensitivity, astrology/mysticism/occult/ESP) and theoretical courses (more standard university type courses—usually classroom and book-oriented). Instructors are generally voluntary, non-paid—that means that you take your chances with the nature of the class and the instructor. . . . People who want a college 'degree' would not be interested in any of the free universities listed. While stemming out of colleges and universities, free universities have more kinship (in practice) with adult education than they do with collegiate education.

"Last time we printed the listing, we got responses from 'experimental colleges' asking to be included. I would like to emphasize that there are no grades, degrees, or job rewards for free university learning. Rewards are primarily internal—instrumental, social, and personal."

—Jane Lichtman

CANADA

FREE UNIVERSITY NORTH
c/o S.C.M.
Box 106, University of Alberta
Edmonton, Alberta

ROCHDALE
341 Bloor Street, West
Toronto 5, Ontario

VANCOUVER FREE
UNIVERSITY
1895 Venables Street
Vancouver, British Columbia

ALABAMA

EXTRACURRICULAR STUDIES
PROGRAM
Union Building—Room 316
Auburn University
Auburn 36830

EXPERIMENTAL COLLEGE
University of South Alabama
Mobile 36608

ARIZONA

FREE UNIVERSITY
University of Arizona
Tucson 85721

ARKANSAS
THE FREE UNIVERSITY
P.O. Box 1608
Fayetteville 72701

CALIFORNIA
ARCATA FREE UNIVERSITY
1628 G Street
Arcata 95521

FREE UNIVERSITY OF
BERKELEY
2000 Parker Street
Berkeley 94704

EXPERIMENTAL COLLEGE
A.S.U.C.D.
University of California
Davis 95616

EXPERIMENTAL COLLEGE
California State College
Letters and Science, Room 78
Fullerton 92631

EXPERIMENTAL COLLEGE
Associated Students Office
University of California
Irvine 92664

EXPERIMENTAL COLLEGE
Associated Students Office
California State College
6101 E. 7th
Long Beach 90801

EXPERIMENTAL COLLEGE
California State College
Student Activities Office
Administration 123
5151 State College Drive
Los Angeles 90037

EXPERIMENTAL COLLEGE
407 Kirkhov Hall
University of California
Los Angeles 90024

EXPERIMENTAL COLLEGE
Associated Students
Student Union 321
University of Southern California
Los Angeles 90007

UNIVERSITY FOR MAN
Room 5A
Monterey Peninsula College
980 Fremont Extension
Monterey 93940

EXPERIMENTAL COLLEGE
San Fernando Valley State College
9520 Etiwanda
Northridge 91324

EXPERIMENTAL COLLEGE
California Polytechnic Institute
Pomona 91766

ALTERNATIVE EDUCATION
ASSSC
Sacramento State College
Sacramento 95819

FAMILY MIX
43 Mariposa
San Anselmo 94960

EXPERIMENTAL COLLEGE
Organizations Center
Aztec Center
San Diego State College
San Diego 92115

ENTROPY
1914 Polk
San Francisco 94109

EXPERIMENTAL COLLEGE
City College of San Francisco
50 Phelan Avenue
San Francisco 94112

HELIOTROPE
21 Columbus
San Francisco 94111

ORPHEUS
1385 7th Avenue
San Francisco 94122

EXPERIMENTAL COLLEGE
San Jose State College
College Union Building
Laguna Seca Room 211
South 9th Street
San Jose 95112

SAN JOSE FREE UNIVERSITY
50 S. 4th, No. 3
San Jose 95113

FREE UNIVERSITY OF SAN
DIEGO
703 N. Rios Avenue
Solana Beach 92075

SHERWOOD OAKS
EXPERIMENTAL COLLEGE
6725 Valjean Avenue
Van Nuys 91406

COLORADO

COMMUNITY FREE SCHOOL
1030 13th Street
Boulder 80302

DENVER FREE UNIVERSITY
1122 E. 17th Avenue
Denver 80218

FREE UNIVERSITY OF
COLORADO STATE
Box 12—Fraiser
Colorado State College
Greeley 80631

CONNECTICUT

FREE SCHOOL OF NEW HAVEN
Dwight Hall
Yale Station
New Haven 06520

EXPERIMENTAL COLLEGE
U-8
University of Connecticut
Storrs 06268

DELAWARE

DELAWARE FREE UNIVERSITY
University of Delaware
Newark 19711

DISTRICT OF COLUMBIA

GEORGETOWN FREE
UNIVERSITY
P.O. Box 2121
Hoya Station
Georgetown University
Washington 20007

NEW UNIVERSITY
c/o Bob Orser
Suite 605
1718 P Street NW
Washington 20009

WASHINGTON AREA FREE
UNIVERSITY
1724 20th Street NW
Washington 20009

FLORIDA

CENTER FOR PARTICIPANT
EDUCATION
247 University Union
Florida State University
Tallahassee 32306

GEORGIA

FREE COLLEGE
c/o Kelly Greene
Emory University
Atlanta 30322

FREE UNIVERSITY
Student Center
Georgia Institute of Technology
Atlanta 30332

ILLINOIS

ALTERNATE UNIVERSITY
Box 4348, Room 317
University of Illinois
Chicago Circle Campus
Chicago 60680

LIVING/LEARNING
Northern Illinois University
DeKalb 60115

SWILC
Southwestern Illinois Learning Coop
c/o Community Involvement Project
Student Activities
Southern Illinois University
Edwardsville 62025

INDIANA

FREE UNIVERSITY
Union Board Office
Indiana Memorial Union
Bloomington 47401

FREE UNIVERSITY
c/o Bethlehem Lutheran Church
526 E. 52nd Street
Indianapolis 46205

FREE UNIVERSITY OF MUNCIE
Student Center—B3
Ball State University
Muncie 47306

KANSAS

KANSAS FREE UNIVERSITY
Student Activity Center
1314 Oread
Lawrence 66044

UNIVERSITY FOR MAN
615 Fairchild Terrace
Manhattan 66502

KENTUCKY

FREE UNIVERSITY
c/o Student Government
University of Kentucky
Lexington 40506

FREE UNIVERSITY
c/o Student Government
University of Louisville
Louisville 40208

LOUISIANA

FREE UNIVERSITY
c/o Student Activities Offices
LSU Union
Louisiana State University
Baton Rouge 70803

FREE UNIVERSITY OF NEW
ORLEANS
1232 St. Mary
New Orleans 70130

MAINE

ABENAKI EXPERIMENTAL
COLLEGE
104 Lord Hall
University of Maine
Orono 04473

MARYLAND

FREE UNIVERSITY
c/o Benjamin L. Henry
Montgomery Junior College
Takoma Park 20012

MASSACHUSETTS

BEACON HILL FREE SCHOOL
315 Cambridge Street
Boston 02114

FREE UNIVERSITY OF THE
FAMILY
68 St. Stephen Street
Boston 02115

TROUT FISHING IN AMERICA
353 Broadway
Cambridge 02139

WATERFIELD FREE SCHOOL
2 Market Square
Marblehead 01945

SMITH EXPERIMENTAL
COLLEGE
c/o Jan Kennaugh
150 Elm Street
Northampton 01060

MINIVERSITY
c/o Your Place
806 Main Street
Worcester 01610

MICHIGAN

FREE UNIVERSITY OF ANN
ARBOR
c/o U.A.C.
Michigan Union
Ann Arbor 48104

FREE COMMUNITY SCHOOL
c/o Project Headline
13267 Gratiot
Detroit 48205

FREE UNIVERSITY
Box 142 University Center, Room 309
Wayne State University
Detroit 48202

MICHIGAN STATE PERVERSITY
U.N. Lounge
Union Building
Michigan State University
East Lansing 48823

FREE UNIVERSITY
Kalamazoo College
Kalamazoo 49001

MINNESOTA

JUDSON LIFE SCHOOL
4101 Harriet Ave. So.
Minneapolis 55409

MINNESOTA FREE
UNIVERSITY
1417 First Avenue South, No. 210
Minneapolis 55403

FREE UNIVERSITY
St. Olaf College
Northfield 55057

MISSISSIPPI

FREE UNIVERSITY
c/o YMCA
Mississippi State University
State College 39762

MISSOURI

COMMUNIVERSITY
UMKC-5100 Rockhill Road
Kansas City 64110

NEBRASKA

NEBRASKA FREE UNIVERSITY
Nebraska Union 331
University of Nebraska
Lincoln 68508

NEW HAMPSHIRE

DARTMOUTH EXPERIMENTAL
COLLEGE
Hinman Box 493
Dartmouth College
Hanover 03755

NEW JERSEY

FREE UNIVERSITY
Seaton Hall University
South Orange 07079

FREE UNIVERSITY
c/o Student Activities
Newark State College
Union 07083

NEW MEXICO

AMISTAD
Room 1060, Mesa Visa
University of New Mexico
Albuquerque 87106

NEW YORK

FREE UNIVERSITY
Kirkland-Hamilton College
Clinton 13323

EMMAUS
241 E. 116th Street
New York 10029

EXPERIMENTAL COLLEGE
343 Finley Student Center
City College of New York
113 St. at Convent Avenue
New York 10031

COMMUNIVERSITY
Genesee Co-op
942 Monroe Avenue
Rochester 14620

FREE UNIVERSITY
LeMoyne College
LeMoyne Heights
Syracuse 13214

NORTH CAROLINA

INVISIBLE UNIVERSITY
King Nyle 1
P.O. Box 294
Carrboro 27510

FREE UNIVERSITY
c/o ASDU
Duke University
Durham 27706

OHIO

NEW UNIVERSITY
Bowling Green State University
Bowling Green 43402

FREE UNIVERSITY
c/o Student Activities
Ohio Wesleyan University
Delaware 43015

FREE UNIVERSITY
John Carroll University
University Heights 44118

OKLAHOMA

FREE UNIVERSITY
c/o Canterbury Center
2839 E. 5th
Tulsa 74104

OREGON

SEARCH
305 Erb Memorial Union
Eugene 97403

FREE UNIVERSITY
c/o Student Activities
Lewis and Clark College
Portland 97219

PENNSYLVANIA

FREE UNIVERSITY
Edinboro State College
P.O. Box 319
Edinboro 16412

PENN STATE FREE U
Hetzl Union Bldg.
Park 16802

FREE UNIVERSITY OF
    PENNSYLVANIA
COS Office
Houston Hall
3417 Spruce Street
University of Pennsylvania
Philadelphia 19104

FREE UNIVERSITY
Box 95, SAC
Temple University
13th and Montgomery
Philadelphia 19122

FREE UNIVERSITY
St. Joseph College
Philadelphia 19131

SOUTH CAROLINA

SHORT COURSES
Program Board
University Union
University of South Carolina
Columbia 29208

TENNESSEE

FREE UNIVERSITY
Student Senate Office
University of Tennessee
Knoxville 37916

FREE UNIVERSITY NASHVILLE
c/o Gregg Thomas
Box 2975, Station B
Vanderbilt University
21st Ave. and West End
Nashville 37203

TEXAS

FREE UNIVERSITY
c/o Student Congress
University of Texas
Arlington 76010

FREE UNIVERSITY
c/o 214 Student Center
Southern Methodist University
Dallas 75222

FREE UNIVERSITY
c/o Oscar Wright
1219 N. Oregon, Apt. 9
El Paso 79902

UNIVERSITY OF THOUGHT
3505 S. Main
Houston 77002

UNIVERSIDAD DE LOS
    BARRIOS
1220 Bueno Vista
San Antonio 78207

FREE UNIVERSITY
Student Government Office
Baylor University
Waco 76703

UTAH

FREE UNIVERSITY OF UTAH
Student Activities Center
University of Utah
Salt Lake City 84112

VIRGINIA

EXPERIMENTAL UNIVERSITY
120 Chancellor Street
Charlottesville 22903

FREE UNIVERSITY
Mary Washington College
Fredericksburg 22401

WASHINGTON
NORTHWEST FREE
    UNIVERSITY
P.O. Box 1255
Bellingham 98225

WISCONSIN
FREE UNIVERSITY
c/o Henry D. Keesing
P.O. Box 965
Madison 53701

FREE UNIVERSITY
c/o Associated Students
620 N. 14th Street
Milwaukee 53233

LIST OF NEW SCHOOLS CLEARINGHOUSES

The following list of new school/free school clearinghouses was compiled by Tom Wilbur of *Outside the Net* and Kat Marin of *New Schools Exchange Newsletter*. It is part of *A New School Tool Kit* being done by Tom, which will include a books and magazine list, national clearinghouse information, and other good stuff. Write *Outside the Net* to find out when it will be available.
    "Many good folks are working to assist the new schools movement around the country by serving as clearinghouses for information and they can be very helpful. If you are going to get involved in a free school you might visit with 'the clearinghouse people closest to you as a first step. Here is a reasonably accurate and up-to-date listing of such groups. (When you write them asking for help or information be sure and send along a dollar or two if you can afford it—they will appreciate it.)"

—Tom Wilbur

East Bay Education Switchboard
805 Gilman Street
Berkeley, Ca. 94710
Serves new schools and new school people in the East Bay area near San Francisco.

New Schools Network
3039 Deakin Street
Berkeley, Ca. 94705
Works with people in the Berkeley area and mimeos a newsletter of happenings, announcements, etc.

New Ways in Education
1778 South Holt Avenue
Los Angeles, Ca. 90035
Mimeos a monthly Southern California newsletter with lots of information and advice on new schools; $5 a year; also connected with daily KMET radio program on education.

Summerhill Society of California
1778 South Holt Avenue
Los Angeles, Ca. 90035
Sponsors conferences, puts out mailings, and works to foster Summerhill-type education in the West.

Bay Area Center for Alternative Education
1385 Seventh Avenue
San Francisco, Ca. 94122
Holds workshops and otherwise helps new school people in the San Francisco area.

Uniteen Switchboard
50 Oak Street
San Francisco, Ca. 94102

Alternatives for Education
P.O. Box 1028
San Pedro, Ca. 90733
Mimeos an excellent monthly newsletter for innovative school people in Southern California.

Unschool of New Haven
P.O. Box 1126
New Haven, Ct. 06505
Mimeos "The Northeaster," with news on educational alternatives in the New England states.

Washington Area Free School Clearinghouse
Sumner School
17th and M Streets N.W.
Washington, D.C. 20036
Mimeos a newsletter with lots of information (including names of people looking for jobs) and generally helps new schools people in and around the Capital area.

Stonesoup School
428 Semoran Boulevard
Altamonte Springs, Fla. 32701
Have had conferences and are in touch with a lot of people in the deep South.

New School News
c/o American Friends Service Committee
407 South Dearborn Street
Chicago, Ill. 60605

Mimeos a monthly newsletter of information for new school folks in the greater Chicago area; $3 a year.

Fort Wayne Folk School
Box 681
Fort Wayne, Ind. 46801
Publishes a newsletter, "Return to Learning," and is generally willing to extend help to Hoosiers working their way out of public education.

University for Man
615 Fairchild Terrace
Manhattan, Ks. 66502
Serves as a free school clearinghouse for the Midwest states of Kansas, Illinois (except Chicago), Missouri, Oklahoma, Nebraska, Arkansas, Iowa, and Tennessee. Would like to hear from people in these states that they aren't yet in touch with.

Innovative Education Coalition
4535 South Saratoga
New Orleans, La. 70116
Mimeos a monthly newsletter and works to get people together in the New Orleans area.

New Schools Switchboard
c/o American Friends Service Committee
319 East 25th Street
Baltimore, Md. 21218
Mimeos a monthly newsletter of notes, new schools, and info for people in the Baltimore area; $2 per year.

Federation of Boston Community Schools
76 Highland Street
Boston, Mass. 02119

Education Center
57 Hayes Street
Cambridge, Mass. 02139
Works to establish communications between public and alternative schools. Their newsletter, "Centerpeace," is mimeoed to provide a forum for innovative education advocates and a channel through which information may be collected and distributed; $3 a year.

The Red Pencil
The Bulletin
131 Magazine Street
Cambridge, Mass. 02139
Excellent Boston-area news sources put out by a collective of people working to change Boston-area education; $4 per year donation.

Michigan Educational Alternatives Collective
P.O. Box 1444
East Lansing, Mich. 48823
A group of people active in Michigan free schools and in publishing *Outside the Net*. They publish an irregular newsletter ($2 per year), get people together at conferences and meetings, and work with people who might benefit from their experience.

Education Exploration Center
3104 16th Avenue, South
Minneapolis, Minn. 55407
Holds regular meetings, helps people get involved in alternative education—both in and out of the public schools system—and mimeos a regular newsletter.

New Jersey Alternative Schools Federation
271 Leonia Avenue
Leonia, N.J. 07605
Works with the alternative schools
movement in New Jersey and
distributes an occasional
newsletter.

Rio Grande Educational Association
Box 2241
Santa Fe, N.M. 87501
Has as its goal the fostering of non-coercive education in the Southwest U.S. Their mimeoed newsletter costs $5 per year, $10 to institutions.

Committee of Community Schools
760 West End Avenue
New York, N.Y. 10025
A coalition of highly regarded free schools working with alternative schools and trying to re-enter alternative schools into the public school system.

Summerhill Collective
137 West 14th Street
New York, N.Y. 10011
Publishes a newsletter and works with alternative education people in the NYC area.

OCEAN (Ohio Coalition for Educational Alternatives Now)
c/o Metropolitan School
444 East Broad Street
Columbus, Ohio 43215
A new, loosely-organized group of people involved with alternative education in Ohio.

Southwest Education Reform Community
3505 Main Street
Houston, Tex. 77002
Helps people in Oklahoma, Louisiana, Arkansas, New Mexico, and Texas get it together. Their excellent newspaper, "The Ark," is printed 6-8 times per year.

New Schools Movement
402 15th Avenue, East
Seattle, Wash. 98102
Holds regular meetings of new schools folks in the Seattle area and mimeos a monthly newsletter on local new school happenings.

Wisconsin Coalition for Education Reform
3019 North Farwell
Milwaukee, Wis. 53211
Works with both public and free schools in Wisconsin and mimeos a newsletter on education reform.

NEW-LEARNING NETWORKS:
See also, Centro Intracultural de Documentation; Consortium for Futures in Education; *Free University Catalog;* Futuristics Curriculum Project; Institute Mountain West; International Cooperation Council; LEARNING EXCHANGES; Michael Marien; Pacific Studies Center; Robert Theobald; Roots, Inc.; *Toward a Guide to Humanistic Education;* World Law Fund.

OVERSEAS WORK/STUDY NETWORKS

INTER-CULTURAL LIBRARY
Student Services
International Services Center
University of California
Riverside, Ca. 92502
c/o Ronald Heinrich, Director
   "We have an Inter-Cultural Library in our office which is used as a reference for students (and sometimes faculty and staff) who are interested in work, study, or travel abroad. . . . We are acting as a reference *only* and cannot distribute quantities of material."

AMERICAN-SCANDINAVIAN FOUNDATION
127 East 73rd Street
New York, N.Y. 10021
A knowledge of the language of the country in which you wish to study is fairly important since most foreign institutions teach in their particular language. One exception, according to the Institute of International Education, is the International Institute for English-Speaking Students of the University of Stockholm, which offers social science courses.

DANISH INFORMATION OFFICE
280 Park Avenue
New York, N.Y. 10017
(212) 697-5107
The Danish Information Office publishes a directory called "Study in Denmark: Courses for Foreigners." It contains information on Danish universities as well as other educational institutions, financial aid, international seminars and other programs which do not require affiliation with an American institution, language courses, and living in Denmark. When enrollment in U.S. colleges or universities is a prerequisite, it is indicated; likewise, language fluency is noted where required.
Some examples: Nine to 14-day seminars in English on Danish design, Scandinavian architecture, Scandinavian education, social welfare, $110-$295. An international ballet seminar for professional dancers, dance students, teachers, and choreographers. International Peoples College, for adults over 19, tuition about $300 per trimester. Short summer courses in Denmark, Norway, or Sweden for adults over 18, with $60 tuition covering lectures, room and board, and local excursions.

INSTITUTE OF INTERNATIONAL EDUCATION
809 United Nations Plaza
New York, N.Y. 10017
The Institute publishes much information on overseas study. They compile lists of various schools of all types in virtually every country that offer programs for English-speaking students, as well as programs for persons fluent in foreign languages. "Please note that the Institute of International Education does not make arrangements or provide information on travel or transportation; does not arrange for admissions to foreign institutions; does not evaluate or recommend institutions or organizations; does not recruit teachers for overseas positions (however, a listing of organizations which place teachers *is* available); does not make living arrangements for students or make arrangements for students wishing to live with families abroad."
Some of their publications include:
General Memorandum for Those Interested in Foreign Study   50c
Study in Mexico   50c
Summer Study Abroad $2
Handbook on International Study for U.S. Nationals $7

LIST OF RESOURCES FOR OVERSEAS JOBS

Kungliga Arbetmarknadsstyrelsen
Luntmakargatan 46
Box 3190
10363 *Stockholm 3*
SWEDEN

Arbetsmarknadsstyrelsen
Viktoriagatan 13
Fact
400 10 *Goteborg 3*
SWEDEN

North American Friends Service Committee
160 North 15th Street
Philadelphia, Pa. 19102

National Employment Service Institute
1700 Pennsylvania Avenue
Washington, D.C. 20006
Publishes "Overseas Employment Guide."

The following organizations publish guides to work camps.

Commission on Voluntary Service
475 Riverside Drive, Room 665
New York, N.Y. 10027
Lists programs in all parts of the world run by agencies based in North
America.

OTU
Jeunesse et Reconstruction
132 Boulevard St. Michel
Paris 5
FRANCE
Guide to work camps in France.

International Student Employment
777 United Nations Plaza
New York, N.Y. 10017
Publishes guide to work camps and employment in England and Ireland. Also
covers "Employment Abroad."

Coordinating Council for International Voluntary Service
UNESCO
1 Rue Miollis
Paris 15e
FRANCE
Listings of non-governmental service agencies in 100 countries on all conti-
nents.

OVERSEAS WORK/STUDY NETWORKS:
See also, Japan Kibbutz Association; Kibbutz Aliya Desk.

THE PEOPLE'S YELLOW PAGES

Mother Bell (the telephone company) has the right idea with the yellow pages, but unfortunately they don't serve most of us with the things we need to know. If you need to know where to get your car fixed cheaply and honestly, want to find out who in your town teaches mandolin, or where to find "good people," you obviously don't depend upon Ma Bell's book.

But, people around the country have been getting together a whole new set of yellow pages, known variously as the *People's Yellow Pages, The Green Pages* or the *Red Pages*, depending on where you stand. Coupled with the switchboards that are all over the country helping people with problems, the People's Yellow Pages goes a long way toward helping the idea of community become a reality.

We've listed the People's Yellow Pages that we know about, and the address of a directory of switchboards and hot lines that is being published. With these, you should be able to find your way round parts of Europe, Canada and most of big-city America. Can small-city America be far behind?

BRITISH COLUMBIA ACCESS
King Edward Annex
500 Block, West 12th Avenue
Vancouver, British Columbia, Canada
   For our friends in Canada, British Columbia, to be exact, there's a guide to resources and people in the B.C. area. Published much in the spirit of the *Puget Sound Access*, it's a good source of information about how, where, what, and who in British Columbia. $2 per issue

BIT INFORMATION SERVICE
141 Westbourne Park Road
London W. 11, England
   They say, "If you happen to need or want a 'hip directory' to the alternative society in England or the Continent, this is the place to go. *Bitman* is . . . packed with information, addresses, news from communes, progressive schools, head shops, radical theatre groups, directory services," etc. Single copies are 50c, or $3 for the next year's issues.
   They also publish a catalog-directory of addresses, contacts, places, and people throughout Europe. $2.50.

THE SOUTH AMERICAN HANDBOOK
c/o Howell Davies
Trade and Travel Publications, Ltd.
19 Leadenhall Street
London, E.C. 3, England
A yearly guide to South and Central America, Mexico, the Bahamas, with all the info on traveling, sleeping, and eating: best, worst, cheapest, shortest, etc. Try Trade and Travel for publications on other areas of the world, too.

COSMIC PAPER
Prins Hendrikkade, 142
Amsterdam, Netherlands
This is an English-language "magazine with a new age approach to the Now; a medium for new currents, multisided information, a preparation for Aquarius, a togetherness of forces . . . a publication of 'De Kosmos,' a new meditation center. It's an impact point for those interested in meditation, yoga, music, painting, and other artforms, macrobiotic, cosmic sciences and sensitivity training."
This would seem to be a valuable contact point for things happening in The Netherlands. Send them a dollar donation, to cover printing and air-mail postage to you.

PARADISO
Weteringschans 5-8
Amsterdam, Netherlands
Phone: 64521-237348
When you're in Amsterdam someday, this a very good, neat and otherwise highly recommended spot to check out. It's a nerve center for all sorts of things happening in Europe, especially Holland. It is an experimental youth center open to all. Membership fees for using the facilities are extremely cheap. They have a program of events that runs from Wednesday through Saturday, including jazz, improvisational theatre, yoga, films, music, macrobiotic restaurant, coffeehouse.
You can't sleep overnight at Paradiso, but they will help you find a place. There is (standing up) room for 850 people in the Paradiso house.

THE ORGANIC TRAVELER $2
by John and Carol Farley
P. Lion and Company
Box 416
North Hollywood, Ca. 92603
The Organic Traveler is a paperback book that offers a guide for travelers on the Pacific Coast. Starting with Bellingham, Washington, and ending in San Diego, California, the Farleys trucked over 12,000 miles doing the research for this book.
"The immediate purpose of this book is to provide a source of information about the Pacific Coast to the traveling organo-freak. . . . We have supplied enough information to lead the traveler to the local organic community in each area. . . .

"There is a long-range purpose to this book—the propagation of the organic community. . . . Our hope is that the organic community will grow and grow (pardon our pun) until every market has pure, wholesome, organic foods, and every community supplies the people with basic, humanly administered services."

Listings include restaurants, food sources, clothing, records, books, arts and crafts, entertainment, media, services and information, and miscellaneous. With helpful and informative notes on the vibrations of each town visited along the coast.

Box 31291
San Francisco, Ca. 94131 $1.50 plus 25c postage
It contains hundreds of sources of medical/legal care, apprenticeships, food, craftspeople, social change work, etc. One of the better ones around so far.

GREEN PAGES   25c
c/o Design Spectrum
2613 De La Vina
Santa Barbara, Ca. 93105
(805) 963-6069
"The *Green Pages* is a directory of the new merchants, service organizations and media in the Santa Barbara, Goleta, Isla Vista, Montecity, Carinteria and Summerland areas. . . . Fundamental to the *Green Pages* is also the belief that the new merchants are not motivated solely by the pursuit of profit, and that they are offering a high quality of merchandise, consideration of the human as well as material needs of their customers and a reasonable rate of exchange. . . . The goals of the *Green Pages* . . . are to . . . connect people who wish to interact on a basis of honesty, cooperation and reason so that they might achieve a maximum of happiness and survival security during their lifetime."

CONTACT
266 State Street
New Haven, Ct. 06510
(203) 865-6141 or 865-1773, ask for Trip or Winston
A project of Number Nine, New Haven's complete switchboard service, *Contact* is a guide to what's where in New Haven, including the radio station most worth listening to, and places to stay for a day or two without hassles if

you're visiting in or traveling through the area.

It's put out and updated every few months, so ask for the latest issue, and send them a donation of 25c.

Listings include crisis numbers, counseling, consciousness raising and personal growth, women's groups, housing and communes, media, political groups, economic alternatives, arts and recreation, day care centers and alternative education. (*See also*, Number Nine)

RED PAGES   25c   or from: Center for Educational Reform
1724 20th Street, N.W.   2115 "S" Street, N.W.
Washington, D.C. 20009   Washington, D.C. 20008

The second issue of *Red Pages* is already out, and it covers the Washington D.C. area pretty thoroughly. Lists information switchboards, local Vocations for Social Change people, and everything else.

*CATALOG OF THE SCHOOL OF THE
ART INSTITUTE OF CHICAGO*
Michigan Avenue at Adams Street
Chicago, Ill. 60603
(312) 236-7080, ext. 260

"The *Catalog* is intended as a resource book and, even more, as stimulus for exploration of this 'wan beeg' city—no one (or catalog) can begin to cover all of the points. All elements of the city have to be thought of as syllabus to what we blithely call an educational experience."

This isn't, properly speaking, a People's Yellow Pages; it's more of a "hip" cultural guide to the city—parks, transportation, restaurants, galleries, films, bicycling, etc. It really is the catalog for the School of the Art Institute, so you can find out about that along the way. But then at the very end (p. 76, to be exact) they slip in a section of hot lines, help, health, legal aid, social services, counseling (draft, abortion, and the usual), and political, community, and action organizations. Also has some nice photographs, in an eye-boggling format. 50c.

PEOPLE'S YELLOW PAGES   75c (free if you can't pay)
351 Broadway
Cambridge, Mass. 02139
(617) 661-1571

Published twice a year by the Boston Vocations for Social Change people, *PYP* covers the Boston/Cambridge area with information on medical/legal help, people who will teach you things, places to avoid, where to find skinnydipping ponds in the B/C area, etc.

CHANGES   50c
529 Cedar Avenue
Minneapolis, Minn. 55404

A project of the Minneapolis Vocations for Social Change people and the Changes, this special issue directory lists primarily groups working for social change in the St. Paul-Minneapolis area.

"So we have this list of alternative institutions. Viewed grandly, one might suggest that they comprise a *soft revolution* in process and still growing. Small, tenuous, rough hewn, and still unstable, they might be considered 'liberated zones' where people are working out experimental forms for a new society. But we have a second kind of list which needs to be noted. It includes the groups who are struggling to dismantle or fundamentally change old institutions—to make room for the new ways on a larger scale." (*See also*, Vocations for Social Change)

NATIONAL DIRECTORY OF HOTLINES, SWITCHBOARDS AND
   RELATED SERVICES $2
The Exchange
131 Cedar Avenue South
Minneapolis, Minn. 55404
   Many towns and small cities have a hot-line or switchboard that functions as a contact point for finding help of any kind in the community. This is a directory of hotlines and switchboards all across the U.S. and it gets updated from time to time, so send in new listings you know about.
   The Exchange also publishes a newsletter monthly, mailed to hotlines, switchboards, and other youth-oriented services in Canada and the U.S. Subscriptions are $10 a year. Also available from The Exchange is an eight-page guide, "Ideas on Starting a Phone Service," and a "Crisis Center Bibliography." Send them a donation, say a dollar or two, for these two items.

CSVA/PLOWSHARES
100 Read Hall
University of Missouri
Columbia, Mo. 65201
(314) 449-8979
   The people at Plowshares know a lot about what's going on in the Columbia area. They haven't published a directory, but they do have a listing of all kinds of places and people to know about in Columbia, ranging from the Help Yourself Center to Veterans for Peace to the Salvation Army.
   Also included are a dope center, Women's Liberation group, Student Mobilization, a crisis line, The Everyday People, legal aid, Columbia Tenants Union, draft information, and more.

LIVINGS
4552 McPherson
St. Louis, Mo. 63108
   This is the guide to St. Louis put together by the people who run the Learning Resources Exchange. Send them a donation of $1 for a copy. (*See also*, Learning Resources Exchange).

FREE UNIVERSITY CATALOG
331 Nebraska Union
University of Nebraska
Lincoln, Neb. 68508
(402) 472-2564 or 472-2581
   Although this isn't properly a directory to Lincoln, it's the one place that we found that has its fingers in the various American pies in the area. The Free

University offers workshops, classes, and discussions on everything, and their catalog lists all the good places and various oases in town: Help Lines, Bitch Line, Women's Liberation, Gay rap line, draft information, recycling, LSD rescue, food and bike co-ops, Dirt Cheap Enterprises, day care centers, and more.

They're the kind of people who welcome newcomers to the community. In places like Lincoln every fledgling people-oriented service is welcomed and they're eager to help build up the community of good folks.

PEOPLE'S YELLOW PAGES
Emmaus House
241 East 116th Street
New York, N.Y. 10029
(212) 348-5622

The New York City *People's Yellow Pages* is jam-packed with information on everything from legal and health care to education, day care, rap groups, media and networks, the elderly, poverty, peace groups, food coops, etc. etc. etc. *PYP* "is one attempt to build bridges . . . of information on alternatives existing in the NY area . . . of people with whom we can connect in working for social change . . . to freedom by making available to more people a spectrum of possibilities from which to choose."

They have no price, ask a donation. Send them at least a dollar for your copy. (*See also*, Emmaus House).

ACCESS: TO RESOURCES FOR PEOPLE IN CHAPEL HILL $1
Box 1005
Chapel Hill, N.C. 27514

A very nice and mellow guide to resources and people in the Chapel Hill/ University of North Carolina area.

Beautifully printed, and very helpful—everything from bookbinders to drug programs to nature walks to mountain music festivals to natural food stores. A second issue, *Access 2*, came out in late 1972. This directory, added to the *Opt* directory from Durham, and *Carologue*, helps define the communities of good people throughout the state.

CAROLOGUE: ACCESS TO NORTH CAROLINA
Box 6739 College Station
Durham, N.C. 27708

This is a comprehensive, statewide resource.

"Expect (hope) to come out in September (1972) and sell for $2. Will include crafts—where to learn, where to buy, sources for materials and tools, apprenticeships, guilds, and fairs. Political stuff . . . alternative communications media . . . ecology/conservation groups and projects. Drug counseling, abortion, birth control, and draft counseling, rap houses, free/cheap medical and legal services, folk festivals, free/freeing schools . . . radical/useful history, good sources for things wherever we find them, homesteading—land, shelter, gardening, and . . . yes, whatever else is going on that might help people to know about."

OPT
P.O. Box 6487, College Station
Durham, N.C. 27708
(919) 684-2909
This is a drop-in center at Duke University, and is also into counseling people about alternatives in working for social change. They've also put together a directory for the Durham/Chapel Hill and Southeast region.

PEOPLE'S YELLOW PAGES   75c includ. postage
c/o People's Information Center
3617 Detroit Ave.
Cleveland, Ohio 44116
More of the same good stuff. A thorough guide to the happenings of all kinds of folk in the Cleveland area.

CHINOOK CENTREX $1.40 includ. postage
c/o American Friends Service Committee
4312 S.E. Stark Street
Portland, Ore. 97215
(503) 235-8954
Chinook Centrex is, in their words, "either a modified phone directory or a modified *Whole Earth Catalog*, depending on how you look at it or use it." It is one of the most comprehensive (142 pages) local directories we've seen, clearly organized and indexed. In addition to the usual People's Yellow Pages-type information on community services, stores, information resources, etc., they list labor unions, professional associations, industrial materials sources, city and state political information, reproduce the city budget, etc.
Resources outside the Portland area are also included: video groups, taped speeches and old radio programs, bibliographers, small publishers, U.S. government publications in many areas, other directories of alternatives.

WHOLE CITY CATALOG $1
4307 Locust
Philadelphia, Pa. 19104
c/o Judy Wicks
(215) 222-3358

Judy Wicks and friends are putting together the *Whole City Catalog* for Philadelphia, published in fall, 1972. *Whole City Catalog* will not be specifically geared toward movement people and places, but will try to appeal to diverse groups throughout the city. "The youth subculture already knows that alternatives exist," says Judy, "but a lot of straight people don't, and we don't want to turn them off." She wants to produce a directory which will be useful to everyone.

DIRECTIONS FOR SOCIAL CHANGE
Office of the Chaplain
Brown University
Providence, R.I. 02912
c/o Beverley Edwards
Beverley Edwards at Brown University has put together a preliminary listing of places, agencies, and some people in the Providence area. It's not as

complete as one might hope, but with it you should be able to find your way around. . . . at least you'll know who to ask for more information.

Some very useful information here that probably isn't available elsewhere in Providence, including lawyers who are sympathetic and willing to answer questions.

PEOPLE'S DIRECTORY OF SKILLS AND SERVICES   10c
University Y
2330 Guadalupe
Austin, Tx. 78705
(512) 472-9246

Now in its fourth edition, the Austin *People's Directory of Skills and Services* lists people throughout the area. Published as a service of the University Y, the *Directory* is one of their several projects.

Skills listed, with people willing to teach them, or practice them for you at nominal cost, include goodies such as how to organize co-ops (with people to come, talk, and help you get started); mechanics: fix-it and how-to-fix-it; baby-sitters, bike repairs; computer programming; candle making; Texas Civil Liberties Union, and more.

THIS PAPER IS ABOUT YOUTH CULTURE
c/o Community Education Office
Dallas Public Library
1954 Commerce Street
Dallas, Tex. 75201

Again, not exactly a People's Yellow Pages, but this is a relatively good, and seemingly complete guide to most of what's what in the Dallas area. Published by the Dallas Public Library (!) it lists resources both locally and nationally in virtually all areas—drugs, education, crafts, draft, pregnancy, information and referral agencies, places of refuge, etc. As a basic "people" map, it's pretty good.

It's published as a newspaper, and it appears to be free, though a contribution of 25c probably would be appreciated.

PUGET SOUND ACCESS $1.25 plus 25c postage
P.O. Box 15301, Wedgewood Station
Seattle, Wash. 98115

A "part-of-the-earth catalog" that covers the Seattle area. Lists local resources for learning about the region, where to find the people who can help you navigate throughout the Pacific Northwest, lists suppliers for snow-shoes, camping gear, kayaks; learning exchanges, free schools, museums, books on the region, etc. Just like the *Whole Earth Catalog*, except they're content to tend their own garden. A very fine guide.

THE PEOPLE'S YELLOW PAGES:

See also, Appalshop; *Black Bart Brigade: Canyon Collective;* Education Exploration Center; Shanti Center; *Toolkit; Win With Love.*

SOCIAL AND POLITICAL CHANGE NETWORKS

Cooperatives

CO-OPERATIVE LEAGUE OF AMERICA
59 East Van Buren Street
Chicago, Ill. 60605
(312) 922-0726
An organization with goals similar to those of NASCO (see below), the Co-operative League publishes three helpful introductory books:
Co-op Depot Manual $3
Introductory Kit $1.75
Primer of Bookkeeping for Co-ops $1.50

North American Student Cooperative Organization

2546 Student Activities Bldg.
AnnArbor, Mich. 48104

(313) 663-0889
NASCO was formed to promote and support the growth of co-ops in Canada and the U.S. "All policies and projects of this organization are designed to strengthen the ability of communities of North Americans to control their economic and social environment." They offer:
technical assistance—including writing and travel; *library resources*—manuals, bibliographies, films, etc.; *conferences*—local and regional; *internships and apprenticeships*—on-the-job training for managers, organizers, and workers; *educational outreach*—encouraging continuous education programs, working for the inclusion of co-op education in secondary and university curricula, and contributing to the development of co-op educational materials; *co-op promotion*—for new and established groups.
Publications include:
Co-op News Bulletin $1 per year (monthly)
Journal of the New Harbinger $6 per year (monthly)
Articles on co-op organizing and operating problems.
Community Market Catalog $1 (annual)
Sales catalog for goods and crafts produced by member co-ops, communes and communities, descriptive articles on co-op stores; and descriptions of activities in member communities and co-ops.
Directory of Student and Community Co-ops $1 (annual)
NASCO also has available a number of pamphlets and articles priced under a dollar or free. They include a bibliography on co-ops, "The Co-op Principles and a New Economy," "On Community Building," "On Incorporating," "Youth, Bureaucracy, and Cooperation," and more. Write for their publications list.
See also, Cape Cod Crafts Cooperative; Highlander Research and Education Center.

Dope Education

DO IT NOW FOUNDATION
Box 3573-C
Hollywood, Ca. 90028
   The Do It Now! Foundation publishes reliable drug information in the form of a booklet called *A Conscientious Guide to Drug Abuse*, recognizing that if people are going to "do" drugs of any kind, including prescribed ones, they ought to know more about them. Their booklet is $1 and is in its second edition. They are working on educational projects dealing with heroin, cocaine, and other drugs, including those not commonly thought of in connection with young people or narcotics addicts. Write for details, newsletters, etc.

NATURALISM, INC.
P.O. Box 3621
Hollywood, Ca. 90028
   Naturalism, Inc., has produced an operating manual for drug rescue services.
   Some guidelines: Staff members should have direct drug experience and, if possible, have resolved their own personal problems. Their specialty is personal communication, not professional help. The telephone is the core of the rescue structure. It makes the service available to anyone, 24 hours a day. Any large flat, preferably with separate rooms for interviewing and coming down from bad trips, will do for a facility.
   The prime piece of equipment is the *Physician's Desk Reference* or the *Merck Index Handbook of Nonprescription Drugs*, since most calls are for information and identification of drugs. The manual also discusses lines to take in dealing with specific call situations (loneliness, anxiety, loss of control, bummers), and gives suggestions on financing, and extensive information on identification and treatment of drug problems ranging from LSD to belladonna and glue sniffing. Naturalism also has other literature available, including a pamphlet called "Study of the Psychedelic Drug User."

STUDENT ASSOCIATION FOR THE STUDY OF
HALLUCINOGENS
638 Pleasant Street
Beloit, Wis. 53511
   STASH publishes reams of newsletters, reprints, pamphlets and generally anything about psychedelics and hallucinogens that anyone could want.
   Most of their material is written by doctors working with them and is constantly updated and revised to be as accurate as possible. Most of the doctors' writings are based on research they're doing with drugs, and is usually remarkably unbiased. Also, check with STASH for bibliographies on drugs. Most of their material is free, but donations are always welcome.

See also, Bio-Meditation Society; CSVA/Plowshares.

Intentional Communities and Rural Living

Communities/communes are everywhere, and anyone wishing to find one for whatever reason, either to visit, join, or to study is going to need some guideposts. One of the best ways is to ask around of people you know. Some-one, almost everywhere, knows of at least one community with which he has a personal contact, or knows someone else who knows someone else, who knows. . . . Other guides to the community "movement" and to individual com-munities are listed here.

Contrary to what many of us may think, communities do not exist solely for the use of travellers crossing the continent. They are *not* crash pads for unan-nounced visitors. Many communities have just enough food and space for their working, contributing members. If you plan to visit, for whatever reason, get permission in advance. Too many spectators at the scene don't leave much air for the "victims." Stewart Brand and friends call it a boll weevil syndrome. We think it's an apt metaphor. Don't bug communities and their people.

NORTHWIND
Maplevale Farm
Cross Creek
New Brunswick
Canada

These folks in the "wilds" of Canada describe their homesteading quarterly as "featuring articles on organic gardening, edible wild plants, herbs, animal husbandry, home building and maintenance, natural foods cookery, and hand-crafts. Sample copy on request." $3 per year.

SURVIVAL AND COMMUNITY FARMING
Free University
c/o The Hall
19 Huron Street
Toronto 133, Ontario
Canada

"There are a lot of people thinking that the only way we are going to make it in this insane world is to somehow get man back in tune with his environment, with nature and the cycle of things. Consequently many people are getting into communal farming, and the sad thing is that many farms don't make it. They struggle on for a couple of months and then fade away in the winter.

"The trouble with a lot of them is that the people who start them, even though they have the best of intentions, are right out of the city and don't have the basic skills or their heads in the right place to seriously farm on a year-round basis. . . . .we find ourselves with a city head in a country environment, a combi-nation which doesn't have much survival potential because a sense of commun-ity, responsibility and commitment has not been developed." So some people have come together at The Hall in Toronto to try to help the learning process along. They act as a switchboard getting people and farms together, and provide a short course in self-sufficiency for people before they go out to the farm.

"So if you are on a farm and have specific tasks which need responsible self-sufficient labor for a specific length of time, write to us and let us know the whats and whens of your needs." Since the need for additional labor is very great at specific times, they'll help match "apprentice" farmers to farms that need them.

JAPAN KIBBUTZ ASSOCIATION
2-5-7 Chome
Akasaka, Minato-Ku
Tokyo
Japan
Tel. 03-583-3280

The Japan Kibbutz Association is run by Tetsu Kishida, who has worked on kibbutzim in Israel and arranges for Japanese to go to Israel for a year's work. He also has a list of Japanese communal farms and will arrange for foreigners to visit, work, and live there. He speaks English, but some facility in Japanese appears to be necessary.

For information, send a self-addressed envelope, with international postage coupons, if possible.

SOURCE CATALOG $2.95
Vol. II—*Communities/Housing*

Swallow Press	Or from:	Source Collective
1139 South Wabash Avenue		Box 21066
Chicago, Ill. 60605		Washington, D.C. 20009

Swallow Press says of *Communities*, "Believing that people are socialized to fear change and unskilled to change fears, the Source Collective is in the process of compiling a 'radical encyclopedia' which provides access to what is being done to rebuild this country and the available tools. *Communities*, to be published in two parts, is a guide to humanizing, transforming the neighborhoods, cities, and towns we live in."

Communities/Housing is an extensive treatment of housing, including tenants' unions, model legal-aid programs, court-watching groups, defend-yourself resources; non-profit housing development corporations; squatters' tactics and urban homesteading; public housing tenants' associations; suburban action on zoning and inequitable property taxes, regional planning; and gay, women, and Third World resources. It is also a "guide to materials and provides comprehensive listings of books, tapes, films, periodicals useful in speeding and spreading community-initiated change."

Since it is as comprehensive as Source's first effort, *Communications* (see Media Networks), it is invaluable to people concerned with local action and change.

ACCESS CATALOG
New Life Environmental Designs Institute
Box 648
Kalamazoo, Mich. 49005

These people have done the *Whole Earth Catalog* one better: they're a readers and researchers guide to alternative life styles. They publish articles about specific aspects of rural living, reviews, bibliographies about alternative skills and technologies.

Access Catalog is published by folks who survived the Haight-Ashbury invasions, and ended up in Kalamazoo, "in possession of our visions, in search of our capabilities. That's when the work began, the hard business of gathering experience. Many ideas were tried and many failed . . . we learned from each. . . . Early in 1970, a group of people got together to decide what could be done to find information and get it to the people who needed it. New Life Environmental Designs Institute was formed and we began to study, think and experiment about communication of information."

What they have is an information service that doesn't just spit it out at you . . . Because it takes information in, digests it and tells others about it if it's good, it's a very basic service, and well done.

THE MOTHER EARTH NEWS

P.O. Box 38
Madison, Ohio 44057

The community movement/rural living *Popular Mechanics*, to say the least. Articles on homesteading, energy sources, individual enterprise, wild food, animal care, etc. etc. etc., plus information exchanges and book reviews. $6 per year for six issues.

COMMUNITAS
121 West Center College Street
Yellow Springs, Ohio 45387
(513) 767-3021

Communitas is a fairly new community journal out of Yellow Springs, Ohio. They began publishing in July of 1972.

"Throughout the country, people concerned with radically changing their life styles are shifting their emphasis from communes to community. It is the intent of *Communitas* to encourage this movement, to help community become a viable alternative and solution to the problems of society. We create new communities to fulfill essential human needs that have been long neglected. We want to live in communities where there is a real sense of cooperating, sharing and belonging. We see community as a healing process that restores wholesomeness and brotherhood to our lives. . . ."

Regular features of *Communitas* are reports of new communities, a section on the philosophy of community, community grapevine with news gleaned from community newsletters, a clearinghouse to put people and communities in touch with each other, and more. $6 for one year, $8 outside the U.S.

Community Service, Inc.

Box 243, Yellow Springs, Ohio 45387

Community Service is a non-profit organization seeking "to promote the interests of the small community as a basic social institution, concerned with the economic, recreational, educational, cultural, and spiritual development of its members."

"As to what we are doing in regard to non-school alternatives, we are in a beginning phase of a program that we have already successfully pioneered on a smaller scale elsewhere. This is developing pioneering groups working together in underpopulated areas and communities and cooperating with the indigenous population desiring new life and educational developments. . . . We have for thirty years and more been working for this, bringing together fragments of ways of life into a viable working whole in relation to the remnants of healthy on-going folk societies. . . . The key, or at least an important key, to success in this kind of development is the coming together of enough adequate people to be a large enough nucleus, and to develop an adequate economic base in the area to become a strong community. . . . One of the prospects we have been exploring is the development of an educational community that would so well concentrate on economic and social competence that 'students' could support themselves and relate to their neighbors. . . . ."

Community Service publishes *Community Comments*, a quarterly journal of essays, reports, and reviews, for $2 a year.

VONU LIFE

Box 458
Cave Junction, Ore. 97523

This newsletter is dedicated to those people who want to avoid becoming America's "new serfs." Issues of the newsletter revolve around articles on how to live in camper-trucks, tents, subterranean living, and more.

"Will you buy land and become a serf: easy to find, tax, regiment? Or will you be more imaginative—and free?" Three issues for $1.

DOME LETTER

161 West Penn Street
Philadelphia, Pa. 19144
c/o John Prennis

At last, another publication about domes. This one is a newsletter and a subscription costs $1. John Prennis, the editor, includes news about domes, ideas, fantasies, people, tools, mistakes, triumphs.

WOOD HEAT QUARTERLY

R.F.D. 1
Wolcott, Vt. 05680
c/o Lowther Press

A very nice and useful publication, geared mainly to the realities of country living in Vermont, but the information often transcends geographical limitations, as does the philosophy behind the quarterly. Hal Hershey, in *The Last Whole Earth Catalog*, said:

Wood Heat Quarterly is Vermont living, simple living, spiritual living. Practical, plain, and poetic, all at once. Its articles on fuel supply, mules, soil care, herbal medicines and water witching are mixed in with the philosophy of Kirpal Singh, Wei Po-yang and the Essene Gospel. They talk about the Shakers and the Population Explosion. It's New England transcendentalism, reborn, redefined and revitalized. $3.00 for four issues.

 SMALL TOWNS INSTITUTE
POST OFFICE BOX 517, ELLENSBURG, WASHINGTON, 98926

"The Small Towns Institute is dedicated to research and educational programs that will revitalize countryside towns and create an environment where the best qualities of human life may be fulfilled. . . . We may ultimately find that it is the town with the will to learn how to maintain its stability at a chosen size, that is finally free from the fears of population loss and economic decline, and which can look to planning a future where the sense of community and quality of life will replace economic expansion as a dynamic force."

Annual membership dues range from $10 for individuals to $50 for chambers of commerce, towns, and local governments. The monthly news journal *Small Town* is included.

ALTERNATIVE SOURCES OF ENERGY $1.00/year
c/o Don Marier
Rt. 1 Box 36B
Minong, Wisc. 54859
A bi-monthly newsletter about solar heating, windmills, water power, and more.

LIST OF PUBLICATIONS
From Alternatives Foundation
P.O. Box 36604
Los Angeles, Ca. 90036
Commune Directory $1.50
Modern Man in Search of Utopia $3.95
Carleton Collective Communities Catalog
$1.50 donation covers printing and mailing

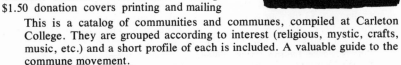

This is a catalog of communities and communes, compiled at Carleton College. They are grouped according to interest (religious, mystic, crafts, music, etc.) and a short profile of each is included. A valuable guide to the commune movement.

NOTE: "We can only offer the catalog in the hope that you will find it useful. . . . We want to mention again that it is assumed that those who receive this information will guard against any improper use. For example, most of these communities do not have facilities for entertaining visitors. Do not plan any visits, at least not without getting consent in advance. Be sure that this information is not put into the hands of anyone who might harm a community."

Alternatives Foundation also publishes *The Modern Utopian* magazine, devoted exclusively to new communities and communes. Articles by communards, interviews, etc.

178   Networks

From Green Revolution
    c/o Heathcote Center
    School of Living
    Rte. 1, Box 129
    Freeland, Md. 21053:
List of Intentional Communities   50c donation
And from all over:

Alternate Society, 47 Riverside Drive, Welland, Ontario, Canada. The primary Canadian commune/intentional community publication. $4/year.

The Appalachian South, c/o Council of Southern Mountains, Berea, Ky. 40403. Monthly magazine, $5/year.

Aquarian Research Foundation, 5620 Morton Street, Philadelphia, Pa. *New Age Newsletter* (see listing in MEDIA CENTERS)

Canadian Whole Earth Catalog, Box 6, 341 Bloor Street West, Toronto, Ontario, Canada. The Canadian version of *Whole Earth Catalog*, with each volume focusing on one topic—industry, healing, shelter, etc. Quarterly, $3 per issue. Beautiful publication.

City of Light, P.O. Box 1804, Santa Fe, N.M. 85701. New Age religious newsletter.

Domebook One and *Two*, Pacific Domes, Box 219, Bolinas, Ca. 94924. Everything you can imagine, and some more, on building domes. $3 for *One*, $4 for *Two*.

Grail Art, P.O. Box 128, Loveland, Ohio 45140.

The Green Revolution, Rt. 1, Box 129, Freeland, Md. 21053. Community newspaper emphasizing decentralization and rural homesteads. $4 per year, free sample.

Leaves of Twin Oaks, Rt. 4, Box 16, Louisa, Va. 23093. Walden Two Community newsletter. Details of how they live and deal with problems. $3.

The Meeting School, 427 Cedar Avenue, Minneapolis, Minn. 55404. Communally free school paper.

Multilateral Relations Study Projects, c/o L. Constantine, 23 Mohegan Road, Acton, Mass. 01720. Papers, research, and counseling services on group marriage.

Natural Life Styles, Box 150, New Paltz, N.Y. 12561. Not specifically a commune/community publication, NLS is an organic guide for living. Information exchanged. $3 for four issues the size of the *Whole Earth Catalog*.

Peacemaker, 10208 Sylvan Avenue, Cincinnati, Ohio 45241. Concerned with the peace movement and communities. $3/year.

Pine Needles, Delton, Mich. 49048.

PreForm, P.O. Box 607, Grants Pass, Ore. 97526. Survival techniques, nomadic living newsletter.

Society of Brothers, Westside Road, Norfolk, Conn. 06058. Information on all Bruderhof Communities.

Trans-Love Energies, 1520 Hill Street, Ann Arbor, Mich. 48104. White Panther Tribe newsletter.

Vocations for Social Change, Canyon, Ca. 94516. Lists places needing people and developments in the movement, including intentional communities.

Walden Three Communitarian, Annex Station Box 1152, Providence, R.I. 02901.

See also, The Life Center; Mankind.

Radicals in the Professions

There are many scientists and professionals who advocate a wider use of their skills and knowledge than the traditional uses of the past. But too often, the feeling of isolation, of feeling that there's no one else who shares your concerns, immobilizes scientists and professionals from acting.

Here are some groups in the New York area that offer information and access to other people sharing the same concerns.

COMMITTEE FOR SOCIAL RESPONSIBILITY IN ENGINEERING
137A West 14th Street
New York, N.Y. 10011
(212) 924-0894
    Publishes *Spark*; is concerned with changing the present orientation of engineering.

COMPUTER PEOPLE FOR PEACE
c/o Dolphin Center
137A West 14th Street
New York, N.Y. 10011
(212) 924-0894

    Workshops and actions against the Indo-China war; publishes *Interrupt*, about radical implications of technology.

META INFORMATION APPLICATIONS
875 West End Avenue
New York, N.Y. 10025
    Group of radical computer technicians "trying to develop human uses of computer technology and to organize scientists in the computer field. They do work for movement folks."

PSYCHOLOGISTS FOR SOCIAL ACTION
c/o Dolphin Center
137A West 14th Street
New York, N.Y. 10011
(212) 924-0894

    "Organizing a loose network of committees working to eradicate militarism, poverty, racism and sexism. Publishes *Social Action*. Memberships are $15 a year, $5 for students."

SOCIAL RESPONSIBILITIES ROUNDTABLE
c/o Jackie Eubanks, Coordinator
Brooklyn College Library
Brooklyn, New York 11210
(212) 780-5335
    "The radical wing of the American Library Association, trying to make librarians more responsive to changing society; organizes task forces to gather information on specific topics such as free schools, gay lib, the American Indian, women's groups, migrant workers, prison libraries, services to poor people, Chicanos, etc. Publishes a newsletter for $1 a year."

Rent Striking

YOUR HOME IS YOUR HASSLE: A TENANT STRIKE HANDBOOK   50c
Metropolitan Council on Housing
2 West 31st Street
New York, N.Y. 10001
(212) WI7-6027
   How-to-do-it for rent strikes against cheap landlords and slumlords is not generally easy information to come by. Thanks, however, to the Ann Arbor Tenants Union and the rent strikers in Harlem of a few years ago, there's some information around on how one goes about it.
   The booklet, *Your Home is Your Hassle*, is a nifty little guide to rent striking in New York City. It's a comprehensive guide that copes with all the New York housing and legal procedures: setting up a tenants union; legal procedures; strikebreakers to avoid; keeping the strike going; and negotiating. With some local research into what your city's housing laws are, this booklet could provide a neat framework for action.

LIST OF TENANTS UNIONS
   This is a listing of Tenants Unions around the country, and the material they publish. We'd like to know more about tenants groups around the country.... does anyone know?

Capitol Hill Tenants Union
1460 Pennsylvania Street
Room 4
Denver, Colo. 80203
   This group shares its information on organizing rent strikes in their booklet: *The Tenant Union Handbook* $1.25

Cambridge Tenants Organizing Committee
595 Massachusetts Avenue
Cambridge, Mass. 02139
   They have experience in organizing over 200 tenants unions. Their handbook is: *A Handbook on Legal Tactics* $1 donation

Ann Arbor Tenants Union
Student Activities Building
University of Michigan
Ann Arbor, Mich. 48104
(313) 763-3102
   The people here have organized one of the most solid tenants unions in the country. Their publications are:
   TU Rent Strike Manual $1
   Trial Handbook: Rent Strikes   65c
   Defend Yourself in Court $1
There's more. Write for details and literature list. They're especially interested in primarily student communities.

Jean Cocteau, *Drawings: 129 Drawings from 'Dessins'*, Dover Books

SOCIAL AND POLITICAL CHANGE NETWORKS:
See also, Canyon Collective, Center for Integrative Studies; Center for Urban Encounter; Emmaus House; Institute Mountain West; International Cooperation Council; Mankind; Minnesota Experimental City; New Jersey Sane; Non-Violent Training and Action Center; Pacific Studies Center; Peace and Freedom Party; The Peace Building; THE PEOPLE'S YELLOW PAGES; Robert Theobald; Roots, Inc.; Shanti Center; Third World Awareness Workshops; The Urban Training Center; Vocations for Social Change.

SPIRITUAL NETWORKS

WIN WITH LOVE $1.50 donation
A Directory of the Liberated Church in America
Free Church Publications
Box 9177
Berkeley, Ca. 94709
    A publication of the Free Church in Berkeley, *Win With Love* is a "comprehensive directory of the liberated church, including peace organizations; youth switchboards; national resource groups; and immigrant aid centers in Canada."
    Listings cover the 50 states, Canada, and overseas (Australia, Belgium, Costa Rica, Denmark, France, Great Britain, Hong Kong, Japan, Lebanon, Netherlands, Okinawa, Philippines, Puerto Rico, Sweden, and Switzerland).
    "We will go on doing *Win With Love* for succeeding years of the People's Peace until we are no longer needed. But we would be glad to organize ourselves out of a job. . . . A solid Movement directory in every U.S. city (such as we have seen for Cambridge and Denver) would make much of our work unnecessary. In the meantime: Be our reporters! Tell us what others are doing. Above all, tell us what you are doing; send your address-change; make sure your newsletter editor puts us on the mailing list."

c/o The Spiritual Community $2.95
Box 1080
San Rafael, Ca. 94902
    From the Campus-Free College newsletter:
    Perhaps the nicest thing about the *Guide* is the way in which information and format are so caringly woven together. The book is not just an accumulation of data. It is itself, as much as a book can be, a spiritual community guide. The central section, "Handbook for a New Age," is composed of brief statements about meditation, mandala, mantra, chakras, dancing, healing, massage, and so on, using the words of men such as Lama Govinda, Baba Ram Dass, Gary Snyder, and Chogyam Trungpa Rinpoche. Also, at the end of this section, is a listing of magazines, periodicals, and books termed "new age publications."
    The first section, a "Guide to Spiritual Centers," includes a sketch of about

88 spiritual centers of all types. These sketches give some idea of the theology of the center, a bit of its history, what it offers and expects from students, and how to contact the center. In addition to the sketches there is an alphabetical listing of about 450 centers with their location and address. The centers sketched and listed cover a very broad spectrum of human involvement and inquiry. There are churches, growth centers, schools, therapeutic groups, meditation societies, and so on.

The final section is a "Community Directory," which lists a large number of communities, groups, and other enterprises broken down by states and then by cities and towns. Using simple symbols as keys, each entry is identified as a "Center"—a school, meditation, or Yoga—or as a "Community"—where people live together to get on with the aims listed under "Center". . . .

The Spiritual Community describes itself as a "non-profit spiritual center," whose purpose is to "channel a flow of information—with your help." They want to do an annual issue and are asking for "additions, corrections, suggestions . . . The book can be had directly from the community for $2.95, plus two bits postage. It is absolutely worth having.

DIRECTORY OF LIGHT CENTERS
International Center for Self-Analysis
I.C.S.A. Press
102 Davis Drive
North Syracuse, N.Y. 13212
This is a 1970 listing of centers interested in meditation, yoga, Vedanta, and "individual and universal Enlightenment for all." It does not claim to be complete, yet includes listing in 33 countries and over 100 entries for the U.S.

LIST OF TIBETAN BUDDHIST MEDITATION GROUPS
    Tail of the Tiger and Karma Dzong provided this list for us.

MONTREAL
3771 Draper Avenue
Montreal, Quebec
Canada
c/o Marie Brewer
(514) 488-9901

TORONTO
75 Binscarth Road
Toronto, Ontario
Canada
c/o Beverly Webster
(416) 920-0162

BERKELEY
1806 B Franklin
Berkeley, Ca. 94702
(415) 843-0050

LOS ANGELES
11027 Strathmore Drive
Los Angeles, Ca. 90024
c/o Leon Schoenfeld

LOS ANGELES
225 Market Street
Venice, Ca. 90291
c/o Carol Smith

SAN FRANCISCO
802 Camelia Street
Berkeley, Ca. 94710
c/o Jerry Grannelli
(415) 525-5157

DENVER
2920 Hudson Street
Denver, Colo. 80207
c/o Al Esposito
(303) 377-1327

CHICAGO
800 W. Altgeld
Chicago, Ill. 60614
c/o Joe Vest
(312) 549-9374

BOSTON
East West Center
105 Marlborough Street
Boston, Mass. 02116
(617) 267-8056

NEW YORK
225 Baltic Street
Brooklyn, N.Y. 90024
c/o Art Bence
(212) 855-8834

NEW YORK
12 East 18th Street
New York, N.Y. 10003
(212) 855-8834, 989-4792

BURLINGTON
University of Vermont
Burlington, Vt. 05401
c/o Bruce Levine
(802) 656-3340

LIST OF ZEN MEDITATION GROUPS

The list below is a geographic sampling of meditation centers. Some of these are informal small groups who are willing to have visitors sit with them; others are formally organized zendos. Most have published introductions to zen teaching and practice.

Toronto Zen Center
569 Christie Street
Toronto, Ontario, Canada

Montreal Zen Center
3664 Mountain Street
Montreal 19, Quebec, Canada

Zen Dojo á Paris (Soto)
59 Avenue de Maine
Paris 14, France
c/o Taisen Deshimaru

San Diego Zen Group
Box 74
Del Mar, Ca. 92014
c/o Rosemary Kiefer

California Bosatsukai (Rinzai)
5632 Green Oak Drive
Los Angeles, Ca. 90028
c/o Mrs. Lily Coffman

Los Gatos Zen Group
16200 Matilya Drive
Los Gatos, Ca. 95030
c/o Arvis Justi
(408) 354-7506

Zen Mission Society (Soto)
Shasta Abbey
R.R. 1, Box 577
Mt. Shasta, Ca. 96067
c/o Jiyu Kennet-roshi

San Francisco Buddhist Church
1881 Pine Street
San Francisco, Ca. 94109
c/o Rev. K. Ogui
(415) 776-3158

Sino-American Buddhist Association
Buddhist Lecture Hall
1731 15th Street
San Francisco, Ca. 94103
c/o Hsüan Hua
(415) 621-5202

Santa Barbara Zen Group
Unitarian Church
1535 Santa Barbara Street
Santa Barbara, Ca. 93101

Washington Group Downtown Zendo
1717 P Street, N.W.
Washington, D.C. 20036
c/o Norman Hoegberg

Koko An of the Diamond Sangha
(Rinzai)
2119 Kaloa Way
Honolulu, Hi. 96822
c/o Betty Earhart
946-0666

The Buddhist Temple of Chicago
Zazen Group (Independent)
1151 West Leland Avenue
Chicago, Ill. 60640
c/o Rev. Gyomay M. Kebose
(312) 314-4661

Chicago Zen Buddhist Church (Soto)
2230 North Halsted Street
Chicago, Ill. 60694
c/o Mike Wise
(312) 348-1218

Washington D.C. Zen Group (Rinzai)
Route 1, Box 604
Accokeek, Md. 20607
c/o John Garges (202) WO6-4878
Lenore Straus (301) BU3-2150

Cambridge Buddhist Association
126 Brattle Street
Cambridge, Mass. 02138
c/o Elsie Mitchell
(617) 864-4554

Zen Center (Soto)
19 High Street
Haydenville, Mass. 01039
c/o Richard Stressurger

Rev. Il-kwon Shin
12 Pembroke Street
Newton, Mass. 02158

Matava Buddhist Temple
2107 California Street
Saginaw, Mich. 48061

Twin Cities Zendo (Soto)
136 Amherst Street
St. Paul, Minn. 55105
c/o Beverly White
(612) 698-9833

Zen Meditation Group (Soto)
6015 Pershing, Apt. 3W
St. Louis, Mo. 63112
c/o Mary Klimik (314) 727-8899
Jerry Siesholtz (314) 862-0178

Rinzai Zen Temple
P.O. Box 1467 FDR Station
New York, N.Y. 10022
c/o Mrs. G. Siegel

Soto Group
440 West End Avenue
New York, N.Y. 10024
c/o Kando Nakajima-sensei

Rochester Zen Meditation Group
  (Rinzai)
7 Arnold Park
Rochester, N.Y. 14067
c/o Rev. Philip Kapleau
(716) 473-9180

Portland Zendo (Soto)
627 S.E. Harrison Street
Portland, Ore. 97202
c/o Ricky Levine
(503) 235-6517

Hui-Neng Zen Temple
R.D. 4 Morgan Hill Road
Easton, Pa. 18042
c/o Abbot Rev. Song-Ryong Hearn
(215) 258-3816

Philadelphia Zendo
217 Wallingford Avenue
Wallingford, Pa. 19086
c/o David Root

煩惱無盡誓願斷

衆生無邊誓願度

LIST OF BUDDHIST PUBLICATIONS
The Bamboo Basket, American Buddhist Order, 135 Ninth Avenue, San Francisco, Ca. 94118 (monthly)

The Triple Gem, Journal of the Tibetan Friendship Group in U.S.A., 11133 Ventura Avenue, Ojai, Ca. 93023.
Articles and news of world-wide activities of the Tibetan Friendship Group. Donations support various refugee/cultural/preservation/monastic activities. No price given; send donation.

Tibetan Society Newsletter, Box 367, Bloomington, Indiana 47401.

Suchness and *Bulletin of Buddhist Temple of Chicago*, American Buddhist Association, 1151 West Leland Avenue, Chicago, Ill. 60640.

Bulletin of Buddhist Vihara Society, 1650 Harvard Street, N.W., Washington, D.C. 20009

Bulletin of the Washington Friends of Buddhism, 4055 Reno Road, N.W., Washington, D.C. 20008

Annual list of books and articles, Cambridge Buddhist Association, 3 Craigie Street, Cambridge, Mass. 02138

The Goji Newsletter, Henpa Hongwanji Hawaii Betsuin, 1727 Pali Highway, Honolulu, Hi. 96813

Home of the Dharma, 940 Post Street, San Francisco, Ca. 94109

Kanthaka, Buddhist Fellowship of New York, c/o Boris Erwitt, 309 West 57th Street, New York, N.Y. 10019

Middlebar Sangha, 2503 Del Rio Drive, Stockton, Ca. 95204

Neo-Dharma, c/o Mr. Baker, 2648 Graceland Street, San Carlos, Ca. 94070

Newsletter of the Buddhist Churches of America, 1710 Octavia Street, San Francisco, Ca. 94109

Scroll Press, 26 Miller Avenue, North Babylon, Long Island, N.Y. 11703

Seattle Betsuin, 1427 South Main Street, Seattle, Wa. 98144

Sokagakkai, World Tribune Newspaper, 2102 East First Street, Los Angeles, Ca. 90033

Western Bodhi, Bulletin of the Universal Buddhist Fellowship, P.O. Box 1079, Ojai, Ca. 93023

Zen Bow, Zen Meditation Center, 10 Buckingham Street, Rochester, N.Y. 14607

SPIRITUAL NETWORKS: *See also*,
Karma Dzong; New York Zendo; Vancouver Zen Centre; Zen Center of Los Angeles; Zen Center of San Francisco.

WOMEN'S NETWORKS

There are more women's networks than anyone could begin to imagine. We gave up the idea of trying to list them all when it became apparent that it was going to turn into a full-time job just trying to keep up with new ones, and with old ones folding.

We've tried to list a few basic contact points that will enable you to go on from there and find your way to the groups and publications that you feel most comfortable with. If we've missed any absolutely crucial listings, such as national groups or publications that act as clearinghouses, please let us know.

MUSHROOM EFFECT
Box 6024
Albany, Ca. 94706

EdCentric says this of *Mushroom Effect*: It "is the most complete listing of women's groups, contacts, magazines, bibliographies, etc. that has been published. It will be updated every few months as additions, deletions, and corrections dictate. Send the following information: Groups—name, address, telephone number, hours open, specialty, newspaper?, cost. Contacts—name, address, telephone number, hours, information and assistance area, etc."

Listings are available for 50c from the above addresses.

WORKFORCE
Box 13
Canyon, Ca. 94516

Every issue of *WorkForce* (formerly, *Vocations for Social Change*) has a full-page guide to resources on Women's Liberation. These are national and local organizations and publications that VSC knows about. Through these listings you can find even more organizations, publications, and other women. Sample issue: 50c donation. (*See also*, Vocations for Social Change.)

HUMAN RIGHTS FOR WOMEN
1128 National Press Building
Washington, D.C. 20004
(202) 737-1059

Human Rights for Women "is a charitable, scientific and educational corporation organized to: provide legal assistance without charge to women seeking to invoke their legal and constitutional rights; to do research, studies and surveys on the economic and social conditions of women, the effect of sexual roles on women and society, and the past and current activities in the field of human rights for women; and disseminate information concerning the extent of denial of human and civil rights to women, sex prejudice, and the feminist movement generally, through various media including conferences and seminars."

"WOMEN IN EDUCATION"   60c
c/o *EdCentric*
Center For Educational Reform
2115 S Street, N.W.
Washington, D.C. 20008
     The *EdCentric* issue for December, 1971, was devoted to the topic "Women in Education" and that's a very wide topic. The special issue is 34 pages, and is absolutely jammed with information about women's groups, women's articles, leads and lists, etc.

NATIONAL ORGANIZATION FOR WOMEN
4445 North Campbell
Chicago, Illinois 60625
(312) 267-1115
     This is the national headquarters for NOW, headed by Betty Friedan and Gloria Steinem, and there are 150 chapters across the country. They are mostly concerned with employment discrimination, abortion repeal, equal rights amendments, child care, and marriage and divorce legislation on all levels.

WOMEN: A JOURNAL OF LIBERATION
3028 Greenmount Avenue
Baltimore, Md. 21218
(301) 366-6475
     This is a quarterly publication, with each issue exploring a single particular aspect of Women's Liberation. Subscriptions are $1 per single issue, $4 for a year.

THE WHOLE WOMAN CATALOG
Box 1171
Portsmouth, N.H. 03801
     "Being a whole woman is like being liberated. Neither is truly possible, but are instead processes of change and growth that can never be completed. Choosing to start that process isolates each of us from what we were before, and removes most of the certainty from our lives. This is happening to women all over the country and the isolation can be broken if we reach out to each other and share."
     This is a central point for information about women's groups and what they are doing all around the country. With articles and organization listings. $2 for individuals, $10 for institutions.

WOMEN: A BIBLIOGRAPHY
102 West 80th Street
New York, N.Y. 10024
c/o Lucinda Cisler
     This is a 36-page annotated reading list, divided into 14 categories with 90 entries; revised in November, 1970. Costs are 50c for one copy, $4.50 for 10, $12 for 30, and $30 for 100. Foreign orders please pay in U.S. funds, and add postage to cover air or surface costs (each copy weighs two ounces). Prepaid orders only, please.

THE WORKING MOTHER
Suite 1-E
46 West 96th Street
New York, N.Y. 10025
   Published by the Maternal Information Services, Inc., *Working Mother* is a "new, national quarterly newsletter which covers day care problems, unfair working hours for mothers, inequitable salaries, unfair taxes, news of funds for day care centers, job training and education."
   Working Mother hopes, by printing any item sent in about local and national situations, to bring women together on a geographical basis to work out solutions to common problems.
   Subscriptions are $2.50, checks made payable to Maternal Information Services.

WOMEN'S NETWORKS:
See also, Gay Women's News Service; The Peace Building; Women's History Research Center.

My mother wanted me to have an education, so she kept me out of school.

—MARGARET MEAD

THE CENTER FOR CURRICULUM DESIGN

An Educational Foundation
for thinking the world together

The Center for Curriculum Design is a non-profit educational foundation, whose projects grow from an ongoing synthesis of many comprehensive metaphors, including, "spaceship earth" (Fuller), "an alternative future" (Theobald), "global village" (McLuhan), and "deschooled society" (Illich).

The Center is exploring ways of developing alternatives, within and outside the school experience; and of communicating whole-earth perspectives on the human/environmental condition.

The center has produced a film, *With Such As These*, which describes for educators and parents the ways in which their young people are dehumanized by conventional classroom practices. This film was designed especially for use by persons and organizations working for alternatives in education.

In addition to *Somewhere Else*, the Center has participated in the publication of *An Alternative Future for America: Essays and Speeches of Robert Theobald* (Chicago: Swallow Press, 1968, 1970); and of *Can Man Care for the Earth?* (Nashville: Abingdon Press, 1971), for use in studying the questions raised by human-kind's gradual assumption of the process of planetary evolution. The Center's own book, *You Are an Environment* (1972), is a guide to the teaching of environmental attitudes.

Further information about the Center is available: P.O. Box 350, Evanston, Illinois 60204.

Acknowledgments

We first became acquainted with networking through our association with Robert Theobald, and our initial limited attempts at it were featured in the "Working Appendix" to his *An Alternative Future for America*. We are also indebted, in our concept of networking, to the ideas of Ivan Illich and Everett Reimer and to such models as *Vocations for Social Change* (now *WorkForce*) and the *Source* Collective.

Several other networkers have been of great help to us: Michael Marien, Kat Marin of *New Schools Exchange Newsletter*, Tom Wilbur of *Outside the Net*, Carolyn Kaye of the Pacific High School Apprenticeship Program, Jane Lichtman of Free-University Clearinghouse, and Tom Linney and his dog Orson.

Unless otherwise noted, graphics in Somewhere Else are from the literature of the entries they accompany, or from: *Design Motifs of Ancient Mexico*, by Jorge Encisco (New York: Dover Publications, Inc., 1953. $2.50) *African Designs from Traditional Sources*; by Geoffrey Williams (New York: Dover Publications, Inc., 1971. $3.00) and are used with the publisher's permission. Cartoon on p. 68 is from "The Wizard of Id" by Brant Parker and Johnny Hart, ©1972 by Field Enterprises, Inc. Cover photo is by Michael Luisi. Back cover cartoon is from Liberation News Service.

We are particularly grateful to Durrett Wagner of Swallow Press, who encouraged us to pursue this project when it was only a dream, and who helped us to make it happen; and to Betsy Brenneman at Swallow Press, who helped us make the book.

A New-Schooling-Leads-to-Deschooling List

Freedom and Beyond, by John Holt. New York: E. P. Dutton & Company, 1972, $7.95

The Underachieving School, by John Holt. New York: Pitman Publishing Corp., 1969. $4.95

School is Dead, by Everett Reimer. Garden City, New York: Doubleday & Company, Inc., 1971. $5.95

Pedagogy of the Oppressed, by Paulo Freire. New York: Herder and Herder, 1971. $2.95

Deschooling Society, by Ivan Illich. New York: Harper & Row, Publishers, 1970. $5.95

The Student as Nigger, by Jerry Farber. New York: Pocket Books, 1969. 95c

Working Loose, an anthology. American Friends Service Committee, 2160 Lake Street, San Francisco, Ca. 94121, 1971. $1.95

Rasberry Exercises: How to Start Your Own School (And Make a Book), by Salli Rasberry and Robert Greenway. The Freestone Publishing Company, Box 357, Albion, Ca. 95410. 1970. $3.95

To Start a School, by Margaret Skutch and Wilfrid Hamlin. Boston: Little, Brown and Co., 1972. $5.95

Farralones Scrapbook, by Farralones Designs, Star Route, Pt. Reyes Station, Ca. 94956, 1971. $4.

Skool Resistance, by Fred Moore, 424 Lytton Avenue, Palo Alto, Ca. 94301, 1971. 25c

Big Rock Candy Mountain, edited by Samuel Yanes and Cia Holdorf. New York: Dell Publishing Co., 1971. $4

De-Schooling: De-Conditioning, edited by Clif Trolin and Johanna Putnoi. Portola Institute, 558 Santa Cruz Avenue, Menlo Park, Ca. 94025, 1971. $2.50 plus 25c shipping.

Sources, edited by Theodore Roszak. New York: Harper Colophon, 1972. $2.95

No More Public School, by Harold Z. Bennett. New York: Random House and Berkeley: The Bookworks, 1972. $2.95

Students Without Teachers, by Harold Taylor. New York: McGraw-Hill, 1969. $7.95

Great Brain Robbery, by Keith Paton. Freedom Press, Angel Alley 84b, White Chapel, High Street, London E 1, England. 50c

Index: Geographical

This index lists, by country and by state, all entries, including both those which are written up and those which appear only in a list. (For example, all the Free Universities in the list starting on p. 148 are included here.) The purpose of this index is to give an overview of a state or geographic area, showing what resources are available and what points there are for further contacts. Publications are not listed here, unless they are Yellow Pages or otherwise concerned with a geographic area. Summer programs available are indicated by (s) after the listing; of course, some folks, such as learning exchanges and community groups, have year-round, ongoing programs.

Index: Alphabetical

This index lists all entries—people, places, and publications—which are written up. A *few* entries are indexed which appear only as part of a list. Lists are noted, however (for example, "Craft associations and guilds"). Summer programs available are indicated by (s) after the listing; of course, some folks, such as learning exchanges and community groups, have year-round, ongoing programs.

What we lack, in the end, is not meaning, not information, not the secrets of the gods; what we lack is the physical world, the world of felt existence—and it is precisely that world that the young are asked to relinquish in return for what they are promised by institutions and authority. Unable in ourselves to tolerate the physical reality of things, the presence in ourselves of the world, we have designed our institutions, perhaps unconsciously, to protect us from all that, and we use them to destroy in the young—in the name of "learning"—what we cannot tolerate in or around ourselves.

—PETER MARIN
New Schools Exchange Newsletter

Supplementing

We have plans to supplement this catalog with a smaller issue which will be published in 1973.

In it, we'll make corrections and publish feedback from people who send us news about any of the listings in this catalog (see Feedback Page below). The supplement will also have new listings that we didn't know about when this catalog went to press, and whatever useful to living and learning comes our way.

If you'd like to receive this supplement issue, send in the form below and $2.00 and we'll send you the supplement as soon as it's out of the printer's clutches.

- -

YES, supplement me; enclosed is $2.00 for the first supplement of *SOMEWHERE ELSE: a Living-Learning Catalog*.
To: Somewhere Else
  P.O. Box 350
  Evanston, Illinois 60204

Name
_____

Address
_____

City   State   Zip
_____

Feedback Page

Please fill out this page and send it to us, and let us know whatever it is we need to know about.

Do you know of other people and/or places that should be listed in the next issue of *Somewhere Else*? (address and phone number, if possible, please) Why? (what do they do?)

Is there anyone listed in *Somewhere Else* that you feel shouldn't be listed? Why?

Have you contacted any of the places listed? How did they treat you? Treat others?

Do the descriptions of the places tell you enough?

What new categories of learning would you like to see in future issues that aren't in this one?

Comments, suggestions, criticisms. . . .

staple here ↙

write more feedback here ↑

fold here ↗

- -

THE CENTER FOR CURRICULUM DESIGN

P.O. BOX 350

EVANSTON, ILLINOIS 60204